Cultural Studies
in the Curriculum

Teaching Languages, Literatures, and Cultures
MODERN LANGUAGE ASSOCIATION OF AMERICA

*Learning Foreign and Second Languages: Perspectives in Research
and Scholarship.* Ed. Heidi Byrnes. 1998.
Cultural Studies in the Curriculum: Teaching Latin America.
Ed. Danny J. Anderson and Jill S. Kuhnheim. 2003.

Cultural Studies in the Curriculum
Teaching Latin America

Edited by
Danny J. Anderson
and
Jill S. Kuhnheim

THE MODERN LANGUAGE ASSOCIATION OF AMERICA
New York 2003

For information about obtaining permission to reprint material from MLA
book publications, send your request by mail (see address below), e-mail
(permissions@mla.org), or fax (646 458-0030).

Library of Congress Cataloging-in-Publication Data

Cultural studies in the curriculum : teaching Latin America / edited by
Danny J. Anderson, Jill S. Kuhnheim.
   p. cm.—(Teaching languages, literatures, and cultures)
Includes bibliographical references and index.
   ISBN 0-87352-802-6 (alk. paper)—ISBN 0-87352-803-4 (pbk. : alk.
paper)
   1. Latin America—Study and teaching (Higher)—United States.
   2. Latin American literature—Study and teaching (Higher)—United States.
   3. Spanish language—Study and teaching (Higher)—United States.
   4. Portuguese language—Study and teaching (Higher)—United States.
   5. Universities and colleges—United States—Curricula. I. Anderson,
Danny J., 1958– II. Kuhnheim, Jill S. III. Series.
   F1409.95.U6C85 2003
   980'.0071'173—dc22   2003016373
   ISSN 1092-3225

Cover illustration of the paperback edition: *Dialogue*, by Rufino Tamayo.
1974. © Estate of Rufino Tamayo. Los Angeles County Museum of Art,
The Bernard and Edith Lewin Collection of Mexican Art, AS1997.LWN.24.
Photograph © 2003 Museum Associates/LACMA

Printed on recycled paper

Published by The Modern Language Association of America
26 Broadway, New York, New York 10004-1789
www.mla.org

CONTENTS

PREFACE TO THE SERIES

The Teaching Languages, Literatures, and Cultures series was created in response to recent transformative changes in these three areas. By curricular necessity or personal choice, many teachers work in more than one area of specialization. Current theories and methodologies encourage them to incorporate multiple perspectives in their courses. This series aims to help teachers meet new challenges by examining how teaching different languages, literatures, and cultures intersects in theory, research, curriculum and program design, and pedagogical practices. The series is intended to reach specialists and nonspecialists and to create cross-specialty dialogue among members of the profession engaged in what were previously separate efforts.

Series Editors

ACKNOWLEDGMENTS

This book is the result of a collective effort that deserves special acknowledgments. Most important, the contributors to this volume deserve a special word of appreciation. For almost three years we shared proposals, drafts, correspondence, and e-mail attachments with them. They were patient when progress seemed slow and prompt as we rallied to meet final deadlines. We thank them for making possible *Cultural Studies in the Curriculum: Teaching Latin America*.

Staff members at the MLA as well as a cadre of reviewers improved the final shape of this volume. Our first contact with the Modern Language Association was with Martha Evans, who encouraged us to move forward with the project. In the final stages, David G. Nicholls and Michael Kandel assumed oversight of the book and helped smooth the way toward publication. The manuscript was read by three editorial panels and several outside evaluators, and we thank them all for their constructive remarks.

At each step, we have enjoyed working on this project. While many Hispanists may be concerned or frustrated by what appears to be fragmentation in our field, we have found that the focus on our shared commitment to teaching and the classroom elicited by this project often changed the tone of the conversation. It shifted our attention to a topic where we readily found points of agreement, and it brought us together in our differences. Technology has dramatically expanded the boundaries of the classroom. For many, the general rubric of "cultural studies" has created exciting approaches that give students new ideas about what can be called a text, offered new answers to the challenge of motivating students to read in the age of the sound bite, allowed us to articulate the centrality of cultural difference in our future, and provided new strategies for promoting critical thinking. In the process of editing this volume, we combined the multiple and overlapping tasks of scholars and teachers that are sometimes frustrating and often exhilarating. We hope that as you read the essays in this collection, you will become aware of the creative energy that our colleagues have invested in linking their scholarship to their teaching and bringing it alive in the classroom through cultural studies approaches to Latin American cultural production.

JSK and DJA

Introduction: From Culture into Cultural Studies in Latin America

Jill S. Kuhnheim and Danny J. Anderson

"It's a flash in the pan." Cultural studies, like many paradigm shifts, has frequently been characterized this way—as just one in a long line of trendy, transient theoretical turns in the academy. Since its inception in England in the 1950s, however, cultural studies has not only grown but has been adapted and applied in many different fields. It has united a variety of analytic practices that, looking beyond canonical texts in literature or history, examine society at large. The various approaches expand conventional disciplinary boundaries; they extend the idea of critical reading to cultural and social phenomena, such as sports, music, and television; and they seek meaning in a range of visual, verbal, and technological forms. Broadly speaking, cultural studies has shifted the focus of literary, linguistic, and historical studies to concerns previously excluded from classroom discussion: the perspectives of marginal groups and the study of expressive forms and social practices associated with popular and mass cultures. The nine essays collected here portray cultural studies in the classroom and demonstrate how its ideas have been incorporated into pedagogical projects.

Many readers may be familiar with the authors who were among the founders of the movement in England—Richard Hoggart, Raymond Williams, and E. P. Thompson—and who collaborated in the Birmingham Center for Contemporary Cultural Studies, established in 1964. In an effort to engage their working-class students more successfully, they examined the meaning of "culture" in relation to the students' own experiences, and they explored the political implications of what officially mattered as culture. Stuart Hall has recounted the waves of theoretical paradigms associated with the Birmingham Center as a series of critical encounters, with first, Marxism, including the work of Antonio Gramsci and Louis Althusser; later, the political lessons of feminism and, then, studies about race and ethnicity; and, eventually, the linguistic models of structuralism and poststructuralism that characterize current understandings of textuality. These theories converged to create what many today think of as British cultural studies.

In the United States, cultural studies has frequently been linked to the interdisciplinary fields of area studies (Brantlinger). Area studies, encompassing such regions as America, Asia, Eastern Europe, Western Europe, Africa, and Latin America, emerged after the Second World War and took on new vigor in the 1980s for many literary scholars seeking to move beyond a bellettristic approach in order to grapple with sociological and often explicitly political characteristics of Latin American cultural production. While the socalled boom in Latin American fiction energized literary studies in the 1960s and 1970s and scholars and teachers were conscious of the political importance of these works, the legacy of the New Criticism combined with the arrival of structuralism and then poststructuralism to focus critical attention mainly on the dazzling formal innovations in the Boom novel. By the 1980s, with Ronald Reagan in the White House and increased United States military action in Central America, the climate was ripe for change among Latin Americanists, especially those who, dissenting from United States government policies and practices, sought to link their disagreements to an understanding of Latin American culture in its entirety. Mary Louise Pratt has chronicled the atmosphere of the 1980s and 1990s as a "culture war," describing, from her position at Stanford University, the struggle in the American academy over what could or should be taught in postsecondary classes. She uses historian Fernando Coronil's phrase to characterize the period as a time of reflection on the "geopolitics of truth" that allowed scholars "to work through . . . a series of important epistemological, methodological, and ethical questions" (30).

Yet the fall of the Berlin wall in 1989, the close of the cold war, and an increasing awareness of globalization were supposedly moving the academy into a postnational era. Some scholars and university administrators, as well as foundations and grant-funding agencies, foretold the end of area studies, because of its focus on specific geographical, cultural, and linguistic sites. Despite such pronouncements, many scholars and teachers continued to see area studies as an opportunity, first, to link literature to other disciplines and, second, to rethink the definition of a nation. The emergence of cultural studies provided scholarship that enabled area studies specialists to examine the links between geography and institutional power more critically and to raise questions about individual; collective; and, especially, national identity. Engagement with Benedict Anderson's *Imagined Communities* became de riguer. Although many scholars had already been working in a cultural studies vein, two conferences in 1990—one at the University of Illinois and the other at the University of Oklahoma—gave cultural studies wide media coverage. In 1992 the MLA's Annual Convention included a major forum, "Cultural Studies and the Disciplines: Are There Any Boundaries Left?" Aggressive manuscript solicitation and marketing at some presses established a clear niche for cultural studies publications; by the early to mid-1990s, introductory readers and anthologies of canonical articles in the paradigm were circulating (see, e.g., Easthope; Grossberg, Nelson, and Treichler; During; Leitch; Storey). At the same time, cultural studies found itself at a crossroads. On the one hand, the rise of cultural studies has been characterized as a postmodern fragmentation of the field into multiple, competing theories and specializations: postcolonial studies, subaltern studies, Chicana/o studies (or US Latina/o studies), critical race studies, performance studies, and sexuality and gender studies, to name some of the most influential. On the other hand, the fragmentation, while dividing scholars into somewhat narrowly focused intellectual camps, has resulted in a number of creative approaches to teaching language, culture, and literature.

As we have collectively played out the drama of fragmentation, some groups of scholars have upstaged others. In caricatures of academic specializations, the comp lit scholars and their French counterparts have often served as the precocious theorists. Traditional Hispanists have frequently been cast as figures of comic relief who disdain theory, defend literature (a word reverentially uttered with a capital *L* and two sharply enunciated *t*s), and visibly shudder at the thought of including popular culture and political concerns in teaching and scholarship. Another group of Hispanists, mostly Latin Americanists, have been seen as competing for space onstage and as sometimes overplaying their roles—they interpret all works from a political perspective, they simplistically reduce literature to sociological models, and they display woefully inadequate aesthetic sensibilities. We do not believe that these caricatures are accurate, but they evoke some of the tensions, in the field of

Latin American literary and cultural studies, that affect the work of all players onstage.

Under the rubric of cultural studies, scholars with more traditional leanings have broadened the scope of their concerns. At the same time, cultural studies has brought together specialists, working from a variety of methodological approaches, who seek to understand the political and social implications of many representations, both literary and extraliterary. As it has arrived and been practiced in the United States, cultural studies is not a single, authentic, or pure methodology; rather, it has evolved by embracing various theories and by reaffirming the interdisciplinary nature of area studies. To Gerald Graff, in *Beyond the Culture Wars*, cultural studies is an "umbrella-concept for connecting and integrating disciplines," as long as it sets aside its connotation as a "euphemism for leftist studies" (169). Among Latin Americanists, however, it continues to be a strongly contested practice because of subtle philosophical nuances and the potential for a progressive political agenda.

The critic Edward Said has noted that "theories travel—from person to person, from situation to situation, from one period to another" and, during their journeys, may undergo "gains or losses in strength" or even become "altogether different for another period or situation" ("Traveling Theory" 226). While Graff suggests that a change in the political orientation of cultural studies is a gain, many practitioners view such a shift as a fundamental loss. As cultural studies with an aesthetic or literary emphasis was becoming institutionalized, John Beverley warned against the loss of progressive political commitment ("By Lacan"). In the twentieth-anniversary issue of the *Latin American Literary Review*, in which scholars provided brief statements on the future of Latin American literary studies, many practitioners echoed Beverley's alarm. Recent books by Román de la Campa, *Latin Americanism* (1999), and Alberto Moreiras, *The Exhaustion of Difference: The Politics of Latin American Cultural Studies*, stress the questions of political commitments and the role of potentially engagé critical activity. At times, the parallel yet related theories of postmodernism, postcolonialism, and subaltern studies are sheltered by the cultural studies "umbrella-concept." At other moments, emphatically separating these perspectives, scholars seek to defend, in the postcolonial and the subaltern, a more politically conscious articulation and to eschew the aesthetic connotations of the postmodern and what they consider to be the

sometimes institutionally hegemonic, and hence politically debilitated, practice of cultural studies.

Today, cultural studies in the United States still reflects the legacies of its
multifaceted origins, but new features have become significant. As a wide
range of practitioners have adopted and adapted cultural studies, the movement has evolved into a variety of sophisticated analytic models and become
institutionalized in academic departments. What characterizes the versions of
cultural studies discussed in this volume is precisely the way in which theories
have traveled and intermingled in the work of teachers and scholars over the
last decade. In colleges and universities throughout the United States, cultural
studies is at home, no longer the interloper that created a stir in the early
1990s. At the same time, globalization has profoundly changed the identity
makeup and motivations of our students. As a result of international migration, many of us may teach classes that are as diverse as the hybrid cultural
formations we analyze in the daily lesson. Employment concerns are also a
prime motivation for our students: Spanish, and sometimes Portuguese, is
often a second major for students in business, prelaw, and premed. In spite
of the predictions of a postnational era, the burgeoning enrollments in Spanish, beginning in the late 1990s, are populated by students avid to gain an
advantage in the job market through certifying their bilingual and bicultural
skills and by aspiring executives seeking a competitive edge by familiarizing
themselves with the language, culture, and history of their potential counterparts abroad. Moreover, these students—who bring to postsecondary education a street-smarts knowledge of film, video games, computers, and the
Internet—often display a resistance to literature and literary reading. Cultural
studies, with its ecumenical embrace of a variety of expressive forms and
broadly conceptualized texts, is one effort to make the classroom experience
relevant to this new generation of students. As the essays in this volume
illustrate, students can more easily grasp the multicultural reality of Mexico
by comparing it with everyday experiences in Hawai'i; they can use the methodology of cultural studies to go beyond the traditional business-Spanish class
to gain insights into imperial and colonial histories; they can benefit from
the wealth of visual culture and varied cultural texts in the classroom that
complement and contextualize the literary texts.

The 11 September 2001 assault on the World Trade Center and the Pen-
tagon by Al Qaeda terrorists under the leadership of Osama bin Laden, which

occurred while this volume was being reviewed for publication, has further dispelled the idea of a postnational era. The dynamics of statehood no longer follow the rules of nineteenth-century diplomacy, when boundaries seem to have been clearer; but the complex notions of sovereign groups, united by language, culture, history, and a desire to stake a claim on a national territory, have not waned. In the months following the attack, questions were raised about why the United States did not recognize, beforehand, the potential for such disaster; qualified area specialists, versed in language, culture, and history, were asked to help explain and negotiate paths for understanding and future action. Perhaps now more than ever in recent decades, the sensitive position of scholars and teachers of modern languages, cultures, and literatures is evident. Far from neutral, we—as creators and professors of cultural knowledge—are profoundly invested in the ways cultural knowledge is structured.

The various contexts that marked the advent of cultural studies make a question posed by John Storey in his anthology *What Is Cultural Studies?* even more compelling. With the academic acceptance of cultural studies, Storey suggests, we no longer need ask, "what is cultural studies?" but rather "whom is cultural studies for?" and "where is cultural studies?" (5, 11). *Cultural Studies in the Curriculum: Teaching Latin America* provides specific answers to these questions. Instead of debating the propriety of theoretical models and the purity of philosophical positions, these essays embody the various ways that teachers in the United States practice cultural studies to impart the language, history, and cultural production of Latin America to students seeking an understanding of a globalized world.

Awareness of the position of teachers, scholars, and students in the United States academy looking toward Latin America makes patent another crucial point about cultural studies. It is not a methodology that is being "applied to" Latin America. In fact, the kind of interdisciplinary scholarship that characterizes cultural studies existed before the 1950s in Latin America. The region has a long tradition of hybrid, or "undisciplined," cultural practices, in large part stemming from colonial legacies, precarious political and economic conditions, and a limited literacy that hindered the production of and support for autonomous literature and art. Intellectuals from the region did not develop a precursor form of cultural studies; they were early practitioners of comparative and cross-disciplinary research that in the twentieth century was joined under the rubric of area studies and has consistently integrated politics into cultural thinking. One has only to think of Domingo Faustino Sarmiento's nineteenth-century cultural analysis of Argentina or the Cuban anthropologist Fernando Ortiz's *Contrapunteo del tabaco y el azúcar* (1940); both works combine features of history, literature, anthropology, and journalism. In his essay "Why I Do Cultural Studies," Abril Trigo of Ohio State University notes the legacy of hybridity and explains that the "difference between current Latin American cultural studies and traditional Latin American thought is that the latter believed in the integrating capabilities of national literature and art, while the former criticizes them as apparatuses of power" (75). What has shifted is the focus on the macro level—on the ways culture is constructed in relation to power.

Like Storey's compilation, most of the recent collections of essays about cultural studies do not include a Latin American perspective. The closest many come is a border perspective, and the border is frequently one that constructs a "Hispanic" United States cultural identity (with Mexico, Puerto Rico, Cuba). This situation points to the fact that the United States is now a primary producer and consumer of cultural studies, as the field has become an increasingly institutionalized practice in the academy (in this volume, Gustavo Verdesio traces changes in its transference from Britain to the United States). The guest appearance of Latin America in these collections may signal the ongoing colonial relations between literary and cultural scholarship in different parts of the world, or it may suggest some trepidation, originating in the Latin American region, over the term. For many Latin American cultural critics, cultural studies is a contested concept. The Argentine writer Beatriz Sarlo prefers the term "cultural analysis" ("Cultural Studies Questionnaire"), while the Chilean Nelly Richard uses "cultural critique." As Ana del Sarto has explained, these terms are not synonymous with "cultural studies" but are related practices that highlight different intellectual and cultural traditions.

To the intricate nuances that differentiate cultural critique, cultural criticism, and cultural studies, scholarship in second language acquisition adds yet another variation. The teaching of modern literatures and languages has always involved culture. In the twentieth century, modern language education experienced a profound shift away from acquisition of basic reading knowledge toward genuine proficiency grounded in speaking; with this shift, the knowledge of culture has become integral to both the learning process and the real-world use of modern languages outside the classroom. The line of inquiry that explores language learners' cultural competency, and strategies for teaching this skill, falls under the rubric cultural studies, and in this perspective "culture" is an ability language learners acquire that allows them to communicate more effectively (see, e.g., Byram and Esarte-Sarries; Byram, Esarte-Sarries, and Taylor; Lange, Klee, Paige, and Yershova). While this utilitarian concept of culture is not negligible, the essays in this volume all presuppose a more analytic approach to thinking about and teaching culture, as an arena in which power is exercised, identities negotiated, and values assessed.

Among language acquisition scholars, Claire Kramsch marks the shift toward the analytic use of the term "cultural studies" that is relevant for the essays in this volume. First in *Context and Culture in Language Teaching* and later in *Language and Culture*, Kramsch uses her thorough knowledge of second language acquisition, pedagogy, and contemporary literary theories to demonstrate the profound importance of a move toward the kind of critical thinking that cultural studies promotes in the language classroom. For, while the term *cultural studies* has been used in a general way to denote approaches to teaching cultural knowledge alongside linguistic competency, many practitioners do not accept the specific methodological assumptions associated with cultural studies as an analytic tool. A cultural studies approach brings to the surface certain assumptions about identity, power, social difference, and expression; it openly questions just what counts as culture and how our concepts of culture are formed and transformed through history. In "The Cultural Discourse of Foreign Language Textbooks," Kramsch examines how textbooks package culture in a certain way and create identities and social difference by positioning language learners vis-à-vis the target culture as certain kinds of consumers. In contrast, the chapters in this volume explore cultural studies as a strategy for teaching college and university students to think critically about culture. Rather than package Latin America for our students as if it were a ready-to-wear garment or rather than encourage them to perform scripted roles of consumers, tourists, or business executives, the writers here advocate guiding students to examine the dynamics and struggles at work every day in cultural life; to become aware, before they consider enacting them, of the way that the roles of consumer, tourist, and business person have been constructed; and to uncover the complex social and historical practices that produced cultural expressions ranging from *Pedro Páramo* and *telenovelas* to the *cholo*.

Learning more about how cultural studies practices can transform teaching experiences will provide readers with a framework for analyzing culture as a socially constructed entity, as well as for recognizing cultural codes and the ways in which they differ among social groups. For example, definitions of what "popular culture" is are not universal. In the United States, a dominant trend equates popular culture with mass culture and views both as arenas in which unseen forces, perhaps conspiratorially, control the behavior of consumers. In Latin America, "popular culture" retains its ties to a folk culture that predates the media of mass culture; furthermore, popular culture and mass culture are often linked to social resistance and cultural dissent. Although specific instances are likely to be more complicated than our neat opposition, juxtaposing these concepts highlights commonalities and divergences in their use. For example, a study of the popular culture associated with *corridos* and *ranchera* music in Mexico, while beginning with the music's origins in oral poetry, rapidly leads to an examination of radio, the recording industry, efforts to promote a national music, and the hegemony of certain forms of music in the national and global imaginary. If we follow the *corrido* into the mass media of the present, the narrative becomes more complex as the *narco-corridos* of the 1990s create folk heroes and an alternative recording-and-distribution industry for a musical form that expresses strong resistance to dominant social values. The boundaries between conceptual categories like folk culture, popular culture, mass culture, and high culture are in continual flux. Similarly, rather than the traditional models that portray monolithic, unchanging Latin American cultures rooted in stereotypes, cultural studies promotes an understanding of Latin American societies as living, evolving, and ever-changing. Studying the processes of change gives students and teachers a dynamic understanding of Latin America, a reasoned approach for analyzing events in the region, and a historical perspective for defining their own sense of culture.

A cultural studies approach also offers teachers ways to transform classroom content and practices and to enhance the study of literatures, languages, and cultures by broadening discussion. Students today are increasingly aware of their position as global citizens, and cultural studies encourages them to think across boundaries—both national and disciplinary—and to make theoretical and practical connections among conventionally disparate categories. This methodology has the potential to respond to the needs of a student body that is becoming more racially, ethnically, nationally, and linguistically diverse and that is frequently attuned primarily to visual and computerized forms of contemporary culture. Cultural studies may provoke curricular changes, such as a shift away from the coverage of classic texts, in courses structured by genre or national orientation in departments of Spanish and Portuguese, to emphasize, instead, the relations among a variety of "texts," as many of these essays demonstrate.

One example that illustrates the pedagogical change that cultural studies introduces is the question of what happens in the so-called culture class. In civilization classes, which may either become obsolete or expand to incorporate additional material and a more self-conscious perspective, the issues that are studied shift. Predictably, many courses in civilization have been organized around the artifacts of cultural pride, either for Latin America as a region or for specific countries. A celebratory history, a review of patriotic heroes, an archaeological overview of indigenous cultures (sometimes with scant reference to living indigenous cultures and languages of the region), an abbreviated cookbook of national dishes, and a short repertoire of major figures in the arts—architecture, painting, sculpture, music, and literature—often constituted the outline for a civilization class. Recently, the options for teaching culture have changed. For instance, teachers of Mexican culture might explore with students the cultural referents their generational peers in Mexico would have—everything from revered historical and cultural objects to global mass media texts. Rather than cultural relics the course is organized around the fragments of everyday knowledge that enable us to understand a joke, realize the charged nature of racial slurs, and catch the competitive local interest in soccer games throughout Mexico. Although many of the texts from a traditional civilization class may be included in such an approach, the purpose is less to teach reverence and more to recognize how the elements are interwoven into everyday contemporary life. A cultural studies approach provides another component to a course on Mexican culture by explicitly positing the nature of representation and power in society. An iconoclastic look at social valorization and political organization can reveal how those in control have justified and partially masked racism; students can also begin to understand the way geography and history have determined the relations between local communities and state authority in the nation. Many other issues are possible.

Viewed through this lens, cultural studies has as its goal not the teaching of a series of dead referents. Instead, it offers an opportunity to explore the social dynamics of power at work in representations; in the creation of national identities; in the negotiation of individual identities related to markers of race, ethnicity, social class, religion, gender, and sexual orientation; and in the question of nation itself as an articulation, in the context of globalization, of collective or individual identity. We have noted that scholars and teachers are downplaying the study of cultural monuments—Mexican muralism, gauchos, and the samba—in favor of more-compelling social practices and cultural acts, such as urbanism and its consequences, migration, and indigenous activism. As Walter Mignolo underscores in his response to the "Cultural Studies Questionnaire" published by the *Journal of Latin American Cultural Studies*, this change represents a shift from the colonial objectification of "culture" as something people "have" in their collective lifeways; it is a move toward a dynamic view of culture as what people "do." Cultural studies employs a broader concept of culture that does away with, or calls into question, conventional values associated with terms like "civilization" and "literature."

Briefly contrasting the ideas of Beverley in "By Lacan" with those of Sarlo in "Los estudios culturales" highlights some of the historic tensions between literary and cultural studies as they apply to the way this approach is practiced in relation to Latin America. Beverley and Sarlo do not represent Latin American cultural studies as a whole; rather, their statements point to two specific positions, one critiquing and the other defending aesthetic values. Moreover, these statements emerge at particular moments; over time, both critics have adjusted their positions in response to new understandings of cultural production. In debates over the meaning and proper practice of cultural studies, however, the antagonism between these positions starkly suggests the range of issues at stake.

Beverley's article, mentioned earlier, serves as the introductory essay for his work *Against Literature*. The essay clearly sets up some fundamental ideas that subtend many conversations about Latin American cultural studies. Beverley grounds his perspective by investigating ways in which Latin America's relation to literature has varied during the area's postcolonial history. Specifically, Beverley notes how literature developed in close association with the state (at times, paradoxically, reinforcing colonialism while at the same time nurturing independence). He signals that the division between a "stylistic will to power" (11) and a desire for Latin American cultural authority appears again in turn-of-the-century modernist texts and continues the struggle between intellectual and popular interest. Later, Latin American literature of the 1960s was idealized as an instrument of national liberation and anti-imperialism, he observes, while the power relations implicit in the literary were naively unquestioned. In the present-day situation of uneven cultural development, Beverley points out, there are democratic possibilities in the fact that mass culture, while distributed globally, is not received in a uniform way. He proposes that testimonial writing, which he sees as an alternative to literature, offers a new link between literature and subalternity that moves North American academics beyond a politics of representation to one of solidarity. *Testimonio's* difference from literature allows us to scrutinize the concept of literature in the act of teaching it.

Sarlo also problematizes literature's role in Latin America. In "Los estudios culturales," she too traces the shifting social importance of literature in the region and agrees that we cannot talk about texts without examining the relations of power that they cover and affect. What stymies her is the question of aesthetic value; art and culture are not the same and, in her view, literary critics need to evaluate what an artistic text should produce. Recalling an incident from her experience as a judge in a Latin American film festival, she observes how critics from outside the region refused to consider in aesthetic terms films produced in Latin American, allowing them entry for sociological or political significance alone. Unlike Beverley, who is willing to do away with aesthetic value and positions the *testimonio* as a model for the relation between First World critic and his other, Sarlo reminds us that Latin American art has consistently been displaced from the category of aestheticism. From her perspective, literary and cultural studies need each other.

In neither essay are aesthetic values neutral. What is important in each case is how context shifts the meaning of the opposition between literary and cultural studies. Like authority (and subjectivity)—which came under scrutiny just when groups who had historically been denied access to human agency had the possibility of speaking for themselves—artistic merit has been a contentious category for Latin American literature. To understanding what is at stake, we have to comprehend and clarify the many paradoxes of a postcolonial inheritance—paradoxes that are far from being arcane details in a scholarly debate. At issue are the conditions that authorize marginalized and silenced groups to speak and write persuasively, or simply to conceptualize and create a worldview that differs from that of their silencers. For individuals, these conditions can be understood as positions, postures, or loci of enunciation that place the scholar, the teacher, and the student within a discourse or regime of truth charged with creating a certain knowledge. Edward Said, drawing on Michel Foucault's conceptualization of discourse, has described the West's vast archive of cultural, linguistic, historical, and scientific writing about the Middle East as orientalism. Following Said, Enrico Mario Santí rightly identifies the discursive practice of *Latin Americanism*. The differences between Sarlo and Beverley rehearse contentions in the field of Latin Americanism that represent a struggle for authority and truth. The two writers are separated by their different positions on the aesthetic and the academic, and even by geographic site and local cultural conversation, as these elements reflect the dialogue among transnational scholars. The debate about cultural studies is fundamentally about the legitimacy of kinds of knowledge, about discursive, national, and institutional positions that define the conditions for creating knowledge. The essays in this volume strive to intervene actively in this debate.

The tension and interdependence between the literary and the cultural becomes clear in significant ways in the essays included here. Some pieces, like Jesse Alemán's treatment of the politics of representation in Chicano writing, deal with literary texts—specifically, Alemán asserts that we cannot simply glean them for cultural facts. Rather, Alemán believes, cultural facts are themselves figurative narratives that invent as much as they represent culture. Other authors, such as Kirwin R. Shaffer, sidestep literature to study how Caribbean film, music, religious expression, and sport respond to and reformulate images propagated by touristic depictions of the region. Gustavo Verdesio, whose expertise is in colonial Latin America, argues that a transdisciplinary approach to this period allows subaltern history to emerge. His pedagogy juxtaposes objects, including codices, archaeological and ethnohistorical scholarship on art, architecture, and religious celebrations with Spanish perceptions (official and nonofficial) of indigenous life. Students in his class become aware of the limitations of their own ethnographic positions as they interpret human relations across cultures.

Joy Logan, Danny J. Anderson, and Robert McKee Irwin all describe how representations constitute identities; in these essays, cultural studies moves between literary and extraliterary representations to consider ethnographic, business, and gender practices. For these authors, location is paramount; they situate themselves and their students in relation to the culture and identities scrutinized in their classes. Logan, who teaches at the University of Hawai'i, encourages her students to link issues of representation in Spanish American texts to those closer to home, by taking on the roles of investigator, informant, and viewer to create their own ethnographic writing. Using literature, film, and anthropology, she works with her students to examine cultural hybridity, multiculturalism, bilingualism, postcolonial experiences, and indigenous rights. Anderson's chapter combines theoretical concepts from both literary and cultural studies in his version of business Spanish. The course he teaches, which probes cross-cultural communication, imperialism, and ethical issues in United States and Latin American business relations, gives his often goal-oriented students more than they bargained for. Irwin offers us some fascinating possibilities for incorporating gender and sexuality studies into the curriculum. Looking at Mexico before machismo, Irwin critiques literary and other cultural works (mass media, photographs, and criminology texts, among others) in confronting assumptions about gender and sexuality.

In two essays, one by Luis Fernando Restrepo and the other by Jill S. Kuhnheim, a cultural studies approach shifts the emphasis from aesthetics and thematics to the broader range of cultural motivations. Restrepo uses the city to bring together historical, sociological, anthropological, cinematic, and literary perspectives that awaken students' awareness of the cultural construction of urban spaces, in their own environment and in Latin America. Kuhnheim's contribution proposes that poetry is emblematic of the balancing act between aesthetic and cultural concerns. Rather than exile poetry from cultural studies, she argues, we should recognize that, when we teach poetry, students come to understand that even this most "literary" of forms (as it has been characterized) participates in the ongoing dialogue about the social and political context of power. These essays take thematic practices one step further by probing the formulation and transformation of their themes and incorporating this investigation into the classes themselves.

Piers Armstrong (like Jesse Alemán), examines Latin America as encompassing areas beyond the Spanish-speaking world. In his examination of the politics of teaching Brazilian studies, Armstrong points out how Brazilianists, who teach a marginalized language and culture, wrestle with the pressures of the educational marketplace. As they compete with Spanish and other languages for students, Brazilianists must strike a balance, in their culture classes, between presenting an "aesthetically stimulating and historically optimistic picture of Brazil" and yielding to what is often a bleak socioeconomic realism.

The essays in this collection were selected from several calls for papers and personal solicitations to cover a breadth of topics, time periods, and places that bear on critical issues raised by the concept of cultural studies.

Most of the authors speak from the mainland United States, with an eye to teaching this audience, and almost all work in Spanish and Portuguese departments. The emphasis on pedagogy evidently attracted younger scholars who are thinking about their teaching in both practical and theoretical ways and grappling with ideas expounded by better-known practitioners in the field. In this sense, the collection creates a dialogue between old and new voices. The authors' institutional positions influence how culture is focused. They all highlight rather than resolve tensions between self and other, between aesthetic values and cultural ones, and between one discipline and another; and they make these struggles part of intellectual inquiry. Each author is aware that no cultural practice is neutral, and each offers the reader strategies for sensitizing students to complex argumentation in their exploration of Latin American cultures. These essays truly question what culture means today and what role Latin American culture may play in a variety of pedagogical settings, as well as in an increasingly global world.

RECOMMENDED READINGS

Many readers of this book, familiar with the theoretical models of cultural studies, may prefer to leap directly to the essays. Other readers may seek guidance in exploring the general bibliography of cultural studies, and this short list suggests some itineraries. For general theoretical introductions, Anthony Easthope's *Literary into Cultural Studies*; Vincent Leitch's *Cultural Criticism, Literary Theory, Poststructuralism*; John Storey's *Cultural Studies and the Study of Popular Cultures*; and Patrick Fuery and Nick Mansfield's *Cultural Studies and Critical Theory* are all good starting points. A variety of anthologies have gathered canonical articles in the cultural studies tradition (During); assembled key studies synthesizing and defining the practice of cultural studies (Storey, *What Is Cultural Studies?*); and brought together examples of cultural studies in practice (Grossberg, Nelson, and Treichler; Baker, Diawara, and Lindeborg; Curran, Morley, and Walkerdine; Garber, Franklin, and Walkowitz).

In their research on Latin America, many scholars and teachers place cultural studies at the center of their interpretive practices. In addition to the works mentioned throughout this introduction, other key texts provide an excellent entry into cultural studies. Jean Franco's "Remapping Culture" charts the shift from literary to cultural studies, emphasizing interdisciplinary methodologies required in addressing the varieties of cultural production or in examining literary creations in a cultural context; her *Critical Passions* portrays a cultural studies analyst at work. Other examples of Latin American scholarship in a cultural studies mode include the compilation by George Yúdice, Jean Franco, and Juan Flores, *On Edge: The Crisis of Contemporary Latin American Culture*, and Marit Melhuus and Kristi Anne Stølen's *Machos, Mistresses, Madonnas*. The essays in the special issue *Cultural Studies and Hispanism* of *Siglo XX / 20th Century* and articles in the *Journal of Latin American Cultural Studies*, struggle with definitions of the field in the light of instances of cultural practice in Latin America. In the latter journal, since 1995, a fairly regular feature has been "Cultural Studies Questionnaire," in which leading scholars self-consciously address their practice of cultural studies: Julio Ortega, Michael Green, Néstor García Canclini, Peter Burke, Beatriz Sarlo, George Yúdice, William Rowe, Walter Mignolo, Neil Larsen, Gordon Brotherston, Luiz Costa Lima, and Jesús Martín-Barbero have offered their views. Other journals, such as *Studies in Latin American Popular Culture*, as well as important books—Ariel Dorfman's groundbreaking essays, David William Foster's study of graphic humor, and William Rowe and Vivian Schelling's *Memory and Modernity*—have demonstrated the vitality of popular cultures in Latin America and their significance in understanding the region. In addition, several journals have emphasized cultural studies scholarship, especially *Arizona Journal for Hispanic Literary and Cultural Studies, Chasqui, Nepantla, Revista de crítica cultural*, and *Revista de crítica literaria latinoamericana*.

Many Latin American scholars have long practiced the socially oriented research that today is associated with cultural studies; only recently have some of these case studies become available in English. Of particular interest are works by Roger Bartra, José Joaquín Brunner, Néstor García Canclini, Jesús Martín-Barbero, Carlos Monsiváis, Angel Rama, Nelly Richard, Beatriz Sarlo, Roberto Schwarz, and Silviano Santiago. Most recently, scholars based in the United States have used the methodologies of cultural studies and critiqued the discipline of Latin American or Hispanic studies as taught in the United States or as practiced in international dialogue. John Beverley's *Subalternity and Representation* and Mignolo's *The Darker Side of the Renaissance* and *Local Histories / Global Designs* add to the conceptual pairing of colonial studies and cultural studies.

PART ONE   *Situating Pedagogy*

Colonial Studies as Cultural Studies: Theoretical and Pedagogical Issues in Classroom Practice

Gustavo Verdesio

In the theory and practice of the humanities, cultural studies is so pervasive these days that we may sometimes forget how recent a phenomenon it is. To refresh our memories about its beginnings and development as an established trend in the academy, we can turn to a work by John Beverley, a longtime practitioner of Latin American cultural studies. In *Subalternity* he looks back at the objectives of the Birmingham school in its early days (104–07). The idea behind the Birmingham Center for Contemporary Cultural Studies was to develop a more or less organic relation between intellectuals and the working class, fundamentally in two ways: first, as an academic project of Marxist inspiration; second, as an academic enterprise in which cultural phenomena originating in the British working class—punk music, gay rights, and immigrant social organization, among others—could be studied. According to Beverley, for the promoters of the Birmingham project—who were sympathetic to the ideas about popular culture advanced by the old Popular Front—mass culture was a form of subaltern agency (106). Neil Larsen rounds out this picture by observing that cultural studies sees in mass culture an emancipatory dimension that other schools of thinking (for example, the Frankfurt school) did not see in it ("Cultural Studies Movement" 191). In this way, the British scholars behind the 1964 founding of the cultural studies center aligned themselves with the working class and attempted to create new ways of relating to it.

The accounts by Beverley and by Larsen provide a good description of cultural studies before its arrival in the United States. Disciplinary theories and practices do not usually remain intact, however, when they travel across boundaries, and cultural studies became something different in the American university. In the 1980s, according to Beverley, some Americans who had grown up in the leftist atmosphere of the 1960s adopted cultural studies—as a tool for implementing the progressive social programs of their youth—when they became teachers in higher education ("Estudios culturales" 48). The American version of cultural studies—understood as an endeavor, from within the academy, for the renovation of the left led by those professors who grew up in the 1960s—coincides chronologically and coexists with a neocapitalist project for the reformation and modernization of American higher education (*Subalternity* 108).

At this point, Beverley asks why, in the extremely conservative political climate of Ronald Reagan's two terms and George H. W. Bush's one term, cultural studies thrived and became, somehow, a dominant paradigm in the humanities ("Estudios culturales" 47). His tentative explanation is that the trustees and administrators of American universities thought that the proposal for changes in higher education put forth by practitioners of cultural studies was more viable than the one advocated by the neoconservatives, who sought a return to the pure, uncontaminated reading of the great books of the Western literary tradition (*Subalternity* 108). In a multicultural society it was evident that the problems stemming from diversity could be better addressed by the cultural studies agenda than by the neoconservative approach. In a similar vein, Idelber Avelar points out that traditional literary studies have little to offer those who are looking for cultural literacy—a key concept in understanding the transformations occurring in the United States humanities curriculum.[1] Cultural studies, instead, has been viewed as promising a more adequate cultural literacy (50).

The new university, developing and flourishing predominantly in the context of neoliberal economics and ideology, shows a cultural diversity among students never seen before in the United States. The United States university system, as Lawrence W. Levine persuasively argues, has always responded pragmatically to the challenges posed by the successive social changes in a country that is in a state of permanent renewal. It is only natural that the institution strove to accommodate the present demographic and social conjuncture (xix, 43, 52). The American university is not a homogeneous place—with regard to ethnic background, class, and gender—anymore (xvii).

For example, in 1994, the student body at the University of California, Berkeley, was composed of 32.4% white students, 39.4% Asians, 5.5% African Americans, and 1.1% Native Americans (xviii). In the new university, then, the notion of cultural literacy has shifted dramatically. That is, the definition of what is useful or necessary to learn does not coincide with that proposed by neoconservatives such as Allan Bloom or Harold Bloom. The curriculum they defend is based on the assumption that Western civilization is superior to all others—an idea that many members of a large, more diverse student body find difficult to swallow (Levine 20). In sum, it can be said that the most recent demographic changes in American society at large have prompted, in the province of higher education, some academic changes (100).

Levine celebrates these changes, yet the shifts that have been taking place in the humanities are not always, and not necessarily, progressive. On the contrary, at least some of the curricular modifications may be inspired not only by a commitment to multiculturalism but also, and perhaps more strongly, by conservative motives. For example, those changes applauded by Levine might have been promoted in part by a certain prejudice against the others—that is, students from nonwhite cultural backgrounds—on the part of university administrators. Their prejudice resulted in efforts to educate students in their own culture—as many Latin American politicians and intellectuals proposed to do with the Amerindian during the nineteenth and twentieth centuries—in the belief that they would have trouble dealing with the Western traditional curriculum. The question Beverley posed about the success of cultural studies during the Reagan era can also be answered by suggesting that, together with administrators' possible prejudice, pressure was exerted by the members of immigrant communities who had had access to a college education and now wanted to see their cultural heritages better represented in the curriculum. Added to those factors might be the one proposed by Avelar: the administrators' search for a cultural literacy that would give a business-oriented touch to humanistic studies and that could be measured against capitalist standards: How much has the curriculum contributed to the expansion or globalization of capitalism? What new markets, internal and external, has it helped to conquer? (50).

The Chilean critic Federico Galende, for his part, would disagree with these musings, because he offers a different answer to Beverley's question: he proposes that cultural studies succeeded because those who practice it today are not the same as they were in the 1960s. Their slogans have also changed:

they have come from demanding the impossible ("Demandez l'impossible!," a typical 1968 war cry) to adopting the less pretentious strategy of accepting, and adjusting to, reality. For Galende, Beverley (who represents here the cultural studies paradigm as a whole) has chosen to play the game with the rules imposed by the system; hence, it should not be surprising that hegemony welcomes the reformed youths from the 1960s (52, 55). Whether one agrees with Galende or not, it is possible to say that among the factors that could explain the rise of cultural studies in the American academic world, the most relevant ones are those indicated by Levine and Avelar: on the one hand, the demographic, ethnic, and cultural pressures on the curriculum; on the other, the instrumentalization of humanistic studies.

In the case of the teaching of Spanish, the instrumentalization translates into a utilitarian, sometimes vocationally oriented curriculum, in which courses like Spanish for Business and lower-division service courses, for completing language requirements, are good examples. A consequence of this trend in Spanish departments is a breakdown into categories that resemble an instructional caste system: on the one hand, tenure-track professors whose job is to produce serious research; on the other, legions of instructors (or lecturers or adjuncts, depending on the institution) who teach a large number of credit hours at the lower-division level (Avelar 55). Thanks to this situation, departments in research institutions often become places where numerous underpaid Spanish instructors teaching language and conversation courses—and, supposedly, the related culture(s)—coexist with a prestigious group of professors who conduct scholarly research, as if there were no need to teach Spanish at the beginning and intermediate levels. Thus most of us who both teach and do research in Spanish or Romance language departments pretend we live in an ideal institutional world; the pedagogical realities we face on a daily basis rarely inform our research. The result is investigation that distances itself more and more from the everyday conditions of its producer. Not surprisingly, the process generates a series of myths and misunderstandings that we, as a community, should avoid duplicating.

For example, consider the way in which academicians often talk, in sophisticated and sometimes obscure ways, about the theoretical problems that cultural studies poses for their traditional object of study. More often than not, the instructor either ignores or forgets prominent theoreticians' lucubrations on cultural analysis and, instead, settles for a more modest practice. In most classrooms, the work by writers such as Beverley, Larsen, and Galende are not discussed. Indeed, what goes on in the classroom has little relation to scholarly conceptualizing. This picture is, of course, a generalization, not an accurate depiction of what happens in every classroom in the United States. However, I believe it is closer to the academic and pedagogic reality than the lofty discursive production, detached from institutional conditions, I described above. In the typical Spanish classroom I am portraying, the professor or instructor may believe he or she is doing cultural studies just by showing a film or playing a compact disc from the target culture, to entertain students while teaching language skills or cultural literacy.[2] The hypothetical colleague is not alone in his or her beliefs but is among a legion of language and literature professors trying to recycle themselves, as well as to adapt to an academic world that expects them to play a utilitarian role by, as Avelar avers, contributing to the propagation of a cultural literacy that may facilitate the conquest of markets in a globalized world. Instructors who are forced to use audiovisual and cybernetic props in their classes must follow, also, the dictates of Spanish programs that mostly advocate what can be called a touristic approach—teaching the Spanish language in an entertaining way that, at the same time, promotes the target culture. In the process, several goals are fulfilled: first, to make the culture interesting to students taking the course as a requirement; second, to encourage them to continue their studies—because, as we know, numbers rule in the neoliberal university (the more majors we have, the better the funding for our departments); third, to offer some minimum knowledge of the target culture (is this the cultural literacy pursued by the neoliberal university?)—an exposure that involves, say, acquaintance with more stereotypical than typical dances and the most traditional meals, perhaps, in the Spanish-speaking world.

One of the reasons cultural studies has degenerated into, or merged with, the touristic approach may be related to the experience of colleagues whose academic training took place before the appearance of that paradigm. Their status as full professors makes them a major force in departmental hiring policies, but they have little understanding of what cultural studies is. As both a candidate for academic positions and a member of search committees, I have noticed that many of those senior colleagues—in spite of their main role in what Avelar (52) and Carlos Alonso (141) call the antitheory fortress of Hispanism in the United States—include, in the job descriptions they elaborate, a sentence like this: "Interest in cultural studies a plus."[3] Most of the time, however, they do not know exactly what they mean by this. Hence the paradoxical situation that can be observed in Spanish departments today: senior faculty members advocating, on the one hand, the most traditional forms of literary criticism and, on the other, expecting the candidates for departmental positions to be engaged in a pedagogical policy that depends on these same high-ranking colleagues' interpretation of cultural studies—when, in actuality, the professors see the paradigm as little more than addition of audiovisual enhancements to traditional classroom practice.

Whether or not my depiction is correct, we are witnessing a moment in which audiovisual culture has made a triumphal entrance into literature departments. For some critics, like Beatriz Sarlo, this development is detrimental to both society and the academy; audiovisual messages, she believes, lack the complexity and profundity of literary discourse. For this Argentinean critic, the most prudent attitude for literature professors is to abandon cultural studies, which, with its emphasis on the audiovisual, contributes to the trivialization of thinking; instead, she proposes to go back to the discussion of aesthetic issues ("Los estudios culturales" 35–36). For Beverley, however, the inclusion of audiovisual products in classroom instruction is a beneficial consequence of the advent of cultural studies; he believes that today it is not literature but mass culture that interpellates the majority of people, both in the United States and in Latin America. For him, the shift in teaching methods is a necessary correction to the left's agenda, especially the Latin American one, that has traditionally privileged literature as a model for cultural and pedagogical authority. He identifies the main accomplishment of progressive scholars: they have replaced literary idealism (which has contributed to the domination of subaltern subjects) with the study of United States–inspired mass culture. Beverley's emphasis is not so much on mass culture per se but on its possible applications in production and consumption. Mass products are not made by, or for, the dominant class, he asserts, and they retain a popular character. In systems of uneven development, the commodification of cultural production operated by the mass media can help democratize society (*Against Literature* 5, 6, 8, 12). A similar opinion is held by George Yúdice, who believes that the mass media have facilitated the social protagonism of new cultural agents ("Posmodernidad" 409).[4]

To disagree with Beverley's and Yúdice's optimism about the democratic potential of mass culture is not tantamount to saying that one endorses a conservative agenda such as the one proposed by Sarlo—who wants intellectuals to return to their role as keepers and transmitters of literary (and academic) heritage based on dominant aesthetic values (36).[5] The problem with her attitude is, as Beverley has pointed out, that such a literary tradition can only perpetuate the structures of domination that determine the subaltern position of most Latin Americans (*Against Literature* x; *Subalternity* 2).

It is important to caution, however, against overoptimism regarding the liberatory potential of cultural studies. A good example of optimism that seems to expect too much from a mere academic trend is Néstor García Canclini's assertion that cultural studies should be the privileged space for reflection on exchanges between the United States and Latin America ("Elaboración" 50)—an opinion that is perhaps as naive as the belief that the aesthetic messages produced by American mass media may play a democratizing role or may have facilitated new forms of cultural agency. As Roberto Schwarz has pointed out, the fact that the nation-state's ideological apparatuses (among them, literary tradition) have been responsible in part for the subalternization of vast sectors of Latin Americans does not exonerate the mass media: "the imposition of foreign ideology and the cultural expropriation of the people are realities which do not cease to exist just because there is mystification in the nationalist's theories about them" (qtd. in Larsen, "Brazilian Critical Theory" 209). Besides, if cultural studies limits itself to the analysis of the mass media, it runs the risk of leaving outside its research agenda some of those cultural and social manifestations that Nelly Richard calls "significant" (Introducción 12). They are what Ricardo Kaliman refers to when he reproaches cultural studies for paying attention to social practices that are "interesting" to the paradigm and not to those that matter to the community under study (262).[6] In this way, critics like Richard and Kaliman suggest that cultural studies broadens its agenda to encompass phenomena beyond mass media aesthetic artifacts. Yúdice seems to be close to this position when he says that literary critics should not limit their research to the study of phenomena traditionally considered cultural but should observe, also, what happens in the realm of civil society ("Estudios culturales" 52). In his opinion, cultural studies should attempt to open and expand civil society, as well as to mediate between it and the state ("Civil Society" 2) through the democratization of social institutions such as the university ("Estudios culturales" 52). However—despite increasing efforts to define the cultural studies research agenda to include nonaesthetic social practices—most of the works on cultural studies still focus on aesthetic phenomena produced, more often than not, by the mass media.

In this essay, I, too, advocate a broader conception of culture—a conception that considers as culture all the manifestations of human activity in a given community. Thus the notion of culture is much closer to its meaning in anthropology than to the one predominant in literary studies. For those of us who study colonial Latin America as well as the pre-Columbian civilizations that took part in the clash between two worlds, the interpretation of cultural analysis as a wide-ranging, multifaceted exploration should provide us with a better understanding of the human groups involved in the exchange that began in 1492. To achieve that kind of insight, we must employ an interdisciplinary approach that may shed more light on our complex object of study than traditional, literary approaches.

As I've suggested, Beverley's belief that global popular culture—understood as that produced or inspired by United States mass media—and postmodernism are more subversive than the Latin American local (pre-Columbian and prenational) and national cultures that preceded them is excessive. Although I do not favor an agenda that privileges the study of Latin American national cultures, I recognize the need to study indigenous cultures, especially of the pre-Columbian era, in order to trace the characteristics and practices that those cultures have maintained to this day and that, often, the indigenous peoples use as weapons for resistance. Despite this disagreement with Beverley's research agenda, I share some of his concerns, especially his view that cultural studies is not progressive per se (*Subalternity* 109) and that the category of the subaltern can help articulate cultural studies in a way that contradicts neoliberal globalization ("Estudios culturales" 50). Here he is proposing, I believe, a pedagogical and research project that has some similarities to the one I am describing.[7] I am not a member of the Latin American Subaltern Studies Group, but I share with the collective both its concern for the oppressed and its interest in the creation of a research agenda that leaves room for subaltern history to emerge. One of the differences between a subalternist agenda and one dedicated to the study of the colonial period is that the latter must delve into the past to locate the foundation of modern-day social injustice. Galende is right when he says that an understanding of the past emancipates the experience of the unjust present by relating it to an earlier, convulsive time. To recover the past, to reprove the present, is, then, a responsibility to the other, to that segment of humankind that suffers oppression in our time (55).

In the following pages, I explain, through a discussion of courses I have

taught and of the materials that I have used (Mesoamerican codices, archaeological and ethnohistorical scholarship on Amerindian ruins, "art," etc.), the
relevance of an interdisciplinary approach that conveys the complexity of the
colonial situation and the contemporary predicament of the marginalized
groups (the losers in the colonial clash). Without a study of certain cultural
artifacts—including monuments, codices, paintings, petroglyphs, dances, the
oral tradition, and other kinds of performance—our analysis of the cultural
clash will not do justice to the specificity of its non-Western elements. I focus
on a less monologic version of the struggle between cultures in Latin America,
in order to explore not only the colonial period but also its legacies in the
present.

Those of us who teach the colonial period in Spanish departments usually
offer a series of courses, both at the undergraduate and at the graduate levels,
that cover a list of sixteenth- and seventeenth-century canonical authors and
texts—for example, Columbus's *Diary* (Colón), Hernán Cortés's *Letters*, Alonso
de Ercilla's epic poem *La araucana*, and El Inca Garcilaso de la Vega's *Comentarios reales*. Only in the last few years has the canon started to admit some
authors—among them Felipe Guamán Poma de Ayala, who wrote and illustrated a manuscript around 1615, and Juan de Santa Cruz Pachacuti—whose
works show an indigenous perspective. These incorporations into the canon
are part of what Walter Mignolo ("La lengua, la letra") and Rolena Adorno
("Nuevas perspectivas") have described as the new paradigm in Latin American colonial studies. The paradigm is characterized not only by the acceptance
of more texts but also by a different attitude among scholars in the field, who
are more aware than their predecessors of the constraints imposed on them
by the Western perspective that has hitherto dominated writing about the
colonial era.

The consequences of this shift can be seen, then, both in the research
being conducted and in the classroom. Hence the inclusion, in some graduate
and undergraduate courses, of authors like Poma de Ayala and texts like *Visión
de los vencidos* (a compilation of Nahua sources about the conquest, edited by
Miguel León Portilla) on the reading lists. However, the ideological orientation
of some of those courses remains strongly anchored in a certain textualism,
despite the changes registered in the field—and despite the fact that one of
the recently canonized texts, Poma de Ayala's *Nueva corónica*, points to the
importance of semiotic systems other than writing, as Adorno's seminal study
of it shows (*Guamán Poma*). Mignolo's book *The Darker Side of the Renaissance*

and many of his articles also explore the possibilities of a research agenda incorporating the study of nontextual cultural objects such as maps, *amoxtllis*, and *quipus*. These advances in colonial studies research, however, do not always have an impact on the way specialists teach.

I, for one, believe we need to bring our classroom practice into harmony with our research agenda. If our explorations in colonial studies reflect the new mode of intellectual production, our classroom instruction should respond to those changes.[8] The courses I discuss here are taught from a perspective that includes the study of cultural objects that are not texts in the traditional sense; the purpose is to present students with an array of texts and objects intended to make them reflect not only on the Latin American past but also on their own experiences as members of a postcolonial society dominated by Western values. One of these courses, an upper-division offering, is The Inca and Other Andean Peoples (see app., syllabus 1). The course starts with *El señorío de los Incas*, by Pedro Cieza de León, a book that portrays Inca culture from a European perspective. In spite of the author's rigor and zeal, his gaze is conditioned, most of the time, by his Western outlook. Reading this work gives students the chance to familiarize themselves not so much with Inca culture as with the way in which it was perceived by the Spaniards. The second text we read is *Comentarios reales*, by Garcilaso de la Vega, whose perspective differs slightly from Cieza de León's. Although the picture of the Inca kingdom portrayed by Garcilaso, a mestizo born of an Inca mother (a princess) and a Spanish father (a captain), follows some European cognitive patterns, its author purports, all the time, to vindicate his condition as an insider. Besides, as José Antonio Mazzotti has suggested in his book about the author, the perspective offered by *Comentarios reales* is not totally European: it includes moments in which the strong presence of Andean elements make it work as a mestizo text.

In both books, one of the main topics is Inca religion. Cieza de León and Garcilaso have distinct views on the fundamental aspects of that religion— views inspired by the informants to whom they had access. After reading those two canonical texts, students face the challenge of reading one of the most subtle and intelligent studies on Andean religion: Sabine MacCormack's *Religion in the Andes*. The author makes an effort to differentiate between Inca religion proper and the religious beliefs professed by other Amerindians who populated the Andes. While chroniclers like Cieza de León and Garcilaso present Inca religion as a homogeneous corpus of beliefs and practices accepted by all, MacCormack characterizes that religion as imposed by the Inca on the Andean peoples they ruled. The contrast between these two representations of religion is understandable, because both Cieza de León and Garcilaso had access mostly to informants from Inca royalty who presented a limited picture of religious practices in the Andes. Distinguishing between official and non-official religions in the area dominated by the Inca allows students to be aware of cultural differences, not only those between indigenous and European but also those within Andean society itself. Given the fact that Western culture subalternizes Amerindians by various means—one of which is their homogenization into a single category (Indians)—MacCormack's book is useful in helping professors transmit a more complex notion of cultural diversity. In particular, the book reminds the reader of the regional origin of some of the religious practices that Cieza de León and Garcilaso attribute to a monolithic and uncontested Inca culture.

Thanks to MacCormack's detailed analysis of an eyewitness's testimony, students can picture the processions during the last celebration (already under Spanish rule) of the Inti Raimi, the most important religious festival hosted by the city of Cusco, the Inca capital. They also learn that Pachacamac was not the principal and most powerful of Inca gods, as Garcilaso would have it, but a divinity worshiped by the Yungas, a group from the coastal regions. This case study is an opportunity to explore the sophisticated negotiations between the Yungas and the Inca with regard to the incorporation of Pachacamac into the Inca pantheon in Cusco. Another case that gives students an in-depth view of Andean cultural and religious life is the Taqui Oncoy rebellion, a dance that took the form of an insurrection led by—according to the possessed dancers who were the promoters of the resistance movement—the ancient Andean *huacas*,[9] and not by the Sun, the main god of official Cusco religion. In other words, students can engage in discussions on a wide array of religious practices that were part of the symbolic universes of several cultures that continuously negotiated meaning and power with each other.

Perhaps the book's rich and varied discourse is possible because Mac-Cormack's effort is not a literary one and does not rely exclusively on texts but uses many sources of information, such as ethnohistory and, to a lesser degree, archaeology. The diversity of sources allows the author, for example, to analyze in detail the meaning of Cusco's sacred space. The city's layout, the Ceque system—four lines that started at the center of the city, throughout which a series of *huacas* were located—had a holy meaning that underlaid the urban structure where social life took place. After they read about the Ceque system, students can examine some of the principles that organized everyday life in the Inca capital and can speculate on the influence that such an urban center, and its structure, had in the provinces dominated by the Inca state. This activity should be supplemented by pictures and other audiovisual aids (such as film) depicting the imperial capital and the ruins of ancient buildings (among which Coricancha, the temple of the Sun, stands out).

One of the effects of introducing students to the type of research MacCormack pursued and to nontextual objects of study—architecture, urban layout, and religious celebrations, among others—in a course that is supposed to be on literature, may be to surprise them. In my experience, once the initial shock has passed, most students seem comfortable with the possibility that texts may be only partially reliable sources. In addition, students are exposed to a culture that was unknown to them before the beginning of the course and that escapes them every time they think they are getting closer to understanding it. Each source analyzed in class both amplifies and casts doubts on the other sources. This paradox represents, perhaps, the main objective of the course: to show students, through its dramatization, the difficult process of knowledge acquisition about the past in general and oppressed indigenous cultures in particular. What I try to do is to shake any feeling of certainty students may have developed about the dependability of sources of information and ideas; I endeavor to replace any expectation of reliability with the concept of learning as a tentative, uncertain, and constant process.

Although the Andean cultures examined take shape gradually in the minds of the students, the class never has the sense that they really know much about those societies. In fact, the only certainty remaining at the end of the semester is that we know little about ancient indigenous peoples. As a consequence, students become increasingly aware that the Western way of representing Amerindian peoples through the homogenization of differences (represented by the construct "Indians") is entirely inappropriate. And they know that those differences—Western culture's efforts to deny them notwithstanding—do exist.

Thus the next step is to have students read indigenous authors who tell the story of the origin of the Inca as well as of historical events from a non-Western perspective. The worldview of the indigenous other is the counterpart of the occidentalized version of Andean cultures produced by authors like Cieza de León and Garcilaso. The letter to the Spanish monarch by Titu Cusi Yupanqui, who continued the rebellion against the Spaniards initiated by his father, Manco Inca, is a complex artifact of the sixteenth century. To begin with, Titu Cusi uttered the contents of the letter in his native language; the contents were, in turn, translated by a Spanish priest who dictated them to a scribe who wrote them down. The incident offers an excellent opportunity both to make students aware of the differences between oral cultures and literate ones and to discuss the issue of communication across cultural boundaries. My experience in the classroom has shown me that students' understanding of the role of translation during colonial times benefits from the analysis of texts that, like Titu Cusi's, dramatize translation as a process—a process that is not usually taken into account in colonial texts of European origin. Many colonial authors seem oblivious of the difficulties posed by contact between different cultures. Rather, the narrators tell their stories about encounters with Amerindians as if communication between the parties developed smoothly and without problems. The consequence of such an approach is that many traits of the indigenous people referred to in colonial texts are lost. One of our duties as instructors should be to remind students of the insensitivity of those accounts vis-à-vis the idiosyncrasies of their others. The reading of indigenous narratives such as Titu Cusi's is an important element in developing a balanced perspective on the colonial encounter.

Another issue that this text enables us to discuss is the way in which different societies keep records of historical events. I usually ask questions about memory and cultural identity, about tradition and the ways to record and transmit it. Questions that encourage students to relate to them at a personal level are more likely to get an enthusiastic response and, therefore, to help students grasp the importance of the transmission of memory from generation to generation. When I ask about the stories their grandparents, or other older relatives and friends, may have told them about long-ago events, students can describe how the memories and traditions of the elders were transmitted to them and how the process may have differed from the types of communication that predominate in the United States today (including TV, print journalism, e-mail, and the Internet). The class can also discuss the local character of occidental conceptualizations of the past, despite the writers' claims to universality.

This text also provides students with another version of the conquest, one claiming that a sector of Inca nobility—led by Manco Inca—collaborated with the Spaniards. Titu Cusi manages to present the events that led to the victory of the Spaniards as a struggle between them and Manco Inca, on the one hand, and Atahualpa (the king the Spaniards encountered at their arrival) and his associates, on the other. This version downplays the role of Huascar, who lost the dynastic wars that took place after the death of the last legitimate Inca ruler, Huayna Capac, and before the arrival of the Spaniards. Both Garcilaso and Cieza de León, informed by members of the Inca nobility that belonged to Huascar's side, presented Atahualpa as a bastard and therefore as a usurper of the throne. The difference between those accounts and Titu Cusi's is that, in the latter's, a third candidate to the throne, Manco Inca, enters the stage. Once again, students are faced with the conflicts of interest among Andean factions, but this time it is not between the Inca and the other populations in the provinces of the empire but between and among members of the Inca royal family.

Next, we study Santa Cruz Pachacuti, an Indian of less noble descent who presents a view of Andean religion that, despite strong Christian influences, still has firm autochthonous roots. Unlike Titu Cusi's, this document is not a translation performed by a native Spanish speaker but an original composition written by Santa Cruz Pachacuti. Thus the class confronts a text that is both culturally and linguistically hybrid: the author did not have a good command of Spanish and includes long passages in Quechua. As students read the works of Titu Cusi and Santa Cruz Pachacuti, the challenge is to interpret documents that, in spite of the presence of Western elements, are mostly vehicles for an indigenous worldview.

The next reading is *Huarochirí*, by Karen Spalding, in which the author studies the evolution of the homonymous Andean province, from pre-Inca times to the eighteenth century. Through a serious analysis of archival material, the author reconstructs a narrative of an indigenous people's alternating attitudes of adaptation and resistance. Thanks to the wealth of documentation, readers are introduced to a cultural world that was very different from the Inca's but that was forced, at a certain moment, to be in contact with it. Aspects of the Huarochirí's social life, the Andean principles for the organization of the world, and the cultural exchanges in the successive periods covered by Spalding's work make students even more aware of cultural diversity among Amerindians. Likewise, the next book in the reading list, *Peru's Indian Peoples and the Challenge of Spanish Conquest*, by Steve Stern, which studies the

Huamanga region, is an evocation of local Andean histories under Inca and Spanish rule. These two case studies help instructors stress the point that ethnic and cultural diversity in the Andes was considerable; they also challenge the European (and Europeanized) chroniclers' views on those regions.

To complete our study of the diverse panorama of regions dominated by the Inca, we finish the course with *Provincial Inca*, a collection of articles edited by Michael Malpass. This volume combines knowledge obtained from archaeological investigations with the data found in the chronicles and documents available at different archives. The main goal of Malpass's project is to determine whether the documents provide a full and accurate account of social life under Inca rule or whether they omit (or add) information about the events and people they describe. Through a comparative study of document sources and recent archaeological investigations, scholars can test the explanatory potential of the two kinds of research. The studies compiled by Malpass target different regions, such as Huanuco Pampa, Huamachuco, and the north of modern-day Chile. Inca occupation of the territory was not the same in all locations. On the contrary, if something stands out in the articles, it is that the Inca state did not exert control in the same way everywhere. Moreover, some of the areas the chronicles describe as very important, from an administrative point of view, were not so, to judge from the results of the archaeological investigations, which focus, depending on the circumstances and the regions, on architectural remains, pottery, storage facilities, and Inca roads. The articles devoted to architectural patterns give us an idea of the number of buildings the Inca built in each occupied region; the figure is used as an index of the administrative importance the Cusco authorities assigned to the province. The number of storage facilities, in turn, permits us to estimate the economic importance of the place under study. In similar fashion, the location of the storage buildings in relation to the Inca roads that linked the provinces indicate the significance of the diverse sites to the central administration. Because apparently the Inca roads connected productive areas but not urban centers, we can conjecture which settlements were economically most important.

We also view a series of films, among them *The Incas*, that show some of the most important archaeological excavations and offer interviews with Andean specialists, such as John Murra. The abundant illustrations in Malpass's compilation help students visualize the structure of buildings, the itineraries covered by the roads, and the patterns and shapes of Inca and Andean pottery.

My students also benefit from a visit to the University of Michigan Anthropology Museum, whose holdings include pre-Columbian pottery from all of Latin America.

Reading Malpass's work enables the class to examine the ways in which the Inca controlled the various regions under their rule. In addition, by portraying society as a highly complex system, the book reminds students that to understand the way a given culture works, they need to pay attention to diverse areas of human activity, such as crafts (pottery), architecture, and engineering projects (roads).

By now, my lack of interest in a definition of cultural studies that characterizes that practice as the examination of American or American-inspired mass media products should be clear. If, instead, we envision cultural studies in the sense I proposed earlier—that is, as the study of culture as a whole—we can identify parallels between the paradigm and the theory and practice of colonial studies. For instance, we may understand other cultures, such as indigenous ones, as complex entities whose conceptions and social practices differ dramatically from ours but are not incomprehensible to us. Moreover, those others—who live geographically and culturally far from our Western imaginary—enter our classroom practice as we teach courses like the one I have described.[10] The colonial legacies that give shape to the present are generally ignored or played down by the educational system. In courses like this one, I both refresh students' memories and help the class discover a cultural and historical reality.

The other course that illustrates my idea of cultural studies is a graduate seminar entitled The Spaniards and the Mexica. I chose the first readings for the course for the same reasons that I selected Garcilaso and Cieza de León for the course on Andean peoples. We started with canonical texts such as *Cartas*, by Hernán Cortés, and the *Historia de la conquista de México*, by Franciso López de Gómara. After studying the cultural clash from the perspective of the winners, we turned to that of the vanquished represented by the compilation of Nahua testimonies about the conquest edited by Miguel León Portilla (*Visión*). Again, the idea is to compare the opposing views of the two societies in conflict, as a way of showing students that history can be told in different ways, depending on the interests and opinions of the narrators. The next text on the reading list is *The Aztecs: An Interpretation*, by Inga Clendinnen, who examines the values, conceptions, and social practices of the Mexica (or Nahua, as other authors prefer) before the arrival of the Spaniards to the Valley of Mexico. It is an interesting approach, because of the scarce sources she chose to work with: the data offered by Bernardino de Sahagún's informants in his voluminous compendium on Mexica culture and society. Although the project has serious limitations, including its thin documentary foundation and the mediated nature of the informants' testimony—produced on request and under the supervision of religious authorities, which conditions, partially, what could be told and what could not—Clendinnen's effort to immerse herself in a world so different from the Western one seems to have an impact on students. When they are confronted with the difficult task of following her lucubrations on religious practices, public and private rituals, the educational system, and the organization of society in its smallest units—the *calpulli*, according to Clendinnen, the *altepetl*, according to Lockhart, as we will see shortly—they embark on an intellectual enterprise in which they must put aside a familiar cultural literacy to observe, as if through new lenses, the other's culture in its idiosyncratic workings. The importance of this book does not lie, then, in the objectivity of its data, or in the certainty of the knowledge it presents, but rather in the experiment it proposes: to interpret human society across cultural boundaries.

Next, we study James Lockhart's *The Nahuas after the Conquest*, a book based on a quite dissimilar research project: the study of the long process through which Amerindians adapted to Spanish domination. The author's sources are the large number of documents preserved in various archives. Lockhart's idea is to obtain a broad picture, through the analysis of testaments and other legal documents, of the ways in which Nahua institutions (he prefers *Nahua*, because it is a less specific and more comprehensive term, to *Aztec*)—such as the *altepetl*—survived, or adapted to the new situation, during the colonial period. He also depicts, in one chapter, the way in which the Nahua domestic space, the household, evolved under Spanish rule. The abundant architectural plans included in the book allow students to examine the actual layout of Nahua houses and to visualize how the Nahuas conceptualized and inhabited domestic space.

Lockhart's intention is not, then, to recover Nahua culture as it was before the arrival of the conquistadors but to follow the evolution of the indigenous societies through the centuries. His thesis is that from the transformations occurring under Spanish rule, we can glimpse the culture as it existed in pre-Columbian times. In my opinion, however, the most important aspect of his investigation is that it offers a strategy for understanding these cultural alterations—a strategy that, if it is pursued to modern times, brings to light the process through which the Indians of present-day Mexico developed their cultural organization.

Beyond this ambitious research project, Lockhart's book offers instructors the chance to discuss with students such notions as cultural change, transculturation, and hybridity. Despite their problematic nature, these concepts are useful tools for the deconstruction of ideas about the Conquest that are still prevalent among nonspecialists—for example, that, after the Conquest, the entire indigenous population fell immediately under Spanish control and that, therefore, the Western way of life was imposed, without resistance, on the aborigines. Deconstructing such assumptions also helps educators challenge discourses that represent the Amerindians from the region—oftentimes referred to as the Aztecs—as a homogenous group. Finally, unlike Clendinnen's work, Lockhart's does not have that exoticist flavor, insofar as it does not seek to reconstruct Nahua culture at its peak—at its moment of splendorous glory—in a state of purity possible only before the Conquest. It attempts, instead, to study a less "interesting" period—from a Western perspective—of that culture: the centuries, following the fall of Tenochtitlán, that produced the masses of poor and oppressed Indians of the present—for whom few seem to feel the admiration they profess for the pre-Conquest Aztec kings. What Lockhart offers, then, are the tools for understanding contemporary Amerindians who, despite their lack of appeal among Western visitors who marvel at the temples and pyramids of yesteryear, are agents of social change and have the same rights as the *criollo*.[11]

Later in the course we read Barbara Mundy's *The Mapping of New Spain*. *The Relaciones geográficas de Indias,* referred to in the book's subtitle, consisted of a questionnaire accompanied by graphic representations, which the crown requested from the local authorities, of recently conquered lands. The questionnaires were easy to respond to, but the *pinturas*, or representations, posed some problems. The main one was that, because of their lack of knowledge about the lands they governed, the local Spanish administrators had to resort to the help of those who were most familiar with the land: Amerindians. The indigenous maps applied representational rules that differed significantly from the ones held by geographers in the metropolis. To Mundy, those *pinturas* are a useful tool for studying the Mesoamerican Indians' perspective. In those *pinturas* Mundy detects spatial conceptualizations that offer us an alternative form of territorial and, sometimes, historical representation. Confronted with hybrid objects that have a profoundly indigenous content, students must make an effort similar to the one required by Clendinnen's book: to put themselves in the shoes of people with a worldview quite different from theirs.

The last part of the course focuses on certain symbolic artifacts of Mesoamerican origin known as *codices*, a Western term for picto- and ideographic documents of differing genres. Before examining one of the artifacts—the *Codex Borgia*—students are asked to read several articles from *Writing without Words*, edited by Walter Mignolo and Elizabeth Hill Boone, which describes what the codices are and how they work. The contributors to the book—including art historians, literary scholars, and ethnohistorians—approach the codices from a diversity of viewpoints that, quite appropriately, reflects the wide variety of genres among codices. They might be juridical documents for the legitimation of dynastic power, "maps" for geographic delimitation, or texts used as calendars. Students also read articles from a special issue of the *Indiana Journal of Hispanic Literatures* devoted to Mesoamerican codices and stelae, or inscribed pillars. The final scholarly work they read is John Pohl's *The Politics of Symbolism in the Mixtec Codices* to get an idea of the political meaning the documents had for the cultures that created them. After consulting and discussing the background materials, students struggle to understand how the codex Borgia functions: they try to read it and decode it. Of course, nobody (including the professor) is able to decipher the document in its entirety, nor is that the purpose of its inclusion in the reading list. What I intend, instead, is to make students more sensitive to those objects that tell us, as Westerners, very little but were highly significant to the cultures that produced them. Objects that occidental marchands have traditionally treated as decorative items or works of art (the complex ownership history of each codex demonstrates this point) become, in the classroom, something completely different: cultural documents that bear witness, at least partially, to indigenous peoples' worldviews.

Another objective of the course is to put students in a difficult cognitive situation, one that forces them to grapple with a new, and completely different, symbolic system. As Sara Castro-Klarén states, "For those born and bred in the 'reading' conventions of the West, 'reading' a Mixtec 'text' represents a daunting challenge," for the process requires interpretive skills that go beyond learning the codes (142)—it entails a wide knowledge of the indigenous culture's outlook. In their efforts to decode an unfamiliar semiotic system, students experience the intellectual diversity of Mesoamerican Indians, the meanings they assigned to images, and their distinctive worldviews. Yet another reason for discussing this indigenous artifact is to offer students a glimpse of the ways in which the symbolic systems worked. The reading of a codex also exposes students to the scarce knowledge we have of indigenous notions of space and time. Discovering the significant differences between their conceptions and ours should help students reflect on the difficulties of communicating across cultural boundaries; it should also encourage them, before passing judgment on other societies, to bridge the cultural gap by examining our others in their own terms.

Finally, for those of us working in Spanish or Romance language departments, the courses I describe provide a chance to present alternative views on Latin American culture. By introducing the continent's indigenous peoples in a nonhomogenizing way that emphasizes their considerable variety, we can avoid transmitting stereotypes and resorting to generalizations. In other words, we can undertake instructional projects that are not dominated by a touristic conception of culture or by a notion of cultural literacy at the service of a neoliberal, global world order. To oppose a pedagogy that privileges the celebration of Mexican food (while forgetting that it is the result of complex historical and cultural processes) or the contemporary dances and music that the media have made fashionable through the glorification of pop icons such as Ricky Martin and Jennifer Lopez, I propose one that focuses, rather, on the diverse histories of the groups that have populated Latin America. I would offer students an in-depth examination of the cultural phenomena that are the outcome of the colonial cultural clash—the historical developments that produced not only tacos and salsa music but the economic and political oppression of present-day Amerindians. I would not try to peddle the delights of Hispanic culture through stereotypical representations of the tropics or Mexico but, instead, would seek to restore some complexity to the portrayal of Latin American culture. The first step should be to make clear to students that there is no such thing as "Latin American culture" but that there is, in actuality, a series of cultures that have tried, through the centuries, to dominate or to resist, to rule or to survive. We have plenty of information about the victorious society—the West—but know very little about the other cultures that took part in the colonial clash. Yet this grim gnoseological situation should not stop us from sharing that meager knowledge with our students: it is better to teach from a position that acknowledges our own ignorance than to contribute to the propagation of myths (such as the existence of "*a Latin American culture*") that serve the cause of those in power, or to comply with the instrumentalizing and touristic criterion that dominates United States university classrooms in the era of neoliberalism and globalization.

NOTES

1. Avelar sees, in departments of Spanish today, the predominance of a notion of cultural literacy that, albeit different, is just as conservative as E. D. Hirsch's. As we will see later, Avelar is referring to academic agendas advanced by teachers and administrators who are not as concerned as Hirsch is with the issue of what corpus of data should be shared by the citizens of a given culture; they are interested, instead, in providing American students with a cultural literacy—that is, a cultural knowledge—that would prepare them to conduct businesses successfully in the Spanish-speaking world.
2. Of course, this does not mean I am against showing films in class. On the contrary: I do so all the time. To show a film or listen to a CD in class does not, however, guarantee that a cultural studies agenda is being put into practice.
3. An earlier diagnosis of the lack of theoretical reflection in Latin American literary studies in the United States can be found in Moreiras, "Secret Agency."
4. As Beverley's and Yudice's arguments in favor of the emancipatory potential of mass culture suggest, Larsen is right when he says that in the American version of cultural studies, mass culture is not disregarded or disparaged but celebrated ("Cultural Studies Movement" 192).
5. For a critique of Sarlo's arguments, see Moreiras, "Order." Another critic who would return to aesthetic analysis, although for slightly different reasons, is Larsen. In "Aesthetics" he advocates that colonial studies scholars continue to explore literary texts; by not doing so, those scholars are "granting to 'Eurocentrism' the exclusive right to make aesthetic judgments." What he does not understand is that for the practitioners of what he calls (echoing Mignolo and Adorno) the new paradigm of colonial studies, aesthetics is a completely Western concept and, therefore, we should avoid privileging it above a colonial semiosis that includes conceptualizations produced by non-Western cultures. By studying the colonial other (Amerindians, Africans, etc.) outside the linear narrative of modernity and progress, Larsen says, colonial studies specialists are suggesting that progress is "a strictly European privilege" (105, 107). Larsen may have failed to realize that for those scholars he criticizes, progress is not a European privilege but rather a European artifact that deserves to be deconstructed. For a more thorough discussion of his argument, see Verdesio, "Reflexiones."
6. In Nelly Richard's opinion, included among those social practices ignored by metropolitan cultural studies are the critical and theoretical practices elaborated in Latin America ("Intersectando" 354).
7. Moreiras's definition of cultural studies as a project that should have a subalternist inflection positions him very close to Beverley's: "Latin American cultural studies is not only the systematic study of Latin American subaltern identities in the global context: it is also, and perhaps primarily, the study of the historical fissures through which the 'valores de la tradición crítica latinoamericana' disappear into material constraints" ("Storm Blowing" 81).
8. I have discussed elsewhere the expressions "paradigm shift" and "new paradigm," used by Mignolo and Adorno to refer to the changes occurring in Latin American

colonial studies. What we are witnessing is not, in my view, a paradigm shift but, as I express it here and in "Colonialism Now and Then," a new mode of intellectual production.

9. *Huaca* is a complex concept in the Andean world, but let us say, for brevity's sake, that it referred to sacred places where divinities were consulted as well as to the divinity itself.

10. At the end of the course, students were privileged to meet Sabine MacCormack, who generously accepted my invitation to come to class and answered questions about her book. Their intelligent questions, the attention they paid to Mac-Cormack's responses, and their familiarity with concepts and vocabulary to refer to Andean cultures were proof that we can help students become sensitive to multi-cultural issues and indigenous cultures.

11. A good example of the social agency I am referring to is the Chiapas rebellion of the 1990s.

The Politics of Representation: Reading Chicano/a Narratives as Cultural Ethnographies

Jesse Alemán

> Too much of the ethnographic work conducted among Mexican-Americans has been aimed at compiling data by the most direct means possible—that of asking people for facts. Every utterance seems to have been received as communicating the information asked for and is duly noted as such, without taking too much into account either the rhetorical and figurative uses of language or the structure of any given speech event, which may demand one response rather than another.
>
> —Américo Paredes, "On Ethnographic Work"

POSTMODERN PREDICAMENTS

Several years ago, when I was at the University of Kansas, I taught a lower-division Chicano/a literature course in the English department (see app., syllabus 2). Literature and nonliterature majors alike enrolled in the class, and even though the Midwest isn't exactly a haven for Chicano/a studies, out of a class of thirty, usually half were Mexican Americans; Anglo students often composed the other half. Both groups, however, took the course to learn about Chicano/a culture. Two earnest Anglo students, for instance, visited my office one semester to ask to be admitted into my already full class. The two students were social welfare majors, and their adviser figured that it was essential for budding social workers to learn something about Mexican Americans. Meanwhile, Mexican Americans, most of them first-generation college students, took the course for the same reason. The small Mexican and Mexican American population that emerged in Kansas around 1917 knew they had to overcome language barriers and the constant threat of being dismissed as "Mexicans," so assimilation was frequently a necessity for their social and economic survival. Three generations later, though, Mexican American students were attending Kansas's largest public university—a testimony to the success of becoming American. And as with the two social welfare majors, they were enrolling in my course to learn about Chicano/a culture.

Most of the students were unfamiliar with Chicano/a literature, except for the few who had read Rudolfo Anaya's ubiquitous *Bless Me, Ultima.* For Chicano/a students in particular, Anaya's novel had established a kind of cultural paradigm. The novel's representation of Mexican Americans somehow spoke to them, despite the vast differences between New Mexico and Kansas, and Antonio Mares's epic struggle between two worlds echoed their own experiences as the first members of their families to go to college. They wanted to read more novels like *Ultima,* they told me, because it taught them about being Chicano/a; they could relate to it, as the saying goes. Their contradictory reasons for taking the course—wanting to learn about Chicano/a culture while simultaneously feeling a kinship with its literature—rested on the assumption that Chicano/a literature accurately represents a recognizable and transcendent notion of Chicano/a culture, a strategic assumption that positions individual identity within a collective one and legitimates both. Imagine their surprise, then, when they discovered that my course examined how Chicano/a literature challenges ready-made narratives of individual and collective ethnic identity and culture. We found ourselves in the postmodern predicament of cultural representation.

Most teachers of Chicano/a or United States Latino/a literature have run into this dilemma. After all, we use literature to elucidate culture, and students often take ethnic literature courses, in particular, to learn about their own cultural heritage or about the social customs of other groups. This is the blessing of multiculturalism and the bane of postmodernity. From English to ethnic studies courses, students and teachers alike often expect a type of ethnographic objectivity from minority literatures, but as Américo Paredes observed of the ethnographies performed on Mexican American communities (see epigraph), we cannot simply open up Chicano/a texts, glean them for cultural facts, generalize those facts, and then walk away with an understanding of Mexican Americans; we cannot view Chicano/a literature as ethnographic fact, with little consideration for the way cultural narratives are themselves figurative moments that invent as much as they represent culture.

What we might refer to as the paradox of ethnic literature has a parallel in what James Clifford calls the "predicament of ethnography" ("Partial Truths" 2). For years, traditional ethnography posed as an objective discipline that represented the cultural practices of others; in the process, it legitimated dominant discourses on race, class, gender, and nation by objectifying the others under the ethnographic eye. According to Edward Said, traditional Western ethnographers reproduced the modes of colonial domination by depicting themselves as the active agents over passive human subjects (*Orientalism*). "Said underscored the links between power and knowledge," Renato Rosaldo explains, "between imperialism and orientalism, by showing how seemingly neutral, or innocent, forms of social description both reinforced and produced ideologies that justified the imperialist project" (*Culture* 42). Armed with poststructuralism, cultural anthropologists are working to dislodge the myth of objectivity and focus instead on the politics and practices that inform contemporary ethnographic writing. "Ethnographic fictions," Clifford writes, offer a narrative form that discloses only "partial truths" about culture (6–7). They are structured narratives that rely on tropes and allegories, include some voices and exclude others, and fashion culture through rhetoric. In other words, as a literary endeavor, new ethnography collapses the distinction between representation and invention, undermining the ethnographer's claim to objectivity and encouraging self-referential cultural critique.

The process of "defamiliarization," for instance, disrupts the usual authority of ethnographic discourse, George E. Marcus and M. J. Fischer contend, by using the culture on the margins to confront the center of ethnographic production. By estranging the familiar, ethnography functions as a self-conscious mode of cultural criticism that invokes and then revokes its own representational authority. As Marcus and Fischer explain, "The challenge of serious cultural criticism is to bring the insights gained on the periphery back to the center to raise havoc with our settled ways of thinking and conceptualizing" (138). We might make similar assumptions about ethnic fiction—the novels we read should serve as counterethnographies that right the wrongs of cultural misrepresentation by using imaginative forms and techniques to resist dominant American culture and offer insight into ethnic identity. By dint of minority authorship, minority literature works as a corrective to ethnic stereotypes. As Alvina E. Quintana puts it, "Because a desire for authenticity motivates the writers of both ethnographic and Chicana creative-writing projects, they share the narrative problems that arise with attempts to 'accurately' portray culture" (75).

If anything, the dialogue between center and periphery calls both into question, since the two participate in each other's cultural constructions. Indeed, the predicament ethnography and Chicano/a literature share is not the problem of accurate representation, as Quintana has it, but their "desire for authenticity," the assumption that there can be a truthful depiction of Chicano/a culture in the first place. In my Chicano/a literature course, I wanted to explore the trouble with using fiction to identify cultural authenticity. The class would read Chicano/a narratives as ethnographic texts that represent culture but also perform a critique of Chicano/a essentialism. That is, Chicano/a literature undermines its ethnographic function by foregrounding culture as a performance, a strategic positioning rather than a birthright. Reading Chicano/a literature with a critical eye, we challenged essentialist notions of individual and collective Chicano/a identity and began to see Chicano/a culture as a useful historical invention. The readings also prepared students to perform their own ethnographies of Chicano/a culture, as a way of understanding the contradictions that shape the development of Chicano/a identity in literature and in life. The goal of the course, then, was to analyze the notion of cultural representation as a construct that confounds itself and to create our own modes of ethnographic writing so that we might arrive at the "partial truths" of Chicano/a culture.

CHICANO/A NARRATIVES AS ETHNOGRAPHIES

While the works of cultural anthropologists such as Clifford, Marcus, and Fischer structured the goals of my literature course, we turned to early Chicano analyses of the social sciences for an introduction to the predicament of Chicano/a culture. Two essays by Nick C. Vaca set the stage by offering an overview of the way social scientists portrayed Mexican Americans from 1912 to 1970. Vaca's two-part study suggests that the ethnography he surveyed was not, in fact, an impartial description of Mexican Americans but a reaffirmation of prevailing, often racist notions of them. Students were especially receptive to Vaca's articles because their copious quotations reveal how Anglo anthropologists relied on theories of biological and cultural determination to explain the presumably low intelligence and poor educational performance of Mexican Americans. As Vaca notes, the emphasis on biology and culture allowed anthropologists to view Mexican Americans as inherently inferior and to ignore obvious factors, such as class status and language barriers, that determine any group's social and educational achievement ("1936–1970" 25).

Paredes's "On Ethnographic Work" continues Vaca's critique of Anglo anthropologists of Chicano/a culture. For Paredes, the social scientists simply misinterpreted Mexican American cultural practices along the Texas-Mexico border. Language, of course, contributed to the misreadings, but even anthropologists fluent in Spanish misunderstood ethnographic moments, especially those involving jokes, storytelling, and subtle linguistic play, sometimes at the ethnographer's expense. Students often delighted in Paredes's examples of informants pulling the ethnographer's leg, responding to intrusive questions with figurative answers and making the ethnographer the butt of a joke he doesn't get. The ironic responses, Paredes notes, are recorded as investigative evidence rather than as Chicano/a cultural play. Paredes offers in effect a useful lesson in reading Chicano/a culture. As interpreted literally by anthropologists, Chicano/a culture seems to reinforce preconceptions about Mexican Americans. Paredes insists, however, that Chicano/a discursive practices, especially folklore and jokes, must be read with a keen understanding of metaphoric language, rhetorical context, and the power relations that undergird Anglo and Mexican American interaction.

In KarenMary Davalos's words, "Chicano/a scholars anticipated a new anthropology and the problems of an apolitical postmodernism by encouraging a decolonized social science" (14). Indeed, Vaca's critique of anthropology precedes the works of Clifford, Marcus, and Fischer by more than a decade, while Paredes's 1977 article echoes the decolonial rhetoric of the Chicano movement. "It was one thing to publish ethnographies about Trobrianders or Kwakiutls half a century ago," Paredes writes, but "it is another to study people who read what you write and are more than willing to talk back" (2). The Chicano movement and the revisionary moment of cultural anthropology thus contextualize Paredes's and Vaca's essays to establish Chicano/a studies as a mode of ethnographic analysis. But the essays offer us an ethnographic moment of their own, a glimpse into the rhetorical and political stances of the Chicano movement. Vaca's seemingly objective, academic analysis of the social sciences, for instance, concludes by calling for a more materialist understanding of Chicano/a culture to account for class status, bilingualism, and racism, and Paredes's study assumes that Chicanos/as in the know, namely Texas Mexicans, share his insider knowledge of border culture. As one student noticed, if we miss Paredes's irony, we're just as bad off as the ill-fated Anglo anthropologists doing fieldwork in Texas.

The essays that began the course demonstrate the ethnographic predicament of Chicano/a cultural studies. "Even the best ethnographies," Clifford explains, "are systems, or economies, of truth. Power and history work through them, in ways their authors cannot fully control" ("Partial Truths" 7). Chicano/a ethnographies are no different. They may function as "oppositional" narratives, as Angie Chabram contends ("Chicana/o Studies" 230), but they are nonetheless vulnerable to the exclusionary politics of ethnographic writing. While the ethnographic impulse of Chicano-movement nationalism fosters a critique of Anglo society, the movement also reinvents Chicano culture along party lines, without paying much attention to the movement's call for a self-reflective examination of identity politics. "At stake in these gestures of inclusion and exclusion," David E. Johnson and Scott Michaelsen observe, "is a policing of the border of culture and of the borderlands in general as the location of Chicano culture, a certain legislation that governs access to culture and cultural identification" (21). What the class often found most exciting about these essays, then, was not that they exposed Anglo ethnography as students had, in fact, expected they would. Rather, students were intrigued by the counterconstruction of Chicano identity the essays developed. One student observed that Vaca idealizes George I. Sánchez, turning the early Mexican American ethnographer into an underdog who champions the cause of correct representation amid a flood of racist Anglo anthropologists. Other students noticed how Paredes positions himself at the center of Texas Mexican border culture without losing his credibility as an academic anthropologist (he becomes an "organic intellectual"). Vaca's and Paredes's essays thus taught students to distrust dominant ethnographies' descriptions of and conclusions about Mexican Americans. From reading the essays, however, students also understood that Chicano/a cultural production, like ethnography in general, relies on discernible narrative strategies that create cultural identity as manifested by, and resulting from, such factors as language, class, gender, and opposition to Anglo America.

Indeed, reading ethnography as literature allowed us to distinguish between the representation of Chicano/a culture and its invention, an idea we traced by comparing two other works by Paredes. Before the publication of *With His Pistol in His Hand*, often viewed as the foundational text of Chicano studies, Paredes wrote *George Washington Gómez*, a novel that did not appear until 1990. A traditional bildungsroman, it fictionalizes the border conflicts that concern Paredes in the 1958 work, but it offers a different vision of the border hero. While the figure of Gregorio Cortez fighting off Texas Ranger injustice with pistol in hand marks a heroic moment of Chicano resistance, *Gómez* has only antiheroes, characters that stand in sardonic contrast to those in *Pistol*'s idealized border community. In both texts, however, Paredes uses irony to critique Anglo America as well as the politics of ethnic essentialism. Reading the two texts allowed us to examine how Chicano/a ethnographic narratives construct and then confound their own representations cultural identity.

Since some undergraduates aren't attuned to the nuances of tone, we began by considering how one scene in particular in *Gómez* uses satire to undercut the "objective" claims of traditional ethnography. Enter K. Hank Harvey, the New York–born "foremost authorit[y] on Mexicans of Texas," who delivers the key address at the graduation of Guálinto Gómez, the novel's protagonist (270). Hired to give the graduates and audience an inspirational speech, he tells the crowd of (mostly) Mexicans and Anglos, "May [the graduates] never forget the names of Sam Houston, James Bowie, and Davey [sic] Crockett. May they remember the Alamo wherever they go" (274). As with many real ethnographers of the Southwest, Paredes's fictional one is an outsider looking in through myopic lenses. Nevertheless, Paredes wryly explains:

> men like him were badly in demand in Texas. They were needed to point out the local color, and in the process make the general public see that starving Mexicans were not an ugly, pitiful sight but something very picturesque and quaint, something tourists from the North would pay money to come and see. (271)

The scene positions Harvey as an expert in Mexican Texan culture, but it undercuts his authority by exposing the ethnographic assumptions behind his speech, assumptions familiar to the class through Vaca's and Paredes's essays. The scene, in fact, illustrates Paredes's irony. Harvey turns out to be an academic anthropologist who packages southwestern culture for mainstream consumption but knows little about the lives he studies. As I ask the class, Does the narrative take Harvey seriously? Generally, students notice that the narrative both mocks Harvey and the anthropological institution he embodies. After all, he resembles Santa Claus with a "slightly vacant face." More pointedly, Harvey gleans his knowledge of Mexican Texan history and folklore from books but avoids works written in Spanish because he doesn't know the language; his groundbreaking research concluded that Mexicans at the Battle of San Jacinto exclaimed, " 'Me no Alamo! Me no Goliad!' before receiving the quietus"; and, as the scene opens, Harvey returns from Mexico disillusioned that Mexicans don't speak English (271–72). Nevertheless, as students often note, Harvey receives an honorary degree and teaching position at a university.

Echoing Marcus and Fischer's belief that "the most effective form of cultural criticism offered by anthropology has been essentially satirical" (140), the narrative's ironic discourse questions the politics of ethnographic assumptions and sheds light on the politics of ethnography in general. Satire and irony, however, cut both ways, and for Paredes, it's not enough simply to criticize Anglo America. His sense of irony extends to the border community as well. "Raised to be the leader of his people," Guálinto, as the young George Washington Gómez is called, struggles between two identities, Anglo and Mexican; eventually he decides to leave the borderlands, marry the daughter of a Texas Ranger, and assimilate. His identity is nothing short of a living contradiction: "Hating the gringo one moment with an unreasoning hatred, admiring his literature, his music, his material goods the next. Loving the Mexican with a blind fierceness, then almost despising him for his slow progress in the world" (150).

In common Chicano/a terms, George is a cultural sellout, a "*vendido sonavabiche*" as another character, Elodia, calls him (294). But irony, as Fischer notes in "Ethnicity," "is a self-conscious mode of understanding and of writing, which reflects and models the recognition that all conceptualizations are limited, that what is socially maintained as truth is often politically motivated" (224). It is thus significant that Elodia has opened a Mexican restaurant for Anglo tourists and is "just raking the money in." Like K. Hank Harvey, Elodia commodifies Mexican culture for Anglo consumption, and the "tourists just love it" (287). George's uncle Feliciano, a border seditionist who fought against Anglo encroachment, also sells out his people. He serves gringo soldiers in a local cantina, rounds up the Mexican vote for an Anglo judge, and gradually ascends to middle-class status as he becomes a landlord and business owner, with the help of money he earns smuggling cattle into the United States. "From cowhand to seditionist and raider," Feliciano reflects, "from there to bartender for Gringo soldiers he had been shooting at a few months earlier. Soon after, a ward heeler whose job was to herd his own people into voting booths for the benefit of Gringo political bosses. And now, party to a smuggling operation. Nothing to be proud of" (82). Even George's "people" sell out. After all, George's parents name him after George Washington so he can grow up "to be a great man among the Gringos," as his mother puts it (16). And when he becomes one, they call him a *"vendido sonavabiche."* In short, no one in the novel becomes a "leader of his people." Instead, the narrative offers a double-voiced critique, one directed at Guálinto's assimilationism and the other at the border community that initiates Guálinto's assimilation and then rejects him for it. Guálinto's contradictory position certainly prefigures Gloria Anzaldúa's relation to her border community: "Not me sold out my people but they me" (43).

As I observed earlier, irony enables Paredes to challenge stereotypical representations of Mexican Americans but also to undermine essentialist readings of Chicano/a cultural and collective identity. Somewhere between essentialism and nonessentialism lies the "partial truth" of Chicano/a border ethnography. Perhaps this notion is best revealed in the naming scene of the novel's eponymous character. Because his family wants the boy to be "a great man who will help his people," they go through a series of possible names for him. His father, a light-skinned idealist from central Mexico, suggests "Crisóforo," which the boy's uncle, Feliciano, soundly rejects. The boy's grandmother, a traditional religious woman, proposes "José Angel," a name Feliciano says will "ruin [the boy] for life." He offers instead "Venustiano," after the Mexican revolutionary politician, Carranza, and draws the grandmother's conservative ire; he then suggests "Cleto," short for Anacleto de la Peña, a border seditionist like Feliciano. Finally, the parents settle on "George Washington," but the grandmother's attempt to say "Washington" leads to the name that actually sticks, "Guálinto" (15–17).

The boy's naming points to the multiple historical and cultural values of the border community, which range from traditional to modern, religious to secular, assimilationist to revolutionary, English to Spanish, American to Mexican. Indeed, in Paredes's narrative, no essential Mexican Texan collective identity exists but a series of culturally constructed categories that define and redefine individual self-perception, in a postmodern process of simulacra layered upon simulacra. Or, as Paredes writes: "It would be several years before he fully realized that there was not one single Guálinto Gómez. That in fact there were many Guálinto Gómezes, each of them the double like the images reflected on two glass surfaces of a show window" (146). Guálinto's identity is merely a reflection's reflection, a commodified self-image refracted in a showroom window but lacking cultural authenticity. As Clifford puts it, "If 'culture' is not an object to be described, neither is it a unified corpus of symbols and meanings that can be definitively interpreted. Culture is contested, temporal, and emergent" ("Partial Truths" 19). And so is ethnocultural identity, Paredes insists in his novel. Guálinto isn't a representative of the Mexican Texan community, but he is symbolic of the cultural contradictions that embody the emergence of Chicano/a culture from the border zone.

Paredes's 1958 ethnography, *With His Pistol in His Hand*, is no different. As most students quickly realize, this work debunks myths of Anglo Texan valor, manhood, and bravery through an ironic tone that glibly pokes fun at the fictions of white racial superiority promulgated by Texas popular and academic culture. Then, as a counterconstruction, Paredes uses Mexican Texan border folklore, the *corrido* in particular, to offer a version of Gregorio Cortez's life and times that situates him and the *corrido* as individual and collective modes of resistance to Anglo culture. In the process, Paredes shifts from an ironic tone to an academic one, relying on newspaper reports, legal documents, oral narratives, and border ballads to present "the facts of the life of Cortez" (108). Even when Paredes recounts the legends of Cortez, the "facts" still remain: his heroic stance symbolizes the Mexican Texan collective resistance to Anglo domination at the turn of the century. In shifting from an ironic to a realist mode of ethnography, Paredes deflates Anglo stereotypes of border culture and offers an alternative portrayal of border life as an authentic representation based on fact and firsthand knowledge. The counterethnographic mode of *Pistol* explains why it has become a foundational text in Chicano studies. It establishes a paradigm of individual and collective resistance well suited to the class, race, gender, and nationalist orientations of the Chicano movement. Moreover, Paredes's analysis of folklore creates a point of origin for Chicano/a literary history as a subaltern form of cultural production. As Raymund Paredes has it, for instance, Chicano literature evolves from the folk base of the *corrido*, and authentic Chicano identity mirrors the masculine image of the working-class *corrido* hero, who, pistol in hand, stands up for the rights of the Chicano community.

But the idealized version of Chicano resistance overlooks how Américo Paredes's irony performs a double cultural critique, as it does in *George Washington Gómez*. In *Pistol*, Paredes targets both Anglo America and the historical changes Mexican Americans experienced in mid-century:

> Brownsville's World War II hero was a border Mexican. Armed with the modern equivalent of the Ranger's Colt, a machine gun, he displayed such Spanish-Indian cruelty toward the German army that he was awarded the Congressional Medal of Honor. And all good Texans in Brownsville received him on his homecoming with festivities and parades. His deeds were not celebrated in *corridos*; legends were not made about him. For he was not the hero of the Border folk but of the American people.   (107)

Unlike Gregorio Cortez, who fought against Anglo Americans, later Mexican Americans fight alongside them against a common enemy, marking the end of border folklore (no *corridos* celebrate the war hero, according to Paredes) and heralding the assimilation of Mexican Americans into mainstream culture. Paredes clearly understands the capacity of ethnography to observe the shifting cultural practices of Mexican Americans, but, instead, his analysis develops an alternative narrative, one that levels a critique of Mexican America for its fall from *corrido* grace. "That was a good singing, and a good song," Paredes writes, as a character imagines the ideal setting to hear *El corrido de Gregorio Cortez*, "Not like these pachucos nowadays, mumbling damn-foolishness into a microphone; it is not done that way. Men should sing with their heads thrown back, with their mouths wide open and their eyes shut" (34).

As José Limón notes, Paredes's ethnography works through a contradictory process that, while holding Anglo America accountable, challenges emergent forms of Chicano/a border identity (85–94). Considered to be proto-Chicano symbols of resistance, for instance, the *pachucos*, as depicted in *Pistol*, vulgarize folk culture rather than respect its traditional performative element. And the *pachucos* are not the only figures who live in "a different world" from Cortez—one of his sons confronts the Germans and the other is in the air unit that bombs Japan (105). The distinctions Paredes creates between Cortez's experiences and the experiences of other Mexican Americans confound the notion of a collective Chicano identity and question whether Chicano cultural expression works as a unified mode of resistance. Indeed, World War II brings an end to the legacy of Cortez's heroic stance and marks a moment when "greater numbers of north-bank Borderers began to think of themselves seriously as Americans" (106). Granted, nostalgia certainly informs Paredes's reconstruction of Cortez's life and times, but it's an ethnographic nostalgia that, by implication, regrets the loss, to later generations, of a commitment to something deeper than acceptance by the mainstream. The book may be about collective resistance in the past, but only because it senses collective assimilation in the present.

Once students discovered the double logic of Paredes's irony, they began to see fissures in his master narrative of Gregorio Cortez as an authentic Chicano hero standing up for the rights of the Chicano community. For instance, while Cortez's flight from the Texas Rangers works as a commentary on the injustice of lynch-mob violence, it also highlights Cortez's individualism, as he leaves his family and community to suffer the mob violence he flees: "Gregorio Cortez, your own people are suffering, and all because of you," one Mexican tells him (48). It often surprised students, moreover, that Cortez is most vulnerable to capture when he enters counties with Texas Mexicans as authorities:

> In Karnes and Gonzales counties his movements often had been an open secret among the Mexicans, but a secret they did not share with officers. . . . On the Border, however, the law was at least partly Mexican, and though sympathy was predominantly with the fugitive the formerly closed circle now had its breaks. When Cortez arrived at the sheep camp, his almost exact whereabouts were known to authorities in Larerdo, and they were riding to intercept him.   (78)

While Texas Mexican sheriffs and marshals begin heading the search for Cortez, a border Mexican finally leads Texas Rangers to him. Legend has it that Cortez gave himself up, but Paredes insists that one Jesús González, who knew Cortez well, cashed in on their friendship and betrayed the fugitive (79). So much for collective resistance along the border: Texas Mexicans sell out Cortez in a cultural contradiction that ethnographically represents the border as a site of competing and contested cultural identities.

We might even call the situation a war of position, in which multiple identities flood the ethnographic scene with so many notions of authenticity that the concept itself becomes merely one of various strategic positions the ethnographer assumes. In fact, Norma Cantú's *Canícula*, another border narrative, stresses the performativity of Chicano/a cultural identity by blending genres in her "fictional autobioethnography." Subtitled *Snapshots of a Girlhood en la Frontera, Canícula* emphasizes linguistic, cultural, and literary hybridity, the fusion of two or more identities that engage in a dialogic process of self-critique. The narrative invents culture rather than represents it, correcting the misrepresentation of Mexican Americans in mainstream ethnography while challenging the reader's desire to interpret the border community as an essentialized cultural entity. Along with combining English and Spanish, fact and fiction, self and community, Cantú's book includes photos that compete with and often question the narrative's authority to provide an ethnographic account of life in the borderlands. As Cantú explains, "The story emerges from photographs. . . . ; the stories mirror how we live life in our memories, with our past and our present juxtaposed and bleeding, seeping back and forth, one to the other in a recursive dance" (xi–xii).

For instance, in the section "Mexican Citizen," the narrator recounts her trips to Mexico, where she feels out of place. Her cousins call her "pocha" (a pejorative term for Mexican American), she misses North American television shows, and she doesn't know the games her cousins play; when asked to show off her English, she recites the Pledge of Allegiance and sings "Humpty Dumpty," "Jack and Jill," and "Little Miss Muffet" nursery rhymes (22–23). Two official documents accompany the narrative, as if to confirm the narrator's dual citizenship status. Yet a closer look at the documents shows they've been altered. The first document, her United States immigration papers, conceals the full name of *el portador,* or carrier of the document, listing only "Ramon," and the signature underneath the photo likewise conceals the carrier's name. Instead, the adult narrator's signature appears but is obviously pasted on, since she is only a year old when the document is issued. The second document, her Mexican citizenship, is also fabricated. We see again a signature pasted over a different one, and the age listed on the document, sixteen, doesn't correspond to the narrator's claim that she was a "twelve-year-old" when the photo was taken (21).

The photos suggest the process of erasure, with the traces of ethnography lingering in the background. They are real photos that have been fabricated for the sake of autobioethnographic fiction. As the narrator puts it, "I must learn to keep secrets," and the secrets she keeps allow for only the "partial truth" of ethnography to emerge from the difference between narrative and photo (23). Cultures may not "hold still for their portraits," Clifford says

("Partial Truths" 10), but because Cantú's portraits do not hold still either, her text questions not only ethnographic authority but also the validity of photographic representation. Cantú sees both as partial modes of identity construction. No wonder the narrator invokes Roland Barthes in the prologue. For Barthes, photos and texts work on the two "cooperative" but "heterogeneous" structures of denotation and connotation; as a result, it is impossible for a text to duplicate the image of a photo ("Message" 194–205). Rather, meaning emerges from the free play between the two structures, both of which are deeply historical. Thus, as Barthes explains, "the reading of the photograph . . . depends on the reader's 'knowledge' just as though it were a matter of a real language [langue], intelligible only if one has learned the signs" (207).

Herein lies the ethnographic component of *Canícula* and its self-critique of representational authority. The book includes photos of collective Chicano/a border identity—family pictures, birth records, passports, and snapshots of community members—that seem to indicate an essential Chicano/a cultural history and identity. But the photos invoke an essentialism only to revoke it, by exposing the fictional quality of photographic representation. As with all photos, the ones in *Canícula* are staged cultural moments. "The photograph," Barthes explains, "allows the photographer to conceal elusively the preparation to which he subjects the scene to be recorded" (200). From the start, however, Cantú's text exposes the scene of ethnic identity as a fabrication: it is a scene that must conceal its own invention to invoke the authority of essentialized cultural ethnography. The give-and-take between the photos and the narrative only compounds the epistemological critique Cantú generates, for while the photos offer one ostensibly authentic narrative of identity, the text offers another, competing ethnographic narrative that challenges the authority of photography. Indeed, as Barthes concludes, it is "literally impossible" to describe photos, because de-scribing (un-writing) means "to change structures, to signify something different from what is shown" (198). Photos and text thus engage in a double self-critique of essentialized representation that often leaves students wondering about the authenticity not only of narrative but of photography as well.

IN THE FIELDS OF CHICANO/A CULTURE

There are, of course, other contemporary Chicano/a narratives to consider ethnographically, including Fabiola Cabeza de Baca's *We Fed Them Cactus*,

Mary Helen Ponce's *Hoyt Street*, and Rudolfo Anaya's mystery novel, *Zia Summer*. All three narratives present quasi-ethnographic accounts of Chicano/a culture. While a contradictory, imperialist nostalgia informs *Cactus*, for instance, Ponce's *Hoyt Street* reconstructs her Pacoima barrio into a quaint Spanish Harlem during the 1940s zoot-suit era. And *Zia Summer* offers a wonderful example of the way mass marketing and a popular genre force Anaya to act as a cultural translator who must essentialize Chicano/a identity to make it readable for a mainstream audience. But the goal of the course wasn't simply to deconstruct Chicano/a cultural narratives. Indeed, I was almost ashamed to emphasize the postmodern problematics of subjectivity at a moment when most Chicano/a students need a cultural and collective identity. José David Saldívar explains the predicament, "It may not be a coincidence that mainstream critics are talking about the end of the subject just when those people who have been cut off from power become aware of their potential role—as subjects—within the historical moment" (qtd. in Chabram, "Conceptualizing" 133). Yet I wanted to entertain the notion that our very location in Kansas, and the histories of Mexican Americans in the Midwest, de-scribed (that is, un-wrote) the narrative of Chicano/a culture. After all, if Chicano/a literature confounds its own constructions of authentic cultural identity, certainly Mexican Americans living in Kansas challenge the usual geopolitical sites— Texas, New Mexico, and California—of Chicano/a cultural production. So we performed our own ethnographic projects.

The course's final assignment sought to break down the assumptions that often define Chicano/a cultural identity and, instead, to encourage students to examine and participate in Chicano/a culture in the making. Recalling what they had learned about the facts and fictions of essentialist Chicano/a culture, students took pen, pencil, or camera in hand to produce their own ethnographic narratives. There were two restrictions on the project: it had to be fifteen pages, and it could not be a traditional report, which might have reproduced the fallacy that observation is objective. In line with cultural studies, revisionist anthropology, and contemporary Chicano/a studies, students were asked to find and analyze meaning in Chicano/a cultural practices or institutions such as family histories, social organizations, restaurants, and media. Of course, students were expected to do traditional research in books, articles, and government publications, but they were also told that interviews, photos, folktales, music, and other forms of Chicana/o cultural production are viable sources of knowledge. Students could use family histories and photos, for instance, to track and understand the formation of Chicano/a culture in the Midwest, or they could examine Chicano/a media or other local forms of expression (murals, fiestas, car clubs or similar organizations) to consider how such cultural developments construct or challenge a sense of authentic Chicano/a identity. Whatever their project, students performed cultural analysis not only to confront cultural essentialism but to experience Chicano/a identity as a fluid and contradictory process of construction.

Two projects in particular are worth mentioning. One student created a family history around a collection of photographs depicting significant moments in her life. Among the pictures were snapshots of her baptism, her first steps as a toddler, her third-grade class, and her and her parents on the university's campus. Taking her cue from Cantú, however, the student didn't arrange the photos in chronological order. Rather, she offered a series of vignettes that built a narrative around each picture. The narrative, moreover, wasn't only about her but included what her family could remember about the moment of the snapshot. In this way, she tried to make sense of her experiences as part of her family. For instance, a self-proclaimed practicing Catholic, the student didn't know that a family scandal had occurred around her First Communion. Originally, her parents did not want her to go through catechism and First Communion, or even to be baptized. They preferred to let her choose her religion, but eventually, the more traditional grandparents had their way. Her parents never told their daughter that family guilt rather than religious piety lay behind the First Communion photo.

While the revelation pushed the student to reconsider why she practiced her religion, it also led her to understand how cultural practices can change over several generations. In fact, the stories framing many of the photos included details about generational rifts—her mother tries to make tamales for a Christmas dinner; an aunt recalls why the student never had a *quincieñera*; her father takes a Spanish night class and barely passes. More than simply conveying family history, the narratives helped explain the student's interest in Chicano/a culture. She wanted to capture a sense of identity that harkened back to the traditions of her grandparents, but her parents' perspective gave her a different glimpse, one of flexibility, anxiety, and performativity. Her parents' choices of which traditions to follow and which to leave behind were influenced by changing times, class status, and personal memories. Indeed, her desire for Chicano/a identity, she concluded, was no different. She hoped to learn at school what she felt she had not been taught at home; instead, she discovered that she had been a part of Chicano/a culture in the making all along, and she had photos to prove it.

Another student offered a critical analysis of Chicano/a culture at large. After examining representations of Mexican Americans in mainstream and in Chicano/a films, he came to the difficult conclusion that there is little difference between the two. He focused on movies that portray Chicano/a gang culture; two movies in particular, he argued, were strikingly similar. Dennis Hopper's *Colors* (1988) works as a culturally conservative film that, by relying on racial stereotypes, presents an unsympathetic view of gang culture. Edward James Olmos's *American Me* (1992), intended in part to shock Chicano youth away from gang culture, in effect reproduces a culturally conservative discourse that demonizes young Chicanos. The student didn't argue that both films are racist; that wasn't his point. Rather, he observed that, as big-budget films, neither could avoid the popular representations of Chicano gang members. In fact, they exploit stereotypes as a way to appeal to a mainstream audience. Although both films, for instance, represent Chicano gang members as fatalistic, neither movie considers how gang culture emerges as a response to poverty in the barrio. Moreover, both films characterize Chicano machismo as a masculinity based on violence and self-destruction—a stereotype, the student noted, with a long legacy in the American imagination. The focus on masculinity, in fact, led the student to see that both films represent Chicanas as figures who redeem Chicano culture. In *Colors*, Maria Conchita Alonso plays a respectable Mexican American woman whose barrio romance with an Anglo police officer (played by Sean Penn) creates a cross-cultural alliance between the Los Angeles Police Department and the Chicano community. In *American Me*, Julie, played by Evelina Fernandez, embodies the last hope for Chicano culture—after Olmos's character returns to prison and dies, Julie covers her *pachuca* tattoo and heads off for college.

Both films, in other words, position Chicanas as cultural mediators, a contradictory position that places them in between Chicano and Anglo cultures and resonates with the narrative of La Malinche. A third film, Allison Anders's *Mi Vida Loca / My Crazy Life* (1994), the student concluded, works as a corrective to both films. Chicana gang members challenge dominant and Chicano stereotypes of women without reproducing the usual stereotypes of gang flicks. Indeed, the film offers a glimpse into the complex culture of gang life as the women decide not only to remain gang members but also to control the cash flow in the neighborhood without the help of the male gang members. Moreover, the student observed, the film demonstrates the contradictory dynamics of Chicana/o cultural production. Anders is not a Mexican American; she's a southern white woman who moved to a L.A. barrio early in her career. The question of authenticity wasn't an issue for the student. Instead, he focused on the politics of cultural representation, concluding that Anders's film offers a viable ethnography of Chicano/a gang culture because it challenges rather than reproduces stereotypes of Chicano/a youth and the vexed relation between representation and objectification.

Admittedly, both projects contained shortcomings, especially in the light of more recent Chicano/a studies. The first project, for instance, didn't clearly consider how the family's transformation reflected the historical shifts in Mexican American communities, and the second project's concluding analysis of *American Me* and especially of *Mi Vida Loca* was directly at odds with most readings of the films by major Chicano/a film critics. The point of the assignment, though, was to have students engage in cultural analysis and criticism that would help them understand and perhaps even challenge the rhetorical formation of essentialist notions of Chicano/a culture that usually excludes midwestern Mexican Americans. The first project, in particular, implicitly argued for a midwestern Mexican American historiography that extends at least three generations; perhaps the second student's geographical and psychological distance from Hollywood allowed him to analyze *American Me* critically and to be more receptive to the hybrid politics of Anders's *Mi Vida Loca*. In any event, the purpose of questioning essentialist notions of Chicano/a society by examining local and national scenes of cultural formation was not to debunk Chicano/a identity but to comprehend how it's made, even in places like Kansas.

Indeed, at the University of Kansas's 1998 symposium marking the 150-year legacy of the Mexican American War and the centennial of the Spanish American War, our panel on Latino/a contributions to United States culture fielded questions after a series of papers on Chicano/a autobiography, Latina literature, and Chicano/a literary history, from *corridos* to novels. An audience member, with a heavy Spanish accent, asked the panel, "Why don't Chicanos learn Spanish so they could learn more about their culture?" It's a question I've heard before from distant relatives or strangers at professional conferences in Mexico. Always, the question seems laced with accusation, and it never fails to evoke feelings of linguistic guilt. In either case, the question was unsettling, and the other two panelists weren't responding; neither was I.

Then, a Chicana in the audience offered her own response: "We can't speak Spanish, but we understand it," she said. "That's our culture." Her two friends, sisters in the campus's Latina sorority and former students of mine, nodded in agreement, and so did I. After all, Chicano/a culture isn't simply a collection of oppositions: English versus Spanish, Anglo versus Mexican, or individual versus community. Most of us already know this, because we know that culture in general isn't as simple as black and white. Yet, as we try to make sense of it for ourselves and for our students, we inevitably fall back on a series of binaries that, at best, enable us to talk about culture and, at worse, reproduce the politics of objectification and exclusion that characterize traditional ethnographic writing. Successful or not, my Chicano/a literature course aimed to introduce students to the messy process of culture making, as a way of challenging their assumptions about authentic culture and of encouraging them to think critically about identity and to urge others to do the same.

Teaching Brazilian Civilization: Interdisciplinary and Institutional Pragmatics in Cultural Studies

Piers Armstrong

SOME CONVENTIONS IN CULTURAL STUDIES

Perhaps the two most formative contexts for cultural studies are postwar Britain and the United States after the civil rights movement. Particularly in Britain, a certain moral momentum on the political center-left contributed to confident interpretations of popular culture, which were considered to be legitimately diverse rather than subversive, progressive rather than canonical and conservative. It is worth noticing the grammatical curiosity that, while a plural subject, "cultural studies" is typically taken—including in the present book—as a singular ("cultural studies is . . . ," not "cultural studies are . . ."), that is, as a movement. The perspective of the center-left tended to conceptually harmonize diverse civil and cultural subjects. The main element facilitating unity was a negative condition: a sense of exclusion from the mainstream of ethnic, sexual, and other social models. The appearance of conceptual unification among marginalized groups, however, masked the substantial differences among the disparate interests of these putative natural allies. If some of the groups become empowered, the tension between the factions will presumably grow. The typical cultural studies perspective has often been naive as to the political potential of an alliance predicated on a previously repressed and now celebrated subalternity.[1]

In the university, another progressive alliance unifies groups whose differences derive from their structural positions in the classroom. Ideally, there is an organic unity among teacher, student, and subject of study and among teaching the students about their world, challenging previous models of cultural authority, and exploring the progressive politics of democratic empowerment. From this point of view, the legitimacy of one's aesthetic *imaginaire* as a positive asset tends to be symbiotic with a negative critical sense as to *imaginaires* imposed in the status quo. Additionally, the contestation of hegemonic discourses in the aesthetic domain links to social empowerment.[2]

The second great reflective moment in cultural studies corresponds to the social configuration of the civil rights movement in the United States, in particular the rights of blacks as imagined by the white mainstream. While the self-empowerment of blacks is consistent with the process of legitimization of a subaltern group, the empathic perception, by nonblacks, of the struggle is of a different psychological order, because it introduces the key motif of the other as a necessary complement to the self (here, the terms *self* and *other* refer to collective cultural subjects and identities).

Enthusiasm for the other, often coupled with doubts about the legitimacy of the self, may counterbalance narcissism in consumer society. An earlier enthusiasm for the other—the discovery, by modernist artists, of aesthetic grace in the "primitive" art of Africa and Oceania—is sometimes now read as the appropriation of an exoticized other, as cultural imperialism. In the postmodern cultural studies narrative of the other, the subaltern other is bestowed with both an inherent moral legitimacy and an analogous arbitrary privilege of aesthetic prestige. Finally, it is often implied that students, as (would-be) subalterns, are in harmony with this other or "co-outsider."

THE MULTIDISCIPLINARY VERSUS
THE INTERDISCIPLINARY

Cultural studies pursues objects of study located between traditional intellectual fields. Film studies, for example, which relies on accepted descriptors of visual data and of narrative data, draws on the discursive repertoire of departments of fine arts and of literature. Because film is a fusion (and not merely a juxtaposition) of visual and verbal elements, the integration of ideas about the plastic arts and about narrative creates a genuine hybrid between two analytic frames. In cultural studies, it is expected that hybrid analytic discourses emerge from the cross-fertilization of disciplines. But it is usually much more difficult in cultural studies than in cinema to verify whether an analytic method has been developed or a genuinely new order of object detected.

We should distinguish between the multidisciplinary and the interdisciplinary. The former refers to the situation in which objects or analytic discourses of more than one order are present; the second refers to a mutated discourse, a distinct analytic method appropriate to a newly designated class of object. In the evolution from traditional disciplines, the multidisciplinary is not inherently better or worse than the monodisciplinary. The multidisciplinary offers the virtue of variety but can lack hermeneutic depth, the specific understanding of a specific type of object: the working subculture of a rooted critical field. The interdisciplinary, meanwhile, is not inherently a conceptual enrichment but rather an intellectual challenge located in intermediary conceptual terrain, a sort of disciplinary no-man's-land. The underlying goal of interdisciplinary initiatives is, presumably, to generate methodologies and disciplines—that is, to cease being interdisciplinary.

The distinction between the multidisciplinary and the interdisciplinary, while rarely noted, is important in terms of what a teacher actually does in a class. Civilization classes that cover diverse objects of study and include analyses from the traditional disciplines that correspond to each of the various objects are usually multidisciplinary. Film studies provides a good example of the interdisciplinary: the distinctiveness of the hybrid object of study has generated its own critical method and even an institutional existence.

Cultural studies as an interdisciplinary field supposes an organic unity between new objects of study, the emergence of new ways of seeing these objects, and increased critical consciousness. This expectation, however, betrays a naive optimism: the assumption that there is a link between aesthetic variety, new analytic discourses, and a progressive social attitude, and that the expansion of the repertoire of objects of study leads to social awareness and perhaps to social improvement, under the mantle of iconic but politically vague terms such as *multiculturalism.*

CONSUMER EDUCATION

While the conceptual journey from more-inclusive study to enlightened social perspective is feasible, it poses problems and may have indirect, unforeseen consequences. The progressive intentions and assumptions may be undermined by the ambiguous effects of cultural consumption. The multiplicity and massive circulation of messages in our media-saturated society dissipates the apprehension of the referential objects concerned. Media saturation leads to an inflation of rhetoric and to the devalued impact of any particular discourse, including that of diversity. Given that the political force for a given project for social justice involves an ensemble of focused moral, material, and aesthetic public attention, sustaining the political energy for a project that is presented as just one possibility in a complex range may be difficult. If projects are psychologically assimilated merely as interesting ideas, the embedded moral and material arguments undergo a paradoxical reduction to the aesthetic plane of abstract contemplation, consumer dalliance, and superficial identity adscription.

How has this conjuncture been translated institutionally? From the 1960s on, the dominant trends in European humanities programs were interdisciplinary; concomitantly, European campuses were traditionally leftist and pro-revolutionary (politically, culturally, socially). American universities were, from the European perspective, politically and culturally conservative. However, while European universities were generally open to cultural studies at the postgraduate level, undergraduate education preserved the pattern of disciplinarity. Thus, for example, humanities and social science students normally took classes in no more than four disciplines (departments). On the contrary, in the United States, in a way independent of both leftist and conservative agendas, the multidisciplinary pattern of general education grew. Students are now expected to take classes in a range of areas (science, social science, humanities, etc.), offered by a large number of departments and bridge programs. As a result, humanities professors compete for student enrollments. Indeed, undergraduate institutions in the United States are organized in a way that views education as a consumer market. They are characterized by disciplinary eclecticism, course innovation reflecting ethnic diversity, the proliferation of leftist maxims in the humanities, and, paradoxically, political conservatism. Somehow, diversity is politically managed, bureaucratically integrated, and economically adapted in a manner consistent with the successful integration, by capitalism, of radical artistic vanguards, as described by Peter Bürger.

TEACHER AUTHORITY AND RESPONSIBLE TOURISM

The ambiguous position of the multidisciplinary can affect teachers in surprising ways. First, for the sake of enrollment numbers, teachers must provide material that appeals to the student mainstream. Second, in moving beyond their discipline, teachers also leave the source of their academic authority. Grading becomes intellectually ungrounded, both because of teachers' lack of specific expertise and because of the lack of assessment criteria in the new terrain. The tendency in education today is to erode the teacher's right to make negative judgments and to enhance the student's right to receive positive judgments about his or her performance. We move toward a hyper-democratic configuration in which, because any discourse of disciplinary legitimacy (in the humanities, at least) can be deconstructed, the right to have an opinion is synonymous with the intellectual legitimacy of the opinion. The dominant criteria are those of the consumer as citizen. Applied to education, the criteria may translate to evaluation of a class in terms of students' sense of their progress in a class, as measured by student responses to questions like "Do you feel you learned something useful?" According to this pessimistic scenario, teachers face the danger of being reduced to cultural tour guides in a virtual culture-scape of discourse. Of course, teachers might reassure themselves that, by determining the syllabus, they have a crucial selective power. In the end, however, just as generous gratuities indicate success for the tour guide, high student enrollments prevail as an index for the teacher.

For the nontenured teacher at least, nothing can be further from the truth than Lawrence Grossberg's noble bravado when he says, "The question of cultural studies is not so much whom we are speaking to (audience) or even for (representation), but whom we are speaking against" (Introduction 9). In terms of self-perception as political subject, the work of the innovative teacher motivated by fears of low-enrollment has little resemblance to the progressive cultural studies project, despite similarities in such areas as the selection of new objects of study, the inclusion of popular as well as high culture, and the role of ethnic diversity. At a pedagogical level, consumer education takes us away from the master-and-disciple model. The teacher, who has become a sort of technician of cultural exposure, is no longer the intellectual master of a discipline (and evidence of a teacher's technological adaptation is more useful than affirmations of the value of the content he or she conveys). In the long run, the source disciplines may be as expendable as the teachers. Interestingly, while conservative views on education and the progressive ethos of cultural studies both endorse the notion of the mission of the teacher, their sense of moral investment is eroded by the consumer education paradigm.

While this essay is in some ways a cautionary tale of the dangerous waters facing the cultural studies interdisciplinarist, I am certainly not suggesting the futility of the endeavor. We must adapt traditional approaches within the cultural studies frame, particularly in the case of Brazilian studies. Further, teachers cannot give up the sense of a mission in which they struggle not merely to facilitate awareness but to present an ideologically loaded version of reality. The role of the cultural studies teacher is political in every sense, and thus as circumstantial as it is ideological.

How does this situation affect teachers as they design a syllabus and thus paint a corner of the world for their students? To answer, we can extend the tour guide analogy. In the following illustration, the guide stands for cultural studies teachers, the group of tourists for their students, and the museum for the classroom. The museum imagined is not the boundless, Borgesian encyclopedia of the Internet but a real museum with a limited number of works. The guide shows the group a picture. Instead of respecting the conventional prohibition against imposing a discursive meaning on artworks (as in the admonition by some contemporary artists that "the picture is anything you mean it to be; once I've painted it, I am no longer its owner"), the guide offers a common-sense interpretation. Let us imagine that the picture is abstract, so that the very act of interpretation is patently subjective. The guide should acknowledge the subjectivity and the genealogy of his or her perspective but, rather than consider all interpretations as equally valid, should invite the tourists to accept this explanation or to justify another.

The syllabus can be thought of as a small selection of pieces from a museum. Of course, like a small gallery in the museum, the syllabus is a selection within a selection. The acquisitions of museums reflect the subjectivity of the era of acquisition more than that of the targeted cultural era and tend to focus on a few favorite issues of perception and veins of expression. From a limited total of texts deriving from traditional and antitraditional canons, then, the syllabus designer must choose an even smaller subset. These discursive icons constitute a mosaic, to represent, for example, a national culture in a civilization class. What becomes most prominent, or centralized, in the picture is some conceptual motif dear to the teacher, whether that be political progress, the identification of gender inequality and racial hierarchies, nonlinear discursive art, or something else. In short, the teacher should consciously and explicitly attempt to *indoctrinate* the students—or, at least, consider the editorial imperative.

At the end of her course outline for the class Latin American Culture and

Civilization (Spanish 331 at Longwood College), for example, Ruth Budd writes, "Throughout this course you will need to constantly analyze the ever-present motifs of religion, violence, male and female gender roles, United States intervention, *mestizaje*, and the 'Other.' "[3] While I might disagree with the selection, I admire the engagé manner in which the culture motifs are openly stated. Clearly, students who opt for the class are stepping onto Budd's turf. Students may or may not accept the ideology; those who don't will have to justify their responses. The evidently subjective selection of topics favors a critical ethical reading of power relations over a developmentalist model, for example. As long as a wide variety of subjective syllabus models are available, there is nothing inherently wrong with the subjectivity; in fact, this approach is more democratic than the earlier domination of a few models, from positivism to dependency theory. As political players, teachers must both expand their expertise to engage in dialogue with cultures beyond their source discipline and defend their power base—preserve their authority despite the disciplinary stretching. What we often overlook, however, is that the confidence with which teachers develop an ethical landscape is related to their assumptions regarding student enrollments and job security—a security that may well erode over the long term. In contrast to teachers of Spanish, moreover, many teachers of Brazilian studies have never had a secure base.

BRAZILIAN AND LATIN AMERICAN STUDIES

Despite the Latin American link, Brazilian studies are in a very different situation from its Spanish (American) counterpart. The enrollments are dangerously low. While Brazil constitutes about forty percent of the Latin American population, there are almost one hundred times as many students enrolled in Spanish language classes as in Portuguese in the United States.[4] The pattern continues in culture classes. Whereas Spanish enrollments have accompanied a general sense of growing Latino/a empowerment in the United States, Brazilianists have remained in a precarious position, at times subject to bureaucratic extermination. Consequently, Luso-Brazilianists experience the issue of developing a course that will secure student enrollments in a radical way. While Hispanicists have enjoyed the luxury of ideological debates about appropriate narratives of civilization, ideology has not achieved a critical mass in Brazilian studies. In short, while identity locations on the self/other axis (such as borderlands discourse) have been explored in pedagogical and academic Hispanicism, the Brazilian camp remains hopelessly other and characteristically powerless. So little debate occurs that one might even suspect that there is no resentment at the unequal representation. But the mystification of a Brazilian aesthetic sublime—the firm conviction of many Brazilians and Brazilianists that, regardless of power and representation imbalances, it's always better to be Brazilian because Brazil is miraculous and wonderful—suggests a process of psychological compensation in the way Brazilians and Brazilianists see their relations with the world.[5]

In the United States, moreover, Brazilian studies has no real student base and does not correspond to an existing ethnic or communitarian group. Few students in Brazilian studies are of Brazilian origin; students do not come to Brazilian studies to learn about their forebears. This situation affects the topics in the multidisciplinary class and its subjective, interdisciplinary trajectory. The Spanish American civilization course usually presents the history of the continent in a semiorthodox way and tends to stress social issues. If a high proportion of students are Latinos/as, or if the school is in a region with a strong Hispanic tradition, teachers may discuss parallels between certain concerns of Spanish Americans and those of United States Latinos/as. For example, in California, the issue of the usurpation of Mexican sovereignty of Aztlán is important; a course taught in the Southwest might stress Mexico, look at the Aztecs in more depth than the Incas, and deemphasize the viceroyalty of the Rio de La Plata. In general, Spanish American classes tend to focus on an authentic mestizo community moving through history, from pre-Columbian roots to relations with *el Norte*.

In the absence of a particular ethnic constituency, there is great interest in creative production and less interest in historical issues. The imagined nation of the Brazilian civilization class relates more to the Brazilian view of miscegenation as a creative, multicultural mixing process than to the continuity of a core group that has been subject to cultural infiltration by the Western other. Students are drawn by a cultural curiosity in which conspicuous aesthetic phenomena are prominent. The study of Brazil is not about "what we were" (for Latino/a students) or about the roots of a number of one's neighbors (for non-Latino/a students); on the contrary, in the United States configuration, Brazil represents alterity (discussed further below).

To further radicalize the situation, a majority of undergraduates who take a course in Brazilian studies—most often as a general education class in English; few students major or minor in Portuguese—do not enroll in a second course in the field, unlike students in Spanish studies. Brazilian studies courses must cover and link a wide range of disciplinary areas and are highly volatile in content and in implicit definitions of "civilization."

Several other characteristics of Brazilian studies (some of which are common to Spanish American studies) mark its relation to cultural studies. The most important point is that Brazilian studies is all but obliged to go beyond the literary. Latin American studies—unlike French studies, for example—has no classical model of induction into the culture through literature. In the majority of extra-European cultures, literature never existed as the norm of cultural discourse except as a Eurocentric indoctrination. Thus, studies of extra-European societies are generally cultural rather than literary. Related to this is the lack of an educational infrastructure (notably, departments and programs in the national literatures) to convey these traditions. Finally, the modern histories of non–North Atlantic nations are basically narratives of ethnic confrontation, of rupture rather than of evolution in economic structures and political power, and of consequent social crisis. As a result, in terms of objects of study and the ways we can explore them, an organic link exists between cultural studies and Third World studies: both are at the margins of power and of representation, in a peripheral zone characterized by crisis and social imperative.

BRAZILIAN CIVILIZATION AND CULTURAL STUDIES

Brazil offers a range of themes for incorporation into cultural studies, including elements from various disciplinary areas: the nation has the world's eighth largest economy by volume; its biogeographic diversity is unique; its population, which constitutes almost forty percent of Latin America, is racially diverse. In general, the aspect that most interests people is the nation's racial and cultural mixing, as manifested in Brazil's socially and culturally successful practice of miscegenation, its religious syncretism, the Africanized *carnaval*, and so on. If we look closer, Brazil continues to be extraordinary. It contains the largest number of Catholics, of practicants of Afro-diasporic religions, and of evangelical and Pentecostal Protestants in Latin America. Its history in the twentieth century represents a series of significant configurations: agrarian oligarchy; fascist dictatorship; early Third World democracy; reactionary military dictatorship; and, finally, a sophisticated but semi-dysfunctional modern democracy, currently and for the first time led by a plebeian president—and a president from a genuinely modern labor party rather than one deriving from the continent's twentieth-century heritage of national populism. It is a crucial country for study in fields from economics to education, religious studies, and ethnomusicology.

Despite the development of its literature, Brazil presents, within the Latin American fold, a singularly sophisticated corpus from the late nineteenth century on. An interesting difference between the Brazilian and the Spanish American traditions is that Brazilian literature has tended to be more individualist and aesthetically oriented, whereas the Spanish American tradition is more sociohistorical. The great novelists of the Spanish American Boom are consciously social commentators and write essays on the national condition from a historical and political perspective. In Brazil, with some exceptions, notably the *romance do nordeste* novelists (a generation that emerged in the 1930s and described social calamities in the poorest part of Brazil), a greater gulf has existed between literary art and broad social portraiture and between novelists and essayists generally. For example, two prominent novelists whose work differs radically in aesthetic terms—Machado de Assis and Guimarães Rosa—share the characteristic that, despite living in a Third World nation, they do not offer social frescoes but restrict their attention to sociopsychological niches. The wave of national awareness in Brazilian modernism in the 1920s, represented particularly in the work of Oswald de Andrade and Mário de Andrade, was also aesthetically centered and oblivious to, or rather deliberately confounding of, materialist thought.

Perhaps the most important case to consider here is that of Brazil's most famous modern writer, Jorge Amado. A former Communist Party member, Amado presents an intellectual trajectory in many ways analogous to that of the Colombian writer Gabriel García Márquez. But unlike García Márquez, Amado eventually deviated from leftist orthodoxy. His solidarity with the downtrodden is based on personal sympathy rather than on objections to class distinctions. Amado adopted an optimistic historical reading in which material and social conditions slowly improved even under capitalism. His greatest works (for example, *Gabriela* and *Tenda dos Milagres*), while retaining a strong empathy for the underclass, are celebrations of miscegenation as a social solution in itself. Amado sees Brazil as a unique culture, taking an autonomous path toward salvation from the inhumanity of racism. Because he does not directly associate racism with capitalism, Amado's work differs from radical readings of Caribbean history that premise the industrial revolution on the accumulation of capital under slavery. To Amado, racism is merely a perverse manifestation of ignorance. Its reform can come from a civilizing influence predicated on such traditional values as charity. Many of Amado's characters consider freedom from racist ignorance to be a humanist virtue and practice it on an interpersonal level, without engagement in a prescriptive political struggle. Finally, miscegenation implies a global mingling and the inherent *alegria*, or joy, of heterogeneous communion. As suggested in the title of Amado's first novel, Brazil is *O país do Carnaval* (the land of *carnaval*). The work must be contrasted with García Márquez's negative reading of Latin American solitude as a perverse isolation (Armstrong, *Third World*).

The triangular racial miscegenation of Brazilians—from American Indian, black African, and European origins—has produced a range of phenotypes that in themselves constitute an aesthetic novelty. The Brazilian obsession with physical beauty suggests the evolution of sophisticated cultural encoding of and adaptations to interethnic power relations. This may justify a culturalist sense of Brazilian difference, because socioaesthetic solutions to structural problems are creative and particular. But miscegenation is also a metonym for cultural cohabitation, a crucial dynamic in metropolitan societies. By this logic, Brazil is a prototype of the melting pot. Further, the much-thematized influence of subaltern ethnicities (notably Afro-) on the Euro-Brazilian elite speaks directly to the seminal issue, in cultural studies, of the relation between high and low culture. In Brazil, cultural syncretism, cultural tolerance, and interethnic/racial relations—which, despite their overlap, should be seen as distinct phenomena—manifest themselves conspicuously and, more important, traditionally. Because of the overlap, these phenomena are often collapsed into a single theme. In Brazil the term *miscegenation* suggests hybridity and *racial democracy* suggests tolerance and equality. Because of the problematic nature of the latter term, I use here an intermediary term, *cultural miscegenation*. It is a process favored in postmodern culture and the hallmark of much Brazilian ideological self-explication.

A deeply felt and widespread imaginative bias locates Brazil as somehow outside the usual materialist sociohistorical rules. Within the culture, the creativity of this force goes far beyond the notion that Brazilian identity ideology is a conscious manipulation by the government or a conspiracy of the elite. This also affects the outsider—including Brazilianists, tourists, and students. Faith in Brazilian alterity links to confidence in subjective autonomy: of the individual, in spite of "the system"; of the aesthetic domain, in spite of socioeconomic constraints; of communal bonds that transcend hierarchic divisions, in spite of the injustice of class inequities; and, generally, of alternative "energies": in short, as an antidote to rationalist materialism.

Even social phenomena that could be read as unifying the United States and Brazil tend to be interpreted in terms of alterity. The institution of slavery, for example, could serve as a link between the experiences of the United States and of Brazil. But it is usually perceived as consisting of two distinct cultural models. Rather than point to the universal socioeconomic processes of racial exploitation, forced emigration, the generation of capital, and other similarities, writers draw attention to the differences in the two forms of slavery, so as to contrast race relations in the two societies. Commentators generally agree that racial intolerance is less of a burden in Brazil than in the United States. To explain the notion that there is less racism, scholars distinguish between the North American binary system (white or black, with no intermediary) and the Brazilian culture, with its gradational color-classification vocabulary, its psychological flexibility, and its inherent subjectivity. But quantitative assessments usually suggest a greater material disenfranchisement of Brazilian blacks; according to this gauge, Brazil is a more racist society. The application to Brazil of conventional historical frames, or of statistical surveys developed by North American social sciences, leads to harsh judgments (Telles, "Race"). These paradigms are, in turn, contested as disguised acts of cultural imperialism. Moreover, the informal impression of harmony, or rather cordiality, is difficult to quantify. Brazilian flexibility fails tests conceived as objective measures; but, by virtue of its creativity, it is not so easily dismissed, since it is not of the same existential order as the quantitative variables. This pervasive, affirmative, and irrational explication of national culture underwrites an informal and pacific social contract. While ever-growing economic inequities have led to increasingly spectacular criminal violence, Brazil is marked by a conspicuous indisposition to mass social mobilization let alone revolutionary militancy.

How this local tradition plays into the cultural studies agenda warrants some examination. The humanist social science of Gilberto Freyre presents an interdisciplinary sophistication (weaving together anthropology, ethnography, sociology, psychology, religion, domestic issues from sexuality to cuisine, political history, literature, and so on) and an encyclopedic density characteristic of postmodern thought. In addition to the work of other writers of his time, like the Mexican José Vasconcelos, Gilberto Freyre's output suggests comparison with that of Foucault (reading psychosexual hierarchies in social history) and with recent multiauthor collections like the French *Histoire de la vie privée*, edited by George Duby, as well as with the cultural studies produced by historians like E. P. Thompson, in the mise-en-scène of specific lower classes. Freyre's work was complemented, in the Brazil of the 1930s and 1940s, by extensive studies on national cultural hermeneutics, including Sérgio Buarque de Holanda's *Raízes do Brasil* (and, later, a less-known but even richer work, *Visão do paraíso*) and Paulo Prado's *Retrato do Brasil: Ensaio sobre a tristeza brasileira*. These three influential writers, and many other Brazilian writers of various periods, incorporated strains of essentialism that, to the contemporary reader, may seem politically primitive. The theoretical suppositions can even be diametrically opposite, as with Freyre and Foucault. Still, given the interdisciplinary character of the writers' earlier thinking and research, the country's self-representative discourse is a sort of cultural studies *avant la lettre* and a good launching pad for cultural studies metadiscussions. The fundamental difference between the work of these earlier Brazilian writers and the contemporary perspective of cultural studies, however, is the former's notion that, regardless of other social evils, Brazil is a locus of social harmony rather than conflict, of expression rather than repression.

Another remarkable stream of self-consciousness that speaks to cultural studies is located firmly outside the academy. Various strains of Brazilian popular music feature lyrics that qualify not only as illustrations of cultural attitudes but also as a metadiscourse on national character. This propensity is already present before World War II in the popular music of Rio, called *samba canção*, notably in the satires and romances of Noel Rosa, a sentimentally lyrical yet socially acute composer of this genre. The most internationally famous and enduring song from this era, Ary Barroso's "Aquarela do Brasil" ("A Watercolor of Brazil"), is a vivid example: "Ô, abre a cortina do passado / Tira a mãe preta do cerrado" ("Open the curtain on the past / Bring the black ma' from out in the scrublands").

The *tropicália* movement of the late 1960s and the MPB (Música Popular Brasileira) of the 1970s represent a conceptual crossroads, possibly unprecedented in popular genres around the world, in terms of an intellectualized contemplation of mass culture. Similarly, Brazilian film's most creative phase, *cinema novo* (1950s and 1960s), is oriented to a metadiscourse on the popular by intellectuals.[6]

In its sophisticated discussion of culture, Brazil resembles Western Europe.

During the struggle between left and right in the early 1960s, the political characterizations of the popular that activists articulated were translated as social interventions and creative initiatives, only to be aborted under the military dictatorship (from 1964 to 1985). The creative mobilizations in some ways prefigured the politicized sociocultural debate of Italian radicalism in the 1970s, for example. But on economic issues, the left, and liberals in general in Brazil, has been unsuccessful in stimulating reform. Though its economy is highly developed, Brazil retains an income-distribution inequity exceeding that of the rest of Latin America and matched only by a handful of the poorest countries in the world. As in Argentina, the contradictory cohabitation of intellectual cosmopolitanism and authoritarian violence consistent with that prevalent in much of the rest of Latin America points to the gulf between cultural discourse and social contract. Brazil shows us how the postmodern proliferation of speculative discourses, which we associate with metropolitan late capitalism, can occur even more radically in Third World societies subjected to inorganic modernization.[7]

Thus, on the one hand, Brazilian culture promises an exhilarating variety of ethnocultural expression. On the other, responsible historical readings and social recommendations are necessarily pessimistic when any rational, quantitative model of social measurement is applied. The problem in approaching Brazil intellectually, for academics and others, is the dominance—and seductiveness—of aesthetically oriented explications of society, which creatively elude rationalist analysis or deconstruction. Attitudes to politics and individual subjectivity hinge on the legitimacy of aesthetic particularism, which is sublimated in the powerful idea of a Brazilian existential alterity.

The Brazilian studies teacher may favor an aesthetically stimulating and historically optimistic picture of Brazil over socioeconomic realism because the former is more likely to increase student enrollments. Such an inclination complements the most famous Brazilian self-referential discourse, from Barroso's lyrical "meu Brasil brasileiro para mim" ("my Brazilian Brazil for me"), in "Aquarela do Brasil," to Freyre's brilliant apologia of the felicitous cultural output of a slave economy (*Casa*). In developing a syllabus teachers can highlight the attractive accessible features of Brazil's culture, or they can stress the country's struggle for social justice. The latter, I think, is at the root of cultural studies. Brazilian studies crystallizes a hidden tension in multicultural and multidisciplinary education. In the consumer economy of pedagogy, cultural studies can either follow Fredric Jameson's insistence to "always historicize"—that is, seek material structures behind cultural extravagance—and increase the social responsibility of the student—or promote a sort of cultural consumption, in which Brazil, for example, is explored as a series of exotic others (Amazon indigenes, *carnaval* revelers, syncretist religions, artful soccer players). Given the ambiguities in the teacher-student relation and in the selection of material, the solitary Brazilian civilization class thus becomes a locus for decisions regarding representation of self and other in the context of cultural studies.

APPLYING A CULTURAL STUDIES APPROACH TO A BRAZILIAN STUDIES SYLLABUS: A CASE STUDY

How, then, is the teacher to proceed? It is not enough for interdisciplinary courses to provide students access to a range of disciplines and texts. Just as students must, in their essays, create their own construction, rhetoric, or identity fiction, so professors must chart a rhetorical course, establish an intellectual trajectory (excluding large chunks of legitimate considerations), make a proposal, offer a loose thesis about reality: they must adopt a political profile and not be merely a museum cicerone.

The teacher's cultural exposition can include disparate pieces of evidence from different disciplines, but it should be classified as circumstantial evidence, because of the deconstruction, inherent in the interdisciplinary approach, of the validity of any single discipline.

The tension between the erosion of intellectual authority that flows from the multidisciplinary approach and the editorial imperative suggested earlier puts the squeeze on us as instructors. On the one hand we forgo the convenient recourse to external authority; on the other, we have to take responsibility for the truth, or at least reasonableness, of our assertions. Such assertions should include both predictions of the future evolution of the phenomena studied—since only through such hypothesis can we test the validity of assertions regarding cultural logic—and recommendations about appropriate steps to achieve social, economic, and cultural progress (i.e., how the predicted turn of events, where negative, might be avoided by the application of alternative policies).

As instructors shape the thinking they aim to foster, they might choose a privileged discipline as essential to a holistic understanding of cultural character. Making such a judgment already draws the teacher beyond the neutral facilitator role. If there is a central axis, an orienting discipline in the interdisciplinary course, I would suggest a humanist historicism (though not the old patriarchal humanism), which stands, hermeneutically, between literature and sociology. By humanist history, I simply mean a narrative of the passage of culture through time, but one asserted as a true and just account of the reality of the past and the present. Humanist history is a paradox appropriate to our pragmatic position. It recognizes the place of culture and therefore of fiction in objective accounts of reality yet preserves a balanced social reality as its ultimate subject and an obligation to read the past in a way that acknowledges inequities and the operation of power in art, from production to the establishment of the canon.

In using the word *humanist*, I am embracing a term that has been discredited in a good part of leftist theory, which holds that humanism is part of a cultural apologia of bourgeois politics. My use of the term is more practical than theoretical. By it, I mean a reading of culture that articulates the broad patterns of material and social development while remaining attentive to creative subjectivity and optimistic about gradual social progress.[8]

We can examine how these considerations may play out in the design of a lower-division (intermediate) class, Brazilian Civilization (see app., syllabus 3). I will discuss the class I taught at UCLA in 1996 and 1997, in ten-week trimesters (quarters).[9]

The models of two predecessors at UCLA present interesting comparisons. The first teacher organized the material primarily as a series of academic disciplines. The topics were an overview of geography, demographics, politics; colonization; indigenous peoples; Afro-Brazil; immigration; modern politics; religion and social movements; music; architecture and plastic arts; media and modern society.

The second teacher preserved some of this model but increased the proportion of topics that are basically themes rather than disciplines: history and economics; human and physical geography; racial issues; tradition and *jeitinho* (finding a way to get something done, typically by subverting official procedures; the word connotes crafty innovation as well as corruption); religion; urbanization and the plastic arts; cinema and mass communication; literature; music and dance; *carnaval* and sexuality. This listing implies a move from the multidisciplinary to the interdisciplinary.

Another good example of an innovative—and subjective—interdisciplinary study of civilization is found in the set of topics for another colleague's course, Comparative Seminar on Brazilian and Spanish American History and

Culture: the Old World and the New; the colonizer, the colonized, and the making of colonial America; the struggle for independence; the dream of reason; Brazil: tropical paradise; eating the Other: a Brazilian recipe; cultures of poverty, realities of oppression; silenced voices of Latin America; *el Norte*. This course focuses on what might be called the subjective moments of a civilization—the ideas, dreams, and ensembles of belief or imagination that shape the cultural psyche of people born into a given tradition. While it represents the move from discipline to theme and thus from the multidisciplinary to the interdisciplinary, there is, as well an underlying conceptual preference. The focus is on generative legends that are rich in narrative depth, and the approach could be characterized as a literary reading of the history of civilization. This class, a seminar, presumes a greater sophistication and knowledge on the part of the student.[10]

For my lower-division course on Brazilian civilization, I organized the syllabus on an orthodox axis of history, alternating with cultural phenomena and issues that, though not necessarily time-bound themselves, for expository purposes symbiotically or contrastively complement the historical period with which they are paired. These topics include indigenous culture; Afro-Brazilian religion and recreation; Romantic Indianism and realist literature; positivist racism; racial democracy; modernism; samba and *carnaval*; social injustice and testimonial literature; Catholicism, evangelical Protestants, *umbanda* (a Rio-based Afro-Brazilian religion, which has assimilated many European and indigenous elements); the Bahian *carnaval*; the Amazon and Amerindians. To compound the relative conservatism in the interdisciplinary context, I used as the central text, covering the drier historical background, Bradford Burns's *A History of Brazil*. Based on economic dependency theory, the work focuses on the executors of power and thus presents a "top-down" view of history— one which, while not intentionally patriarchal, gives dead white males prominence. The book does not, however, glorify national leaders, who are associated with subjugation and servitude; it is, rather, a pessimistic work, one that expresses regret for the unjust experience of the masses in Brazil. The book is not restricted to economics, however, and describes several novels that Burns considers illustrative of Brazilian society.

My syllabus was cautious in two ways. First, it assumed that students' acquisition of an orthodox history of Brazil is fundamental for locating, in hierarchies of power, both achievement and oppression. Second, the cultural presentations corresponded, generally, to specific historical and social developments. This approach is less innovative than positing, as the floating parameters of what might be called interdisciplinary studies in Brazilian discourse, topics such as *jeitinho*, Brazilian sexuality, and *antropofagia* (anthropophagy, or cannibalism, practiced by Amerindians to acquire the victim's strengths and taken up allegorically by the modernist Oswald de Andrade as a celebration of the Brazilian capacity to reread and adapt foreign techniques and discourses ["Manifesto"]).

Since the cultural and contemporary material in the course focused on subaltern groups and thus presented contestations of the hierarchy, the juxtaposition of the two themes, history and culture, suggested both polarization and symbiosis. The pessimism of the dependency theory occasioned emotional and intellectual challenge by the students, for whom the cultural material provided support. As an interdisciplinary enterprise, however, the course offered a "salad bowl" (cluster of diverse elements) rather than a melting pot of materials, and in that sense it did not innovate; in the terms outlined in this essay, it was multidisciplinary rather than interdisciplinary.

In terms of asserting a clear thesis regarding the historical, political, or social character of Brazilian culture, the course's manifesto—as I argue in this chapter, my responsibility—remained unwritten. Neither was there any anticipation of a particular process of development likely to emerge as dominant. The message I presented was an insistence on the constant tension between, on the one hand, elitist, paternalistic forces nevertheless creditable with nation building and, on the other, a fertile interaction of popular cultures.

This course design in a sense, corresponds to the actual power relations at work in Brazil: A positivist project of nationhood moves forward through economic and political phases, basically in step with Western history but threatened by the plight of existing primarily as a copy of the North Atlantic model. A heterogeneous series of local configurations militate against such conformity. Popular culture has evolved with its own dynamic, and its very suppression has often generated new sorts of imaginative dissidence. Nevertheless, attempts to contest power have consistently been quashed with relative efficiency by the regime. As Marshall Eakin has noted, the continuity of power in the hands of a limited number of families in Brazil is so solid as to constitute a peculiar feature of the country. In the course, the patriarchal monopoly was structurally confirmed, though Brazilian cultural contestatation was explored and student intellectual contestation was solicited.

Another failure of my course, in the terms of this essay, was the absence of a proposal regarding an appropriate direction for social development. How might this be undertaken in a new course? The *Movimento sem Terra* (MST; Landless Peasant Movement, which encourages peasants to occupy under-utilized land so as to win title to it) offers promise as a political endeavor built on a popular base. It establishes a bridge between the concerns of poor farmers and the power struggles at the top of the hierarchy (the successive failed attempts by politicians to implement *reforma agrária*). The MST is significant in forcing recognition of the widespread social trauma that has largely been neglected in the utopian discourse of the artistic mainstream. North American students can visit the organization on the Internet (www.mst.org.br).

The MST's position in contemporary politics affects our understanding of Brazil's past. The link can be seen, for example, in the emblematic historical period called Canudos, a favorite theme of teachers and researchers. Canudos was a millenarian, antirepublican Catholic community founded in the backlands of Bahia in the 1890s by an itinerant preacher, Antônio Conselheiro. In a few years, the community swelled to ten thousand people. Perceived as a threat by municipal authorities and then the state and federal governments, the community was attacked by troops. After drawn-out resistance, the entire community was annihilated. The site was later submerged when a huge dam was constructed. The episode was the subject of a seminal book, Euclides da Cunha's *Os sertões* (*Rebellion in the Backlands*), ostensibly an account of the military campaigns but, more significant, a cultural exploration of the *caboclos* of the *sertão*, the mixed-blood inhabitants of the dry interior. The incident has become an icon of Third World polarities between poor and rich and between past and future. The cataclysm of Canudos, which can seem almost like a biblical event rather than modern history, resurges in the newly dynamic struggle of the rural poor under the MST.

A new course on Brazilian civilization might feature the MST as a symbol of progress—a social and political outlet after centuries of repression. The shift in the strategic agenda, from millenarianism to opportunistic socialism, reflects a radical modernization within the subaltern stratum, despite the permanence of brutal hierarchies. A new course will also factor in the first Workers Party presidency, problems in rural-urban relations within the progressive fold, and the need to de-essentialize notions of regions such as the Amazon, which is often represented only in terms of nature and the traditional lifestyles of the indigenous population.

While preserving history as the backbone of the syllabus, instructors might employ a "bottom-up" view to replace the "top-down" approach. The cultural themes that corresponded to events on the mainstream historical axis, in the course I taught, might now be juxtaposed with aspects of the new subaltern axis. Thus, in the unit on religiosity, the class could look at folk Catholicism at Canudos and at evangelicism as sources of material empowerment for the urban poor, and perhaps contrast these movements, in turn, with the political characteristics of Afro-Brazilian religions. A unit on popular music might compare the lyrical themes of *forró* (the traditional rural popular music) with those of Rio Samba and of *música sertaneja* (a popular rural and urban music, reminiscent of country music of the United States) in terms of implicit social values.

Perhaps my interest in the MST also derives from the fact that, in many ways, it forces our attention away from the "bossa nova viewpoint"—consisting of urbane aesthetic motifs and the notion of racial democracy—that dominates Brazil's self-image and the world's way of imagining Brazil. In focusing on the MST, teachers and students must think against the grain, stressing social conflict rather than aesthetic harmony, a rural rather than an urban context, and the continental interior rather than the coast, and redressing the underrepresentation of ethnic *caboclos* (like Spanish American mestizos, of predominantly Euro-Amerindian extraction, as distinct from mulattoes of predominantly Euro-African extraction).

HISTORY AS A CENTRAL DISCIPLINE; MARKETING CIVILIZATION; THE TEACHER AS A POLITICAL ANIMAL

While the proposal sketched here is appealing, we must be aware of the difficulties of course design and management. For Brazilian studies, there is no text in English that adequately examines social and state structures while foregrounding the popular classes as the protagonists in the cultural history that gives the country its character. To adapt Gayatri Spivak, we might ask, Can the subaltern be portrayed efficiently? In the absence of an appropriate text, I may well stick to the top-down history. Before abandoning Burns's *A History of Brazil*, I would need a clear sense of the rhetorical and pedagogical implications of a replacement. The research now being done in social and cultural history should occasion, I hope, more innovative texts.[11]

Is history indispensable as background knowledge? If so, should this point be reflected in the syllabus? I would argue that it is better to privilege history than to arrange disciplines democratically, or to meander freely among themes or concepts. It is easier to proceed from a traditional discipline to the multidisciplinary than to develop an interdiscipline that adequately covers the traditional material. Within the multidisciplinary frame, the class I taught (see syllabus) centralizes history and juxtaposes against it a variety of cultural expressions but not other disciplines. The more innovative class I sketched out focuses on a subaltern historical current, and, again, sets against it various issues and expressive genres rather than disciplines. In both the actual course and the proposed one, history remains central, whether "top-down" or not. I think that this way of knowing the (national) other—familiarity with major events and power configurations of the past—affords a better (implicit) social contract between student and Brazilian culture than accumulating a wide range of data through any number of relevant disciplines. In fact, this perspective is consistent with my own literary bias: the master narrative of a people is their epic, the story of how they got where they are and why they do what they do. Certainly the challenge is to develop an alternative epic, but it must be historically substantial and politically apt. In short, designing a cultural studies civilization course depends on the preparer's global reading of the historic and political character of the society being examined. The strategy must be teased out gradually rather than imposed arbitrarily—whether the teacher's bent is subaltern or academic.[12]

Brazilianists have no interest in condemning their object of study; their dedication necessitates an optimistic reading of society. In this sense, there is an interesting dialogue between Brazilian studies and Spanish American civilization classes. The Brazilian studies teacher can learn from the ethical imperative that is commonplace in the latter. The Spanish American civilization teacher might note that trends in the educational market are volatile. The focus on area studies from the 1960s on (which may now be in decline because of reduced government funding), the swelling Spanish enrollments, and the growing Latino/a presence in the United States have created a false sense of security—a marginalized community has finally received recognition, but the privilege could also be removed at any time by the vagaries of cultural politics.

The teacher must first distinguish between the ideological impulse behind the design of a cultural studies course and pragmatic issues, including the need to provide some unifying intellectual principle and to appeal to student interest. Instead of taking a neutral role as the "facilitator of access to diverse material," the professor should consciously *profess*. The teacher must chart a philosophy of cultural politics—both a broad vision of the world's future and a strategy of self-preservation. The classroom is not a place where contradictory social pressures are abstracted away so that we can think clearly. The volatility and negative identity of the situational locations explored by Stuart Hall and others apply no less to teachers than to those subaltern cultural subjects they place on the pedagogical stage.

NOTES

1. A useful overview of subaltern studies—addressing the emergence of cultural studies in Britain, the south Asian specialist theorists of subalternity, and the contemporary Latin American studies field—is provided in Beverley, "Hybrid or Binary?"
2. An unfolding theoretical critique of the field—or, rather, an unfolding of the theoretical field as it accompanied praxis through the 1990s—appears in works written or coedited by Henry Giroux: *Impure Acts; Between Borders* (with Peter McLaren); and *Education and Cultural Studies* (with Patrick Shannon).
3. This course outline appears on the Duke University Outreach program Web site, which includes many sample syllabi: www.duke.edu/web/las/Outreach/syllbus99. The weekly themes are "Orígenes de Latinoamérica; Conquista, colonización, independencia; la importancia de la raza y la etnicidad; el mundo de las drogas; las guerras sucias en Chile y Argentina; la arquitectura de Latinoamérica; las artes plásticas; guerrillas y gringos; tierra—vida y muerte; celebraciones—la música de Latinoamérica."
4. According to MLA statistics, Spanish enrollments (606,286) in 1995 constituted 53% of all foreign language enrollments at institutions of higher learning in the United States; they had increased by 13% from 1990. Portuguese enrollments had grown more modestly, by 5%, to 6,531, or 0.6% of the total. Thus there were about 92 Spanish enrollments per Portuguese enrollment; there were also more than twice as many enrollments in ancient Greek as in Portuguese.
5. The work of Brazilianists (researchers on Brazil, based mostly in the United States), as well as general trends, is comprehensively examined in the anthology assembled by Paulo Roberto de Almeida, Rubens Antônio Barbosa, and Marshall C. Eakin. It provides a historiographic survey of social sciences and humanities scholarship; it also maps the presence in the United States of Brazilian subdisciplines in specific departments.
6. MPB has come to refer to the mainstream of Brazilian pop music since the mid-1960s. Because the mainstream reflects the influence of Anglo-American pop music, as well as the heritage of bossa nova, MPB also infers an internationally hybridized Brazilian popular music, rather than traditional genres, many of which are very much alive. Perrone looks at the ideological subcurrents of the internationalization of MPB during the military regime (1964–85). For an international perspective on the expressive dissidence of *tropicália*, see Dunn (*Brutality*). In Dunn and Perrone's *Brazilian Popular Music and Globalization*, Brazilian and international scholars cover a range of contemporary styles. Johnson and Stam provide an overview of aesthetic ideologies in *cinema novo*.
7. See Yúdice—in particular, his comments on the seminal Brazilian essayist Silviano Santiago ("Postmodernity")—in Yudice's discussion of tradition and vanguardism in Latin America. Santiago is a professor of literature and a cultural studies theorist. Unfortunately his rich body of work is not available in English; the bibliography gives Brazilian publication references for essays by Santiago on the relation between

Brazil and Latin America and Europe and the United States ("Apesar de dependente" and "O entre-lugar").

8. For a discussion of the problems of such a mainstream perspective as the one outlined here, see Mowitt. His essay, which covers an eclectic theoretical base from a leftist perspective, describes the challenges of imposing an ideological consciousness in the classroom.

9. This description of the civilization course draws on an essay in the BRASA bulletin, *Fagulha* (Armstrong, "Interdisciplinary Discipline").

10. This class was designed by Rodolfo Franconi and Beatriz Pastor at Dartmouth College. It was intended for Spanish and Latin American studies majors and other interested undergraduates. It is taught in English and focuses on the multicultural history of Latin America. This essay describes a Brazilian civilization class. For teachers who wish to design a class on Afro-Brazilian culture, an indispensable resource is John D. French's *Sharing the Riches of Afro-Brazilian History and Culture*.

11. A recent textbook that includes diverse subaltern discourses and accounts of key historical events is *The Brazil Reader*, edited by Robert M. Levine and John J. Crocitti. The range is extraordinary, and the excerpts are fragmentary, so that the book works like a verbal slide show. The text would function as a rich corollary to either a conventional history book or to a packet of material, prepared by the teacher, on Brazilian history.

12. The question of the role of literature in the civilization class, crucial for teachers from language departments, is beyond the scope of this essay. However, in the course I taught, literature was covered extensively, in two ways. First, excerpts from various writers are read as the cultural counterpoint to the history. Second, one text, Jorge Amado's *Tent of Miracles*, was read in its entirety. The theme of this witty novel is the political construction and social manipulation of ethnocultural images; its dramatic conflicts illustrate, with an uncanny felicity, many of the course's topics.

PART TWO

Thematic Practices

The Latin American City: A Cultural Studies Approach

Luis Fernando Restrepo

In *Constructive City with Universal Man* and other paintings, Joaquín Torres García's constructivist aesthetics draws attention to the essential forms of the modern city. For this Uruguayan painter, art has a fundamental function in the modern city: "un arte férreamente *vinculado a la ciudad*: comentando o cantando su vida; poniéndola de relieve; mostrándola y hasta como guián-dola" ("an art strongly *linked to the city*: commenting or singing its life; high-lighting it; showing it and even guiding it") (Torres García, "Escuela"). To represent the Latin American city, Torres García uses simple, geometric shapes, suggesting both pre-Hispanic symbols and children's drawings. An experi-mental visual language seeks to capture the images of the city—multitudes, avenues, vendors, trains, skyscrapers, noise. Emphasizing its own texture and expressive forms, modern art depicts the city in its own terms, not subservient to realism or reduced to imitating reality. To imagine indigenous societies as simple and infantile, however, is to reproduce the prejudices of nineteenth-century imperial anthropology, as James Clifford has argued in *The Predica-ment of Culture*. Ironically, this painting evokes the reality of many cities, like Mexico, Bogotá, Lima, and La Paz, where thousands of indigenous people live (García Canclini, *Consumidores*). Perhaps unintentionally, Torres García's art reveals the conflicts and contradictions of Latin American cities and society.

From the pre-Columbian cities in the Andes and Mesoamerica to present-day megalopoles, Latin America's urban societies are vibrant and complex. The city encompasses not only architecture but the human experience of

Constructive City with Universal Man, by Joaquín Torres García (1942). Collection of the Art Museum of the Americas, Organization of American States. Used with permission.

urban space. A cultural studies approach can explore how Latin Americans have endowed their cities with meaning.

This essay discusses the relevance, conceptual and methodological complexity, and potential of the cultural studies approach to urban Latin America. The reflections offered are based primarily on my experience developing and teaching a course on the topic for the Latin American studies and Spanish MA programs at the University of Arkansas, Fayetteville. The article also draws on my research project on colonial Latin America.

BUILDING A CULTURAL STUDIES CURRICULUM
FOR THE AMERICAS

Today, when more than half the world's population lives in cities, it is important to understand what cities, past and present, represent. We should not be deceived by the apparent transparency and universality of the concept of city, nor assume that life in New York, Istanbul, Rio de Janeiro, Paris, Los Angeles, and Mexico City is the same. Gaining insight into the experiences of cities around the world can help us and our students become more aware of urban issues at home, such as sustainable development, the privatization of public spaces, increased police surveillance and repression, and the power of real estate corporations over the future of our cities. Creating an urban critical discourse is one way to achieve democratic, just, and humane societies. It is the kind of intellectual project in which cultural studies is becoming engaged.

There has been plenty of discussion about precisely what cultural studies is. The concept seems to be an umbrella under which to group investigations from different disciplines, approaches, and intellectual traditions. It unites such pursuits as cultural critique; sociology of culture; cultural anthropology; legal critical studies; postmodern philosophy; gender, ethnic, and religious studies; and similar critical examinations of culture and society. The complexity and broad scope of the concept of culture has been an epistemological concern for a quarter of a century, from Raymond Williams's *Keywords* to the recent book by the English critic Terry Eagleton, *The Idea of Culture*. Acknowledging the productive debate on the value of cultural studies, I would like to highlight three aspects of this field that make it a useful foundation for an innovative curriculum in Spanish and Latin American studies.

First, cultural studies considers all social practices as valid objects of inquiry. Thus, for example, the humanist tradition, which focused mainly on high culture, is replaced by a more comprehensive, less elitist social viewpoint—one that does not expect us to abandon literary works but simply to examine other texts as well. Second, cultural studies has defied traditional paths of inquiry. Its transdisciplinary or antidisciplinary thrust includes questions, perspectives, and connections whose implications extend beyond a single discipline. Finally and most important, a distinctive characteristic of cultural studies has been its insistence on producing politically relevant scholarship and pedagogy and on devising an engaged curriculum that will generate social change. As a result, some authors consider cultural studies more a movement and an intellectual tradition than a discipline (Richard Johnson; Peter Murphy; and Jameson, "On Cultural Studies"). We must realize, however, that it is hardly a monolithic movement. Rather, it has developed differently in different contexts. The Marxist approach that was established in England by Richard Hoggart, Raymond Williams, and E. P. Thompson—and that focused on class issues—contrasts with the emphasis placed on gender and ethnicity in the United States. In Latin America, issues of subalternity, globalization, and postcolonialism have been important concerns of cultural studies projects.[1] In each case, the intellectual traditions and the sociopolitical context are the key factors determining the kind of projects that are undertaken. Another consideration is the complex transnational production, exchange, and appropriation of theories. The British-based *Journal of Latin American Cultural Studies*, for example, brings together European, Latin American, and North American perspectives on Latin America.[2]

Cultural studies—in its theoretical and thematic versatility and its desire for political engagement—is generating a more relevant curriculum for Spanish programs in the United States. If in the early twentieth century, Spanish programs focused primarily on the Golden Age, peninsular high culture, and Spanish philology, the main thrusts now are the cultural, social, and political issues of present-day Latin Americans and United States Hispanics.[3] With NAFTA and the globalization of the economy, increased immigration rates, and the growth of the United States Hispanic population, Spanish is becoming the second language of this country. Today, Spanish touches the fabric of North American life in innumerable ways. For these reasons, our field is at the center of historic change: once again, the Americas are thought of as neighbors in a hemisphere that has much to gain if north and south cooperate. Social justice, however, remains an elusive goal: almost half of Latin America's 500 million people live in poverty (earning $2 or less a day). In this country, although living conditions improved in the 1990s, United States Hispanics are far from achieving equality in income, health care, education, and cultural and political participation. Forging a socially relevant curriculum is a step in building a just and more inclusive hemisphere, expanding the reach of what the Cuban poet José Martí called "nuestra América"—an integrated continent.

THE LATIN AMERICAN CITY: A BRIEF HISTORY

In the United States, Latin America is often viewed as a rural or tropical landscape. The rural image was accurate about a century ago, when the region was primarily an agricultural society. Cities, however, have always been a major element of the area we now call Latin America. Today, Latin America is primarily an urban region (70% of the population live in cities), with several megalopoles of five million people or more—Mexico City, Buenos Aires, and Bogotá among them. Three good introductory books on the continent's urban history are José Luis Romero's *Latinoamérica: Las ciudades y las ideas* (1976), Ramón Gutiérrez's *Arquitectura y urbanismo en Iberoamérica* (1998), and Alan Gilbert's *The Latin American City* (1998).[4]

Let us take a quick look at Latin America's urban history. The chronological order followed here is not intended to suggest an *evolution*, although urbanization has traditionally been associated with the rise of civilization and a higher moral development. Latin America's urban history began more than a thousand years before the Christian era. The Olmec constructed two centers, San Lorenzo (1200 BC) and La Venta (700 BC), on the coast of what is now Veracruz, Mexico. In the Andes, one early settlement was the Chavín de Huantar (1000 BC) (Hardoy and Hardoy 60). Other major urban areas emerged during the first centuries of the Christian era, the classic period of Mesoamerican civilizations (250–900). In Oaxaca, Mexico, the Zapotec built two impressive cities, Monte Albán and Mitla. Likewise, the Maya developed urban centers in the Yucatán peninsula and in Central America. Their city-states encompassed a complex urban system that spread far beyond the monumental, ritual architecture. The anthropologists David Fash, Michael Coe, and Linda Schele and David Freidel provide a broad view of the Maya urban centers. In Mexico's central valley, the city of Teotihuacán, known for its colossal pyramids, may have had up to one hundred thousand inhabitants by the sixth and seventh centuries (Meyer 54). Later, the Aztec (Mexica) empire built the great Tenochtitlán, a commercial and cultural center of about two hundred thousand residents, that mesmerized Spanish invaders. At the time, the largest Spanish city, Seville, had about sixty to seventy thousand people (Clendinnen 18). Hernán Cortes's Second Letter to Charles V (1521) and Bernal Díaz del Castillo's *Historia verdadera de la conquista de la Nueva España* (1568) vividly describe the great Aztec capital. The monumental architecture and the ritual use of public spaces presented an image of the city that legitimized the imperial claims of the Aztecs (Clendinnen 28).

In the sixteenth century, Spanish colonizers introduced their ideas of the city; they often built urban structures over existing Amerindian settlements, as in Tenochtitlán (later Mexico City) and Cusco, Peru. Native Americans throughout the Spanish empire were forced to live according to European settlement patterns, as Francisco Solano has documented. Iberian colonialism created a hybrid urbanism that combined, reinscribed, and juxtaposed

Spanish and Amerindian spaces. For example, in Cusco, the Inca Qori Cancha, or Temple of the Sun, was turned into Santo Domingo's Christian temple (Hyslop 44).

A distinctive feature of Spanish settlements was their chessboard layout. The main plaza was the ritualistic and symbolic center of the city (Hardoy and Hardoy). The plaza was the site of public events, including bullfights, fairs, farmers' markets, processions, and the Inquisition's *autos-da-fé*. During the following centuries, the emergence of Latin American cities was slow and uneven, but neither uneventful nor peaceful. Social historians have documented an often conflictive and difficult urban experience: riots, rebellions, excommunications, crime, famine, diseases, earthquakes (F. Castro; Cook; Arrom and Ortoll).

The centralization of the Spanish political system was a major cause of the region's unequal development. The primary administrative centers became the most important cities. For example, Mexico City and Lima, the two original viceroyalties, were the largest in the area until the nineteenth century. Below the viceroyalties were the lesser administrative centers, the *audiencias*, which displayed considerable development: Santo Domingo, Santa Fe de Bogotá, Buenos Aires, and others. Some mining centers, like Potosí (now in Bolivia), prospered, as did important port cities like Cartagena de Indias (Colombia), Havana, and Portobello (Panama). Nineteenth-century laissez-faire policies and immigration practices favored the use of port cities like Buenos Aires and Montevideo.

Not until the first decades of the twentieth century, however, did Latin American cities, boosted by incipient industrialization and numerous migrations from the countryside, begin to grow rapidly. In the following decades, the urban population soared. Bogotá, for example, had 350,000 people in 1938; by 1964, it had 1.7 million; today it has over 8 million. Most cities could not provide housing and basic services (water, electricity, transportation, health care, education) to the migrants. As shantytowns developed, government administrators called for national projects to halt urban migration. In 1950–60, population growth rates in Bogotá, Caracas, Lima, Mexico City, Rio de Janeiro, and São Paulo ranged from 4% to 7.2%. In 1980–90, the rates ranged from 0.9% to 3.3% (Gilbert 31). Clearly, growth has been slowing down. Today, these cities and others have much in common with metropolitan centers around the world, although they differ in many ways from cities in North

America, Europe, Africa, and Asia. Our task is to explore the history of Latin American cities and to relate it to the history of human societies.

URBAN STUDIES: LINKING THE OLD AND THE NEW

The region has theorized and understood its urban societies in a number of ways. Jeff Kowalski's *Mesoamerican Architecture as a Cultural Symbol* discusses several indigenous perspectives. The Spanish idea is depicted in Philip II's *Ordenanzas de población* (1573), which presented a rigorous urban design. During the Enlightenment, some two centuries later, Creole intellectuals began to examine the city within the framework of European epistemology. Many ideas of what constitutes urban life reflect imperialist conceptions of society, because of the link between the emergence of social science and the rise of Western hegemony. For a critical account of the development of the city as object of study, therefore, we should adopt a postcolonial perspective.

Enlightenment attitudes toward the city as object of study were, and to some extent remain, ambivalent. On the one hand, the ethnocentric, elitist, and universalizing vision monumentalizes the city by focusing on public architecture (plazas, palaces, cathedrals, office towers), not on the marginalized inhabitants, including slaves, artisans, the poor, and the ghettoized, whose lives archaeologists and other scholars have started to document. Although many urban dwellers have lived in misery, the city continues to be depicted as the embodiment of civilization. In glorifying its cities, Western capitalism seeks to validate itself. The notion of city as humankind's brightest achievement is represented in our time by works like Lewis Mumford's *The Culture of Cities* and Christopher Hibbert's *Cities and Civilizations*. On the other hand, the darker side of the Enlightenment, with its contempt for disorder, distrust of emotions, and desire to control nature, engendered its own conception: cities are to be disciplined, ordered, sanitized, and embellished.

In Latin America we also find an ambivalent vision of the modern city. On the one hand is the desire to emulate the great European architecture—opera houses, theaters, government centers—by erecting such buildings as the Teatro Colón (1857) in Buenos Aires. Its architect, Carlos Enrique Pellegrini, employed an iron structure imported from Great Britain. According to Pellegrini, "[E]l adelanto de los pueblos se mide ahora por el consumo de hierro" ("a nation's development is now measured by its use of iron") (Gutiérrez 394).

On the other hand, late-eighteenth-century scientists like José Celestino Mutis and nineteenth-century positivists such as Miguel Samper raised the issue of urban public health and social control (vagrancy, crime, cholera, waste management). Julio Ramos's essay examines how the discourses on public health sought to manage subaltern populations in nineteenth-century Cuba.

Since the mid-twentieth century, social scientists have redirected their investigations to stress demographics, housing, transportation, economic development, poverty, and crime. Although some of the prejudices of nineteenth-century positivism made their way into many of these studies, their findings are an important contribution to scholarship on urban life. The focus, however, has proved inadequate in explaining some of the cultural and symbolic practices of city life. In *Culturas híbridas*, for instance, Néstor García Canclini rightly points out that anthropology was ill prepared to understand these complex processes because it had primarily examined traditional rural societies and other groups thought of as closed corporate communities (neighborhoods, associations, sodalities). Sociology, for its part, was historically concerned with industrialization and urbanization. It tended, therefore, to see the persistence of practices such as the *compadrazgo* (a social-bonding tradition employing the god-father figure) as obstacles to modernization (228–29). For historians the many facets of the modern-day metropolis cannot be accounted for by looking at its ancestor, the colonial district. In the humanities, art history and literary criticism focused on elite practices and generally failed to understand the influence, on city life, of the mass media (film, radio, TV, newspapers, Internet, and the like). In the city, the traditional and the modern, high culture and popular culture, the local and the global come together in no simple fashion. As a result, we need multiple ways to explore urban societies in which the regional and the multinational collide or are juxtaposed—in which we can find, for instance, traditional herbs and handicrafts sold next to video arcades, Internet cafés, and foreign-movie houses.

RETHINKING THE LATIN AMERICAN CITY

Cultural studies does not simply select information and ideas from different disciplines, as a way to accumulate knowledge. As stated earlier, it is a field with a strong antidisciplinary thrust that seeks new paths of inquiry. It is a highly reflexive scholarship that questions the generation and dissemination of knowledge in any field; it assumes knowledge itself to be a cultural and historical product. Emphasizing the mediating role of language in the understanding of the world and ourselves, cultural studies takes, as primary objects of analysis, the major discursive and symbolic practices—scientific, legal, religious, artistic, literary.

The proposed approach is therefore not a cumulative study of related fields (anthropology, urbanism, architecture, history, sociology, geography, and others) but a strategic revision of the many discourses produced from and about the Latin American city. Most important, we should remember that the production and reception of such knowledge takes place in specific social contexts marked by gender, power, and ethnic differences and inequalities. The discourses about the city endow it with meaning and value, define its boundaries and its people. The material city has long been inscribed with changing, often competing meanings.

In the remainder of this essay I discuss my experience teaching the course for the first time, in the summer of 1998, and offer additional recommendations for implementing a cultural studies approach to the Latin American city (see app., syllabus 4). The course was a special-topics, intensive seminar taught at the graduate level. In planning the course, I had to decide what to include and what to leave out. As I soon found out, there is an ample variety of materials from which to choose—films, art, novels, and more.

SUMMER 1998

The University of Arkansas, Fayetteville, has a small Spanish MA program—about twenty students, many from Latin America. Most of our students will teach at the secondary level or at community colleges. Only a few continue toward the PhD elsewhere, since we do not have a doctorate programs in Spanish; some may pursue a PhD in our comparative literature program. With this student population in mind, I offer summer courses to help them teach languages and cultures, including film and art, and to highlight pedagogical issues. In one such course there were about seven graduate students and one advanced undergraduate student. We met four times a week (three-hour sessions).

First week. We read three articles on the semiotics of urban space. Foucault, in particular, was helpful, since his article on heterotopias explains space as a historical concept. After discussing the cultural construction and meanings of urban space, we turned to readings about the Latin American city from the pre-Columbian era to the present. Several works by anthropologists (Meyer; Schele and Freidel; Fash; Hyslop) provided information on indigenous urban centers. Texts such as Nahuatl poems on the defeat of Mexico-Tenochtitlán (in León Portilla's *El reverso de la conquista*), Cortés's Second Letter, and descriptions of Andean cities by the seventeenth-century historian Felipe Guamán Poma de Ayala helped us examine representations of the city. For example, Cortés's bird's-eye view of Tenochtitlán is based on Renaissance perspective; Poma de Ayala emphasized virtue as a key element of civility and urban prosperity.

Second week. We discussed the utopian city of the Renaissance and viewed *Quilombo*, by the well-known Brazilian film director, Carlos Diegues. It portrays the heroic maroon (runaway slave settlements) society of colonial Brazil as an ideal society. The depiction of the historic *quilombo* is somewhat problematic, because Diegues's emphasis on music and dance tends to turn maroon society into an aesthetic object. Next we read about the colonial city. Mario Sartor's article provided a good historical overview; Jorge Hardoy and Ana Hardoy include examples of city plans. We compared the importance of the plaza, during the colonial period and today, with the role of shopping centers. For example, the plaza is an open public space, while many malls are enclosed, private structures. We also considered the baroque architecture and its sense of space.

Third week. We looked briefly at the city from the eighteenth to the twentieth century, highlighting such elements as public health discourse (Julio Ramos), the *costumbrista* representation of the city (Casimiro Castro), and the reemergence of the classic topos of the city as a corrupt space (Martí, *Ismaelillo*). We concluded the week with *Los olvidados*, a powerful film that offers no easy solution to modern urban violence—neither repression (the blind man's desire for the "good old days" of the dictator Porfirio Díaz) nor liberal reform (the naive efforts of the experimental farm director) can halt the brutality of modern life. In addition, we read poems by Jorge Luis Borges on Buenos Aires and its streets, as well as selections from the work on the Argentine capital by Julio Cortázar and Alicia D'Amico-Sara Facio, and Alejo Carpentier's description of Havana in *La ciudad de las columnas*.

Fourth week. Readings from works by Néstor García Canclini (*Consumidores*) explained the difficulty of studying the modern city. We read selections from *No nacimos pa' semilla*, by Alfonso Salazar, and saw Victor Gaviria's *Rodrigo D: No futuro*. The film's stories about Medellín's *comunas* (shantytowns) generated discussion about youth culture and poverty. We concluded the course by examining carnivals and expos, as well as the disappeared in Argentina.[5]

Overall, I had included too much material. Although the long syllabus allowed us to explore the multiple dimensions of the Latin American city, we couldn't discuss any historical period or city in depth. When I later taught a similar class, at the undergraduate level for the Latin American studies program, I ran into the same problem, especially because I had to provide more background on Latin America. At any rate, a comprehensive approach to the city is beyond the limits of a semester. A viable strategy is to focus on specific aspects of the city.

CULTURAL STUDIES AND URBAN SPACES: ADDITIONAL SUGGESTIONS

The following sections discuss four topics that exemplify how the city can be analyzed from a cultural studies perspective—popular culture, urban temporalities, urban imaginaries, and urban subjectivities—and suggest materials for each topic. My goal, however, is not to provide a ready-to-use syllabus but to reflect on aspects of urban space that can serve as starting points. Because these themes are not defined by any academic discipline, a cultural studies approach seems appropriate.

Popular Culture

Cultural studies has significantly enriched our understanding of popular culture. The folklorist vision tended to see popular culture as traditional, rural, simple. In reality, it is highly complex, if we consider the intricate links among the cultural industry, the growth of cities, and the emergence of social movements. For example, the gramophone, photography, radio, television, film, newspapers, video, and the Internet have rearticulated social relations at the local, national, and global levels. Key introductory readings include Jesús Martín-Barbero's *De los medios a las mediaciones*, García Canclini's *Culturas híbridas* and *Consumidores y ciudadanos*, and William Rowe and Vivian Schelling's *Memory and Modernity*. In literature, topics to examine are the Romantic vision of the city in the nineteenth-century *cuadros de costumbre*; the city in the newspaper chronicles of modernist poets like José Martí and Rubén

Darío; the Afro-Caribbean language and music of *negrismo* poets like Nicolás Guillén, Julia de Burgos, and José Luis Pales Matos; and such novels as Manuel Puig's *La traición de Rita Hayworth* and *El beso de la mujer araña* and Guillermo Cabrera Infante's *Tres tristes tigres*. Students can compare and contrast the ways these literary works look at and incorporate popular culture.

The city can also be seen through popular culture such as film and music. For film, John King's *Magical Reels* and Michael Chanan's *Twenty-Five Years of the New Latin American Cinema* are good introductory material. The analysis should go beyond examining content or the accuracy of the representation— for example, how the film's narrative and visual language give form and value to urban spaces. Most of these films can be borrowed (at no cost) from the Stone Center for Latin American Studies, at Tulane University.

As I mentioned, I have used Buñuel's *Los olvidados* and Gaviria's *Rodrigo D: No futuro* for portrayals of youth culture and urban violence. Other choices are María Novaro's *Danzón* and Jorge Fons's *El callejón de los milagros*, for gender perspectives on the city; Italian neorealism's view of the Latin American city in Jorge Sanjinés's *Yawar Mallku* (*Blood of the Condor*) and Marcel Camus's *Orfeo negro*, based on Vinicius de Moraes's 1956 play *Orfeu da conceinção*. Moraes's play has recently been reworked as *Orfeu*, by Diegues. (Unlike the low-budget, experimental films of the *cinema novo* of the 1960s and 1970s, *Orfeu*, the new version, was funded by the Brazilian media empire Globo and by Warner. Such transnational, multimillion-dollar ventures are themselves an important topic of inquiry.) Two films that provide opposite views of the Latin American city are Sergio Cabrera's *La estrategia del caracol* and Alejandro González Iñarritu's *Amores perros*. In the first, Cabrera tells a story of the urban poor's optimism, creativity, and solidarity. The second one, without moralizing, sheds a disturbing light on a corrupt urban culture in which incest, murder, and violence against animals are part of the everyday life of both the rich and the poor.

In music, one genre often associated with traditional Latin America is in fact a product of modern urban society. The bolero, or love song, emerges at the end of the nineteenth century, incorporating modernist poetry, combining high culture (operatic tenors) and popular rhythms, and giving form to the sensibilities of a growing working- and middle-class society. The history of the bolero is intertwined with that of the gramophone, the radio, and the cinema. Iris Zavala's *El bolero: Historia de un amor* and Carlos Monsiváis's "Bolero: A History" are good introductory readings. Monsiváis explains how

Agustín Lara's songs dedicated to prostitutes, like "Noche de ronda" ("Night Games"), challenged patriarchal Mexican society and articulated new ways of life: "Agustín Lara (the man and work) represents the transition between a closed society to one characterized by fissures, infiltrations, [and] zones of permissiveness. 'Perjura' ["Swear"] caused a scandal in 1910 because it cele-brated the existence of lovers and sex outside ecclesiastical law" (184). With the advent of the gramophone and radio, these profane songs entered "good" homes, described by Monsiváis as "centers of devotion." The genre expresses the contradictions of urban life. It is not surprising, therefore, that a large audience for these songs of tenderness, happiness, and endless love emerged from an environment of poverty, low-paid jobs, and discrimination (Monsi-vaís 169, 177).

Urban Temporalities and Rhythms

Reexamining such basic concepts as time and space can give us new perspec-tives on the Latin American urban experience. Once considered a priori cat-egories, time and space are now thought to be culturally and historically determined. We cannot take for granted that assumptions about time, say, were and are the same throughout Latin America's diverse population. Many varibles—age, gender, ethnicity, and class, among them—have led to signifi-cant differences in the perception of time. The urban youth culture of the working-class *comunas* of Medellín, for example, has a particular death cult that expresses, through metropolitan and native heavy-metal music, an aware-ness that many of these young people are likely to die young. Salazar's *No nacimos pa' semilla*, mentioned earlier, includes several *testimonios* from mar-ginalized urban youth.

In a larger context, colonization itself made the European (Christian) no-tion of time hegemonic. Thus to understand conceptions of time, we need to question European teleology and an assumed sense of progress. To found cities in the Americas was one of the civilizing missions that are used to justify the Spanish invasion. But the assumption that greater degrees of urbanization equal cultural superiority or moral progress cannot be sustained, especially if we look at the violence that makes the city possible. Violence began the mo-ment the Europeans appropriated the land in the founding rituals.[6] To some extent, forced labor and slavery were used in building the core of the city. Today, violence is institutionalized in the exploitation of workers of late (savage) capitalism. As Manuel Castells has argued in *La cuestión urbana*, the city has been fundamental in the production and reproduction of the colonial and neocolonial order—the accumulation of capital, the maintenance of an available workforce, and the consolidation of the political system.

Many texts examine the relation of time to the city. The European notion of cities as civilization is present in Columbus's writings in passages in which he longs for the great cities described by Marco Polo. Many chroniclers, European and Native American, describe the colonial cities in detail (see the selection of primary descriptions in Joseph and Szuchman). Students can compare Cortés's description of Tenochtitlán with the Amerindian *Florentine Codex*. Poma de Ayala provides descriptions and drawings of several South American cities (2: 811–75). Three good sources of colonial maps, paintings, and codices are Manuel Toussaint's *Pintura colonial en México*, Javier Aguilera Rojas's *La ciudad hispanoamericana*, and Serge Gruzinski's *Painting the Conquest*.

The notion of utopia is also worth exploring. Some works are Thomas More's *Utopia* (1516), Francesco Patrizi's *La citta felice* (1553), and Tommaso Campanella's *City of the Sun* (1602) (for analysis, see Manuel and Manuel; Imaiz). In the nineteenth century, José Joaquín Fernández de Lizardi's *El periquillo sarniento* reworks the utopian island in the novel. Three decades later, Domingo Faustino Sarmiento's *Facundo* presented a nation-building project based on urbanization. The story of Macondo in Gabriel García Márquez's *Cien años de soledad* (1967) is a parody of the civilizing pretensions and sense of progress that have characterized Latin American cities.

The urban experience of time encompasses different rhythms: ritual time, working time, and leisure time, and so on. For example, festivals and carnivals occur at certain times and are of a particular duration. Our perception of time also includes an awareness of the past, such as the traces of the past that are present in the city. Pierre Nora calls these the "places of memory" (*lieux de memoire*)—locations that have symbolic meanings. The city has been the site par excellence of collective memory: museums, monuments, libraries, and archives. A commemorative nomenclature of streets, plazas, and districts tells the story of the official memory—Plaza Bolívar, Plaza San Martín, Avenida Juárez, Ciudad Colón, Avenida de la Independencia, to name only a few. There are, as well, many marginalized places of memory. For instance, the urban memories of indigenous and African people merit greater recognition. In this context, two useful works are "Alturas de Macchu Picchu" from Pablo Neruda's *Canto general* and Diego Rivera's National Palace murals, reproduced in Dawn Ades's *Art in Latin America*. And there are places of memory where the past has been suppressed, or eliminated, such as Punta Carreta prison in Montevideo, Uruguay; a site of torture during the dictatorial regime, it was later turned into a shopping mall (Jelin 27). Differences in what the places of memory—official, subaltern, or suppressed—represent are fertile grounds for a cultural studies approach. Awareness of the memory-keeping facilities available at particular moments in history—writing, engraving, lithography, photography, film, phonograph, video, CD-ROM—helps us understand Walter Benjamin's reflections on the way technological innovations change our perception of the world and of ourselves (222). We can use the insights as a point of departure.

Urban Imaginaries: Spaces and Communities

The city is a rich tapestry of spaces—private, public, enclosed, open-air, convents, parks, gardens, avenues, prisons, brothels, zoos, cemeteries—that can be defined by their function: workplaces, leisure places, and the like. The functionalist approach, however, reduces the many meanings a diverse population has historically given to these sites. Roland Barthes's seminal essay "Semiology and Urbanism" is good background reading for a cultural approach to urban space. Totalizing visions of the city fail to capture the urban landscape as it changes continuously and imperceptibly. Michel de Certeau suggests that there is a radical difference between the city designed by the urbanist and the city experienced every day. Urbanists are like grammarians; they impose the rules. But the city, like a language, is a living entity that constantly transforms itself. The unmeasurable itineraries of its people alter the significances of the spaces they traverse. Certeau illustrates this idea with a suggestive analogy between language rules and language usage (what he calls "speech-acts"). To walk the city, Certeau affirms, is to write a poem. Each step taken links urban spaces in creative, unexpected ways, as poets link words. The grotesque, bodily language of the marketplace may not sound poetic, but it, too, provides a vivid urban image. This language also finds its way into high culture (challenging its loftiness), as Mikhail Bakhtin has demonstrated in his analysis of Rabelais. From another perspective, Armando Silva's *Imaginarios urbanos* explores the symbolics of the city. Examining the narratives, concepts, and images that city dwellers associate with urban spaces, Armando Silva stresses that it is in those mental and symbolic processes that their experience of the city becomes real for them.

Literary texts can offer perceptions of the city at a particular point in history. Benjamin's work on Baudelaire in *Illuminations* and Raymond Willams's *The Country and the City* are two inspiring examples. In Latin America, Fernández de Lizardi's novel *El periquillo sarniento* (also referred to under Urban Temporalities) conveys a nineteenth-century experience of urban spaces in Mexico: schools, shops, churches, and prisons. Cirilo Villaverde's novel *Cecilia Valdés*, which describes in great detail the neighborhoods and avenues of Havana, contrasts the homes of the elite and those of the poor. Agustín Lara's boleros, as discussed above, are lyrical depictions of city life. A more recent example of the rethinking of urban space is the work of the Argentine artist Guillermo Kuitca. As Marzena Grzegorczyk has shown, Kuitca challenges the limits of public and private spaces by painting city maps (the public sphere) on mattresses (private spaces).

Different spatial conceptions have dominated the region historically. In pre-Columbian and colonial cities, for example, space was hierarchically organized, with everything in its proper place (Foucault 22). There were high and low places, sacred and profane; the earth was seen as the center of the universe. Renaissance astronomy challenged the hierarchical ordering of space, but in Spain and Spanish America, Counter-Reformation politics sought to retain the medieval scheme. As the city changed, the effort became unsustainable. The expansion of the city, the skyscrapers that dominated the landscape, the noise that drowned out the church bells, the removal of cemeteries from the church's courtyard to the city's outskirts—all undermined the centrality of the colonial churches. The modern city sought to eradicate the past, demolishing old buildings, making way for vehicles, highways, and housing projects. The postmodern city, which has a more ambivalent relationship with the past, turns historic buildings into shopping malls, offices, and restaurants. The historic strata, of course, are mere surface. In the nineteenth-century prison that today houses the Museo Nacional in Bogotá, for example, a café stands in a patio where the structure of confinement is evident in the old building's materials (prison walls) and the small windows with bars. The café has been designed as a glass cage with metallic frames and floors—an ironic transparent confinement. There is no nostalgic appeal to emulate the prison architecture, but neither is it ignored. The sites of torture and confinement become places of leisure. One can argue that the Museo Nacional represents the triumph of culture over violence—but only if references to present-day prisons are suppressed, as is the case here.

The postmodern city conveys a certain anonymity and emptiness. Between urban spaces like avenues and subway lines are what Marc Augé calls "non places" (*non lieux*) (41). It is the city we encounter in Jorge Luis Borges's poems of solitary streets, Julio Cortázar's "El perseguidor," Ricardo Piglia's *Ciudad ausente*, and other literary works. Strikingly, the "non places" often act as magnets for street children, the homeless, prostitutes—those whom right-wing death squads, known for brutal campaigns of urban cleansing, call *desechables* (disposable).

Although, in particular historical eras, certain notions of space may prevail, they are not the only perceptions of public and private environments. At any given time, there may be several, sometimes competing, conceptions of space. In shantytowns and working-class neighborhoods, for instance, we may find subaltern imaginaries—ways of thinking about the city that are radically different from the official, or bourgeois, perspective. Populist cultural politics can also appropriate marginalized perspectives; the tango, for example, became the Argentinean national dance, although the music originated in the brothels and poor migrant quarters of Buenos Aires (Rowe and Schelling 35–36).

The experience of the shantytowns (*favelas, barriadas,* or *comunas*) is a topic with many possibilities. Alan Gilbert explains that the negative vision of marginal and emerging neighborhoods is changing. Once seen as a threat to the (bourgeois-controlled) establishment, they are now viewed more positively. City administrations, for example, are providing support for squatters who seek to claim unoccupied property. An introduction to this topic is the documentary video *Recuerdos de mi barrio,* which highlights the collective efforts that made possible a self-help neighborhood in Cali, Colombia.

In literature, the Peruvian anthropologist José María Arguedas's novel *El zorro de arriba y el zorro de abajo* depicts events in the port city of Chimbote, Peru, including the occupation of land for a self-help community. This narrative is interpolated by passages from Arguedas's journal outlining the challenges of writing an ethnography of the Latin American city in which the ancient collides with the present—the world of the sierra (the Andes) and the coastal region. *Child of the Dark,* the diary of Carolina María de Jesús, an Afro-Brazilian woman who lived by collecting scrap paper, provides insight into marginalized urban communities. Several films, including *Los olvidados, Rodrigo D: No futuro,* and Gaviria's *La vendedora de rosas,* portray the struggles of urban youth. *La estrategia del caracol* can be seen in conjunction with Manuel Castells's essay "The Dependent City and Revolutionary Populism," which describes tenants forming an alliance with the working-class movement.

Urban Subjectivities: Identity Narratives and Social Control

Cultural studies can shed light on the relation between identity and urban space. Many factors influence our identity: place of birth, gender, age, nationality, class, ethnicity, religion, occupation, political views. Where we come from and where we live are often important elements of our identity, in a paradoxical way: we live in spaces that are cultural constructs but serve as determinants in the development of our identity.

To grasp the intricate relation between space and subjectivity, we can examine the city's social interactions. A close look at social groups and their milieu is a good place to start. Louisa Hoberman and Susan Socolow's *Cities and Society in Colonial Latin America* is a well-documented study of landowners, the military, churchmen and religious women, merchants, artisans, and the lower class.

For another perspective, we can consider the roles gender plays in shaping urban space and endowing it with specific meaning. Although some studies have examined gender in the city, like Silvia Arrom's *The Women of Mexico City*, it is also important to question how the city itself is gendered—that is, how particular spaces are coded, for example whether as male or female spaces. There is also a growing scholarship on religious women's writings in colonial Latin America; many editions are becoming available, including Electa Arenal and Stacey Schlau's *Untold Sisters,* Kathleen Mayers's *Word from New Spain,* and Angela Robledo's *Jerónima Nava y Saavedra.* Since convents were always in urban settings, these texts allow us to examine one aspect of the link between the city and its inhabitants. A critical look at the convents themselves is also useful. Architectural designs can structure the world according to class, gender, and ethnicity, sometimes below the level of consciousness, as Pierre Bourdieu has rightly argued. For this reason they can be effective in maintaining the social order.

Special attention may be given to the relation between the body and architectural designs—for example, symbolic manipulations of bodily experience that integrate the body's space with cosmic space (Bourdieu 91). Working, praying, singing, and fasting are experiences that can be analyzed in this context, since these activities took place in a range of designated spaces (chapel, chorus, locutorio, cells, etc.). In contrast to the lack of privacy in the rooms of colonial residences of Spaniards and Creoles, the individual cells of the convents offered nuns a space of their own, strengthening their sense of individuality (Arenal and Schlau 3).[7] At any rate, the cityscape was marked by large cloisters, a sign of an urban center's power and prestige. To understand why Latin America invested so much energy in constructing convents, we need to comprehend the ideas such buildings embodied. Seclusion did not mean that nuns were cut off from the outer world. On the contrary, they took part in the making of the city in numerous ways. They participated in the economy, as bankers (*censos*) and owners of real estate (houses, stores, and rural properties). They sponsored lay brotherhoods and played a role in public religious celebrations. In the convents, the Latin American elite educated their daughters and buried their dead. Considerable endowments, or *capellanías*, ensured that their patrons' souls would be ritually remembered. In short, the nuns' rituals and purity were considered essential for the material and spiritual well-being of the city—they represented the ordering of bodies and spaces in the cosmos.

The city as a theme has many ramifications beyond those explored here. The city in itself can easily be the topic of a semester course. It can also be a unit in a Latin American culture course. The key element, in either case, is to encourage students to take a critical look at the cultural construction of urban spaces. Connections with students' own urban experience are crucial. In upper- and graduate-level courses, I would examine some of the methodological quandaries that arise from confronting a topic as complex as the city. Rather than simply memorize facts and ideas, students will become participants in the adventure—the promises and dilemmas—of the search for knowledge. The project should be rewarding, because the urban experience is a vital part of the human story.

NOTES

1. See, for example, García Canclini's work on global culture in Mexico City (*Consumidores*); Barbero's focus on cultural politics and communication in Colombia; Sarlo's work on postmodernism in Argentina; and the postcolonial cultural studies *from* Latin America in the electronic journal *Dissens*. Latin Americanists in the United States have said that the institutionalization of cultural studies in this country has

significantly watered down the radicalness of the British project, and they have been accused of using the positivist, bourgeois concept of culture without much rigor. Beverley and other Latin Americanists in the United States decided that, to maintain the spirit of early cultural studies and to incorporate postcolonial theory, they would focus on subaltern politics. Thus in 1992 they produced the Latin American Subaltern Studies Group Founding Statement, which emulates the Indian postcolonial group led by Ranajit Guha. From another direction Neil Larsen expresses distrust of the popularity of cultural studies in the United States and Latin America ("Questionnaire" 247).

2. This global dialogue is evident in genealogies of the field, appearing in introductory essays, and in the cultural studies questionnaire of the *Journal of Latin American Cultural Studies* (*JLACS*). Common references include the early-twentieth-century Italian intellectual Antonio Gramsci; the Frankfurt school (Walter Benjamin, Theodore Adorno, Jürgen Habermas); Louis Althusser, French poststructuralism, and psychoanalysis (Michel Foucault, Jacques Lacan, Slavoj Žižek); and the Birmingham Center for Contemporary Cultural Studies (Raymond Williams, Stuart Hall, and others). See Simon During's introduction to *The Cultural Studies Reader* and responses in the *JLACS* by the literary and cultural critics Sarlo, George Yúdice, and Walter Mignolo. In Latin America, there is growing identification with the region's intellectual tradition (the nineteenth-century Cuban poet José Martí, the early-twentieth-century Peruvian writer José Carlos Mariategui, the Uruguayan critic Ángel Rama, and others) that stresses continuity rather than rupture in the left.

3. This shift is evident, for example, in Beverley's *Against Literature*, in which he discusses the appropriateness of studying *testimonio* instead of the Western (European) canon.

4. Additionally, Aguilera Rojas's *Fundación de ciudades hispanoamericanas* offers a comprehensive view of the colonial city.

5. Persons abducted and often killed by security forces (police, army, and paramilitary groups) are referred to as *desaparecidos* ("disappeared") in Latin America.

6. The founding ritual of the Latin American city was described in 1599 by Bernardo Vargas Machuca. With a dagger in hand, the chief Spanish conquistador threatened to kill anyone who challenged the city's being founded.

7. Reflections on the cultural dimensions of architecture by Jean Franco, Armando Silva, Fredric Jameson, Guillermo Kuitca, and others can be found in the collections edited by Cynthia Davidson, *Anyplace* and *Anybody*.

Cultures of the Lyric and Lyrical Culture: Teaching Poetry and Cultural Studies

Jill S. Kuhnheim

A colleague who teaches in an English department tells me that her students frequently comment that reading poetry is like reading a foreign language. This may suggest that my students, who are most often nonnative speakers of Spanish, are doubly challenged when faced with understanding Spanish American poetry. They read a strange language made even stranger, and they do so with some hesitation. Poetry's perceived complexity has led to its valuation as the most literary of literary forms, for literature is a field in which density of meaning has been more highly esteemed than clarity and directness. Many definitions of poetry depend, in fact, on a concept of its distance and difference from everyday speech, but even as these borders are constructed, they begin to leak. Roman Jakobson, in his famous mid-twentieth-century linguistic study of the poetic function of language, for example, founds his observations on instances from commonplace speech (anyone who has read Jakobson's essay is not likely to forget "Joan and Margery" and "I like Ike"). Jonathan Culler, who investigates poetry's specificity in *Structuralist Poetics*, follows this fundamental work with an exploration based on the concepts of "babble and doodle"—the playful and figurative use of language grounded in quotidian speech ("Changes"). Our perception of poetry's particular work shifts even within essays attempting to fix its cultural meaning.

It may be because poetry has been given this primary role of upholding "literariness" that its boundaries crack in the process, for poetry cannot be separated from the cultures, the languages, and the histories within which it is constructed. As Cary Nelson reminds us in his compelling study of marginalized poetries in the United States, "No purely literary categories exist: there are merely different ways of constructing the textual and social domain of literariness." There is no transcendent meaning to, or definition of, what poetry does and how it does it. Nelson defines poetry in contention with other speech and writing and asserts that it "gains meaning from its struggle with various discourses trying to win the credibility to serve similar cultural functions" (56, 132). Poetry—however closely connected to literary aesthetics—is social. Situating poetry as a cultural object allows us to see how the genre changes, just as poetry's shifts reflect, in turn, on other cultural transformations.

A late-twentieth-century interest in cultural studies is one such transformation that certainly has affected poetry's work. Poetry has been marginalized within cultural studies—the result, perhaps, of cultural studies' cross-disciplinarity and poetry's historical association with literature. Within the genre, the lyric's particular post-Romantic ties to the expression of subjectivity and lack of reference to historical reality have stimulated readings that isolate much poetry from the world. When poetry enters the discussion, it often does so only to the degree to which it can be transformed into different, though associated, cultural objects, such as song lyrics, slogans, advertising jingles, greeting cards, posters, rap, or MTV versions of the poetic. These are all valid and often provocative areas of study that indicate poetry's penetration into the everyday world and cross the divide between high and low cultures, yet these examples leave more generically pure poetry untouched. Students can easily see that an examination of these objects grounded in popular or mass culture differs from a conventional approach to poetry. Exploring the popular manifestations of poetry is only the first step, however. We must unsettle traditional notions of poetry by providing readers with new tools that illuminate both aesthetic and cultural facets of the texts. Poetry, with its high cultural baggage, in fact provides us with an opportunity to teach students to examine how every cultural intervention participates in the dialogue about power in its particular social and political context.

It is customary to teach poetry for its literary qualities—meter, rhyme, symbols, connotations, among them—sometimes introducing elements of sociohistoric significance (such as the changing role of the artist and concurrent privileging of the literary voice in Spanish American modernism). That this information is often presented as supplemental maintains the hierarchy of aesthetic over contextual. If history is made primary, though, the result can be an interpretation of the poem that does not account for poetry's engagement of issues in aesthetic terms. A cultural studies reading attempts to bridge the gap between these tendencies by analyzing all elements of the poem as inscribed in culture. Instead of marking the poem's distance from ordinary language, we can ask, How does it use this language, and when? What kinds of discourses are incorporated into the text? How does it include the "cultural noise" of society, or how does it oppose it?[1] Approaching poetry this way necessarily includes aesthetic elements, for poems contextualize one another, but looking at these traits alone circumscribes the kind of information we receive.

As readers of poetry, we have frequently been too respectful of disciplinary boundaries. Cultural studies aims to challenge the ways in which traditional disciplines and categorizations (such as genre) are constructed to resituate poetry as one of the ways people structure and express their self-understanding and location in the world. Putting Jakobson's and Culler's theoretical observations into practice, new readers might break established boundaries by returning to the origins of poetry. They may become poetic anthropologists, uncovering how poetry occurs in everyday life, how people use language poetically (does someone in their household talk in a poetic way?), discussing the ideas behind found poetry, and thinking about what makes language poetic. In this way they may begin to see that poetry does not exist just in the classroom or as text (the traditional object of study) but is oral, alive, in transformation, and participatory. Sending new readers of poetry to poetry readings or slams and encouraging them to observe when and where poetry occurs in their cultures give them another context for the form as practiced today and remind us that the poems we read and teach have existed in a variety of settings on their way to the classroom.

Lyn Hejinian has said that poetry is a "barnacle-encrusted cultural text," an image that concretizes the sedimentation of meanings poetic texts accumulate. One of the authors in the Spanish American canon whose texts exemplify this layering of cultural signification is José Martí. After discussing with a class some of the basic ideas behind cultural studies, as briefly outlined above, I assigned students to small groups and gave them Martí's poem "V," from *Versos sencillos*, with no author or book title referenced, and asked them to analyze it in cultural terms as much as possible. The poem begins:

Si ves un monte de espumas,
Es mi verso lo que ves:
Mi verso es un monte, y es
un abanico de plumas.   (Jiménez 90)

If you see a mountain of foam,
It is my verse that you see:
My verse is a mountain, and it is
a plumed fan.[2]

The absence of contextual information produces a thematic reading, and students readily identify the topic as poetry. The natural images encourage them to elaborate on poetry's role in expressing humankind's conception of nature, and more-advanced students may identify the speaker's problematization of the way poetry mediates between public and private worlds. The regular rhythm and strong rhyme suggest song and, since it is from a well-known collection, some students recognize the writer as Martí. This context-blind reading encourages students to incorporate aesthetic aspects into a cultural framework; it also signals the limits of a text-only focus.

To decipher what else Martí's poem does, we need contextual information. Listing possible questions and lines of investigation that arise when we identify the author demonstrates that the poem is embedded in Cuban culture (and other cultures) in a variety of ways. Some possibilities: How does our understanding of the poem change when we study the prologue to the *Versos sencillos* (which sets up the author's expectations about the book)? How has the meaning of the poem changed from Martí's time to the present? What is the poem's relation to modernism, to other modernists, to other Cuban modernists (e.g., Martí vs. Casal)? These literary preoccupations lead to others: What has Martí meant in Cuba at different moments? Why is this poem part of Martí's canonized production (and what is not)? What happens if we read this poem in relation to Martí's prose (both well-known and lesser-known examples, such as his letters and his novel *Lucía Jerez*)? We can pose a question based on the poem's rhythmic qualities: How have *Versos sencillos* been turned into song—when and by whom? Because Martí is frequently anthologized, we can also provide a context by investigating the poem's publishing history. When does it appear in which anthology and what other poems accompany it? Following Nelson's lead as he analyzes the ways in which individual volumes of poetry can constitute acts of cultural intervention, we might study different editions of Martí's text—its illustrations, typeface, and accompanying material—to discover its contribution to the cultural dialogue.[3] We can read the poem as representing the journal in which it appears: Who are the journal's anticipated audience? How does the journal aim to participate in culture? (Nelson 181, 219). How has Martí been rearticulated outside Cuba? As I write this piece, United States television is running an ad for bottled water using "Guantanamera," with Martí's lyrics, to sell tropical escapism.

The example of Martí illustrates another idea that is central to the practice of cultural studies: that readings are constructed between texts and contexts and that they change (Easthope 33). There is no single reading of "V," and pursuing one or another line of investigation will probably yield different results. A cultural studies approach, then, leads us away from a hermeneutical model of reading poetry and allows us to explore alternative aspects of the text. Some poems also teach us how to read them; their effect may be to produce different readers as well as different readings. In his "Indian poems" Ernesto Cardenal offers several examples that guide us in our understanding of specific cultural information in the texts. His collection *Los ovnis de oro* ("Golden UFOs") consists of poems about various indigenous groups. Cardenal incorporates, in his poems, facts and ideas that shed light on their cultures and histories, but his culture-crossing also occurs at the level of language. The poem "Nezhuacóyotl," for example, includes Nahuatl-inspired metaphoric, two-part language that infiltrates the Spanish and, at the same time, functions as a translation and an enactment of the lexicon of his autochthonous referent: "canto florido" ("flowering song") can be interpreted as poetry, while "labrar rostros" ("sculpting faces") suggests education. Cardenal's references to native hieroglyphics, in his parenthetical explanations of indigenous culture remind his readers of the multiple translations performed here and of the transition from pictographic to alphabetic writing, with its inevitable link to colonialism:

> Cambió su nombre "León-Fuerte" por "Coyote-Hambriento"
> (una cabeza de coyote con un nudo; el nudo quiere decir *ayuno*)   (30)

> He changed his name "Fierce-Lion" to "Hungry Coyote"
> (a coyote's head with a knot; the knot means *fasting*)

The translation process is not hidden; it is part of the poem.

In "El secreto de Machu-Picchu," another poem from the collection that focuses on Andean groups, the position of the speaker points to our limitations in reading this poem; he is a cultural outsider, as we are too, and it is a perspective we cannot transcend. Led by a "native informant" (his guide, Fernando), the first-person speaker continually reminds us that he is translating both temporally and culturally, and he inscribes his difference and distance from the cultures he observes. He is our guide, at least twice removed from the Inca cultures he traces, and his readers also serve as problematic ethnographers, unable to penetrate the reality of the other. Poetry is a partial bridge here, providing access while reminding us of the boundaries of that access. Indian culture, like culture in general, is shown to be not a monolithic, centralized, and coherent entity but a series of relations between societies entangled in past and present narratives of dominance and resistance.

These examples come from my experiences in teaching as well as in reading, for I regularly incorporate poetry into my cultural studies classes and vice versa. The intermingling of poetry with other cultural practices (sports, films, essays, *telenovelas*, music) crosses the high culture–popular cultural divide and illustrates how poetry, rather than producing "culture" (emphasizing a hegemonic, elitist inflection of the term), is one of many practices generated by the social systems we also refer to as "culture."[4] Reading lyric poetry within this more ample sense of culture will, in fact, demonstrate the interdependence between poetic and cultural knowledge. A segment of a recent graduate seminar on contemporary poetry will provide an illustration of this affiliation.

In this section, I draw on the contemporary tradition of poetry that textualizes the city. I historicize the theme by discussing its association with early-twentieth-century modernization and change in Spanish America (the nostalgia of Jorge Luis Borges's *Fervor de Buenos Aires* is a good departure point). We segue from issues of modernity to postmodern ones via the Chilean Nicanor Parra's midcentury poem "Los vicios del mundo moderno" ("Vices of the Modern World"), a piece that usually strikes readers as surprisingly contemporary. The quality of modernity in Parra's poem—in which "modern," like "vice," is a relative term—prepares us to compare the work with more recent examples of urban poetry, from the Chilean authors Clemente Riedemann and Carmen Berenguer and the Mexican writer Efraín Huerta. Reading these poets in conjunction with theoretical essays by Michel de Certeau and Beatriz Sarlo brings together distinct approaches to urban modernization. It also illustrates how the poetry relies on its readers' "geosocial" knowledge: we cannot read any of these poems for language or technical traits alone; we must be familiar with the social meaning of place in order to understand what the poem *does*.[5] We discover that the urban poetry of these Chileans incorporates urgent contemporary issues, for it confronts the neoliberal economic success of Chile in the 1990s and the country's past and present colonialism; the work also demonstrates how both poetic language and style change to meet expressive needs.

In his well-known essay "Walking in the City," Certeau uses walking as a metaphor for the reading process. He relates spatial practices to signifying ones to demonstrate how alternative, contestatory readings are produced. Reading and walking through the grid of a city use given forms in different ways. The panoramic view of New York that he observed from the World Trade Center acted as a kind of master narrative for Certeau, providing a totalizing perspective of the city that does not account for the variety of walkers/readers and their transformative "pedestrian speech-acts" (97). This vision of the city is complemented by that of Sarlo, who, in the "Ciudad" section of *Escenas de la vida posmoderna*, scrutinizes the shopping mall. Like Certeau, Sarlo spatializes reading practices and explores how space affects our use and reading of the mall. Noticing that we are controlled by the mall's structure, she comments on our lack of orientation or connection to the outside (the mall is like a space capsule). The mall may exist in an urban environment, but it produces an extraterritorial culture that has no history, is disconnected from chronological time and the city, and envelops us in an amnesia in which it is difficult to make sense (15, 20–23). It is a postmodern "no-place,"[6] evincing an absence of history that corresponds to Certeau's concept of the "nowhen," created by the totalizing discourse on the city (Certeau 94).

Reading these two pieces together makes the differences between their theoretical perspectives apparent. Students have readily seen that, in Sarlo's essay, the mall leaves us subject to postmodern disorientation, while Certeau offers us possible strategies of resistance, ways to reorient ourselves and regain or obtain agent status in the urban landscape. Adding yet another element, Riedemann's poem "Parque Arauco" also challenges us to decipher our roles in urban terrain. With the ideas of Certeau and Sarlo in mind, readers must decide whether Riedemann's poem positions us as potential agents of resistance or as subjected objects of history in the city.[7] We might contrast the ahistoricity of Sarlo's *shopping* and Certeau's ideological discourses on the city with Riedemann's poem. Reinserting us into history, the poem stresses the incongruity between the history of Araucano people, Native Americans

renowned for their resistance to conquest, and the Parque Arauco, an up-to-
date shopping mall in Santiago, emblematic of public pride in modernization.
The poem begins

> *Cash*, cheques a treinta / sesenta hermosas bolsas de empaque
> con gobelinos en los flancos.   (72)

> Cash, checks for thirty / sixty pretty shopping bags
> with gobelin tapestry on their sides.

The vocabulary situates us in a commercial venue, and the use of English
globalizes the principal activity here: consuming. The accumulation of references to merchandise in the first stanza (bags, cars, cosmetics) makes the
function of the Parque Arauco clear. Playing on associations between the Aru-
acanian past and the present, the poem depicts this shopping mall as a temple, a contemporary "no-place" that has supplanted holy places:

> Falsos han de ser los dioses de esta época, pues asisten tantos,
> todavía, a las iglesias. Bautizan a sus retoños con ternos de
> seis cuotas. No dan limosnas. Ni abren, el corazón, a quien
> les llora.

> The gods of this epoch must be false, since so many go,
> still, to churches. They baptize their offspring with six timed
> payments. They do not give alms. Or open, their hearts, to who-
>   ever
> cries to them.

A mercenary culture of spectacle has inverted traditional religious values. Instead of generosity, greed reigns (the commas around "el corazón" literally
cut it off from the surrounding text). The visual aspects of the mall emphasize
the difference between those who have access to this consumer utopia and
those who are excluded from it—those who can look but not touch.

"Arauco, qué domadura" ("Araucano, what a taming") begins the last
stanza, an exclamation, or perhaps an address, to an absent indigenous lis-
tener, in either case signaling that the Araucano has been tamed through
transformation into a symbol of consumption. At the same time, this line
ironically inserts Riedemann's poem into literary and national history by its
reference to Ercilla's colonial epic poem, *La araucana* (published in three parts
in 1569, 1578, 1589), and to Pedro de Oña's later elaboration of the conquest

and conversion of native populations, *Arauco domado* (1596). But "Parque Arauco" does not simply record a loss; its irony makes almost every image two-edged: "El Parque, con todas sus luces, en la mañana enceguecida" ("The Park, with all its lights, in the blind morning"), like the lights that both blind and illuminate. The irony turns us into more than oblivious consumers, for it historicizes the shopping mall and allows us a double perspective; we may be victims of a society that thinks of us as clients, but we can resist that treatment by seeing through the repackaging of neocolonial values.

In "La especulación de lo pretérito" ("Past Speculations"), Riedemann continues to highlight the connections between past and present. The speaker's voice is that of a sideshow hawker marketing Santiago. The city as product is an unlikely appeal to visitors (because of the Chilean capital's peripheral location and its smog), but the metropolis attracts ironic "tourists" who will arrive burdened by their possessions: "Traed vuestros bártulos a cuestas" ("Bring your things on your back"). These are poor travelers who shoulder their goods to market or carry their belongings in a Christ-like manner. The visitors are encouraged to participate in a peculiar kind of big-game hunt, where they are spurred to annihilate "las pulgas del tigre tuerto, sordo i mudo, que ingresa al zoológico de Wall Street" ("the fleas of the one-eyed, deaf and dumb tiger, who enters Wall Street's zoo")—a thinly veiled allusion to cleaning up the impaired economic miracle of Chile. (Chile is often referred to as "el tigre sudamericano" because of the success of neoliberal economic programs in the 1980s and 1990s.) The hawker's anachronistic use of the second-person plural recalls Spanish presence in South America, a colonial association that is reinforced when he urges the travelers to abandon "vuestras ciudadelas aguachentas, donde la conquista de SUDAAmérica aún no se ha consumado" (60) ("your sodden fortresses, where the conquest of SUDAAmerica has yet to be consummated"). Consumerism perpetuates colonialism in another guise. Naming the region "SUDAAmérica" ("South/SweatAmerica") reinforces the poem's humor and calls attention to the geographic position of the area and, perhaps, to the idea of physical labor. Riedemann also reminds us of his writing process through this shift, which, like the use of "i" for "y" throughout this section, is primarily a visual rather than an aural alteration. Breaking with convention makes the author's writing consistent with the rhetoric of the text, which urges us to break step, not to follow rules blindly.

These works demonstrate how poetry performs a variety of functions in present-day Chile. They probe the economic success of the end of the

Pinochet dictatorship and its accompanying social complacency, and they offer us another option: a position from which to criticize neoliberal economic and cultural achievements. Riedemann engages issues such as colonial and contemporary politics, religion, development, modernity, and the changing relations between the cultural and the economic realms. He employs what could be called postmodern irony but relies, as well, on an avant-garde–inspired link between art and life, in order to demonstrate that literature is not separate from other cultural concerns.

The physical and sociological changes in urban life that Riedemann charts are complemented by technological transfigurations—the fragmented glimpses we catch on television, video clips, or from speeding trains, for example—that alter the ways in which the city is constructed and experienced in all forms, including poetry. We find an example of this in Berenguer's collection *Huellas del siglo* ("Century's Footprints"). Her poem "Santiago metro" is a series of vignettes structured around the names of metro stops. The titles of the fragments lead us to expect scenes—neighborhoods briefly seen through windows or represented by a metro stop. Yet the visions here are personal, inner-focused:

REPUBLICA
Es el único
hablo contigo: y vivo

MONEDA
Estaríamos comiendo una sopa
de letras
                              Dios

EL LLANO
Toda la noche camino en llamas
Lenguas de paraíso
                              contigo.

REPUBLICA
It is the only thing
I talk about with you: and I live

MONEDA
We would be eating an
alphabet soup
God

EL LLANO
All night I walk in flames
Tongues of paradise
with you.

The metro stops appear to interrupt an interior monologue that, rather than García Canclini's city as video clip, an "effervescent montage of discontinuous images" (*Consumidores* 100), is disconnected from its surroundings. The train rider passes through diverse moments and spaces marked by signs that spark poetic free association. Yet the name of each metro stop, a word with no referent, in capitals, stops us in our tracks. Narrative impulse is impeded, and Berenguer uses the fracturing of the lyric form to emphasize the inner fragmentation of contemporary society. She moves us through the city in a reading experience analogous to our mode of experiencing urban life.

In poems from his 1974 collection, *Los eróticos y otros poemas*, Efraín Huerta also uses urban transport—the bus and the metro—to structure his experience. "Meditación y delirio en el metro" ("Meditation and Delirium on the Metro") is similar to Berenguer's poem: in both works, traveling on public transportation in a metropolis provokes an interior journey. Huerta's textualization of the experience is less fragmented, not interrupted by metro stops. He describes passing them as he ponders:

Hoy desperté y anduve pensándolo bien:
padecí en la Ruta 1 durante Chapultepec-Insurgentes,
Insurgentes-Salto de Agua,
sin encontrar a nadie parecido al dios de los enigmas.   (299)

Today I woke up and walked around thinking about it
I suffered on Route 1 during Chapultepec-Insurgentes,
Insurgentes-Salto de Agua,
without meeting anyone resembling the God of Enigmas.

Unlike Berenguer, Huerta uses the station names as part of his text rather than as pauses in it. They are segments of daily life for metro users, and they flow into the speaker's thoughts. But the routine progress of the train, accented formally by the poem's repetition ("Chapultepec-Insurgentes, / Insurgentes-Salto de Agua"), goes against his desire for divine intervention. The movement of the metro and the presumed presence of other people contrast here with the speaker's desperate meditation on a static situation: democracy and the state of electoral power in Mexico. This referent does not become clear until the end of the poem, however, when the speaker breaks out of his isolation and announces to his readers (and his implied listeners in the metro) the results of his contemplation:

> Sí, señoras y señores, víctimas y verdugos,
> gente azul, morada o tricolor;
> sí, de verdad, una noche de cualquiera
> haré un montoncito de cenizas
> con mi despiadada y cínica
> credencial permanente de elector.   (300)

> Yes, ladies and gentlemen, victims and tyrants,
> blue, purple or tricolored people;
> yes, really, one of these nights
> I will make a little pile of ashes
> with my merciless and cynical
> permanent electoral credential.[8]

Nevertheless, this revelation does not easily resolve the ambiguity of the source of his desperation, for his reflections reveal the speaker's social situation; in the course of the poem we have learned that he talks to friends who are absent because they are in jail, and his melancholy appears to be tied to the transportation system as much as to the electoral one. Still, by moving his meditating man through the city, Huerta makes public this often private intellectual exercise, creating a communal aspect that is reinforced when the speaker announces his desire to destroy the permanent emblem of his citizenship. The metro in this poem isolates yet brings people together; like the speaker's meditation, it is an individual experience made collective.

"Juárez-Loreto," another poem by Huerta from the same collection, embeds its social commentary in a contemporary love poem. The situation of the speaker, a bus rider on Route 85, allows him to spatialize his desire for an unknown woman on the bus and associate it with the city: "empiezo a amarla en la diagonal de Euler" (301) ("I begin to love her on the diagonal street Euler"). The speaker employs tropes and rhetorical elements of classical love poetry, calling his unknown "beloved," "beautiful," "golden," "unattainable" as he bestows on her several powerful names: "debe llamarse Ría, Napoleana, / Bárbara o Letra Muerta o Cosa Quemada," and later, "Alabada seas, bandida de mi lerda conmiseración / Escorpiana te llamas, Cancerita, Cangreja" (301–02) ("she must be called River, Napoleana, / Barbara or Dead Letter or Burned Thing," and later, "Praised be, bandit of my useless pity / Scorpiana you are named, Little Cancer, Crab"). She is distant, untrue; he is in her power, for she is a thief of his heart (his bad luck and his pity) and one of the perpetual thieves who work the buses in Mexico City. Huerta mixes discursive registers, poeticizing daily life on mass transport in a rhetorical display that complements the theatricality of public life. In the process he engages the "literary" space of the Distrito Federal. The ride on Route 85 not only dramatizes a scene of unrequited love; it moves us through a city of literary markers, streets and bus stops named for Western cultural heroes: Maimónides, Hesiod, Dumas, Poe, Molière, Horacio, Homero, Miguel de Cervantes Saavedra. Incorporating these place names, Huerta restores them to their literary sources while calling attention to the intersections of literature and life. His speaker is a "viejo-príncipe-poeta (soberbiamente idiota)" (302) ("old-poet-prince [arrogantly idiotic]"), whose movement through the literary/literal city unifies our perception of it as he transforms the distance and disengagement of the city into imaginative intimacy.

Huerta uses his poetic vision to repossess, to reconquer aspects of urban life. He rereads the city and resemanticizes it through literature, transforming his conception of it from one of meaninglessness or imposed meaning to that of creation of meanings. In "Meditación y delirio," this process happens through the speaker's musing on the destruction of his official, nonfunctional identity and his public declaration that he intends to live outside the law. Yet the action remains hypothetical; he does not destroy his voter's card and, like the political discourse he disparages, his language is ineffectual. Rather than renew language corrupted by political abuse, this poem reveals the irony of its speaker's own false promises. In "Juárez-Loreto," Huerta reidealizes the urban environment through literature, but not without irony. His would-be lover never speaks to his princess-thief, and there is a clash in his invented world between Western cultural allusions and urban Mexico (they do not translate smoothly). The political and romantic irony in this poem is supplemented by a democratization of vision because the speaker, though striving to be different, is one of us, riding on public transport, a space available to all. In broader ideological terms, it is also a socially useful space subverted by the collusion of government and capitalism to function as an instrument of exploitation—another level implicit in Huerta's poetic ride through dystopia.[9]

In the poems I have discussed, there is no totalized vision of the city but, instead, a focus on the interior of the bus, metro, or mind of the speaker in public gathering places. In this respect, the poet, taking advantage of the lyric's traditional association with a subjective voice, communicates an individual experience that in many ways represents how every traveler survives the "human hyperdensity" of mass transport (García Canclini, *La ciudad de los viajeros* 11). Public transport all over the world brings people to and from urban centers and connects commercial, industrial, and residential spaces that have become separated. The metro and the bus are in-between places, no-places, like the shopping mall, yet they are significant locations on the cognitive maps of the city's inhabitants, as these poems demonstrate. In the poems of Berenguer and Riedemann, these transitional spaces provide a forum for the speakers to express alienation and disorientation in contemporary Santiago—a response that opposes the social optimism, conformity, and acceptance of neoliberal success that dominate the public sphere in postdictatorship Chile. Mexico has become a megacity, and Huerta's poems register the change in scale through their speakers' alienation and futility. The poet embodies the explosive urban expansion through the acceleration and the fragmented perspective of public transport; the speaker-passenger paradoxically reasserts both the importance and generality of specific experiences. At the same time, his irony checks an unselfconscious celebration of egoism and individuality, which cannot compensate for the lack of genuine collectivity in the distended city.

Lyric poetry, with its brevity, its stanzas surrounded by white space on the page, emphasizes the partitions between its elements. Poetry thus has more in common with the single visual image of a painting or a photograph than with a series of images gathered together in a film. In *La ciudad de los viajeros*, García Canclini provides photographs of the city that complement these poems (particularly those of Huerta, since the images are of Mexico). He remarks, "Hay una correspondencia entre las operaciones de recorte y encuadre que hacen las fotos y el conjunto de experiencias desarticuladas que se obtienen en una megaciudad" (109) ("There is a correspondence between the cutting and framing that photos enact and the gamut of disjointed experiences that happen in a megacity"). García Canclini's comparison leads us to consider how a poem uses its formal elements to frame an image, which then alters its readers' vision. As we have seen, poetry constructs a perspective that could be compared to that of a photograph, except that it frames our view through language. Reading beyond the text, we might ask students to find other photos of Santiago and Mexico City, as well as postcards and maps of metro and bus routes; the class can compare linguistic framing with visual cropping and other literal or symbolic representations of urban space.

After providing examples of how poetry can be read within a broader definition of culture, I return to the question subtending this essay and offer a straightforward response: Why read poetry in a cultural studies class? Why not simply study the lyric through music (or study mass culture, working-class culture, etc.)? My clearest answer to this question is that, as we observed in the opening example of Martí, poetry plays a distinct role in a wide array of cultures and, as such, it too must be accounted for. As we have seen, contemporary poetry can provide students with depictions of experiences with which they may be familiar—shopping, taking public transportation, feeling the impact of social and economic conditions—yet the lyric defamiliarizes these places and activities and re-creates them in its own terms. As I noted at the beginning, poetry makes language strange, and in the process can also make history, politics, economics, gender, sexuality, ethnicity, class, race, and myriad other cultural elements strange. Contemplating poems in terms of various characteristics of human society, then, demonstrates how students can use their knowledge of poetic techniques to re-view other cultural objects, to see them differently.

Reading poetry in a broad cultural context reinforces the notion of meaning as a social construction made up of contingent conventions. As Nelson puts it, poetry is not a "transcendent realm of atemporal values" "available [only] to those deserving access to it" (238) but a set of specific practices rooted in the world. In contemporary Latin America, as in much of the West, there has been a hegemonic investment in the perceived split between "political" and "aesthetic" functions of poetry and in maintaining a distance between high and popular cultures. Reading poetry as one of a number of cultural practices makes us recognize this split, examine it, question its validity and its function in distinct times and places. Poetry simply provides us with another means of access from which we can question the changing construction of culture and what it does.

NOTES

1. I borrow the term "cultural noise" from Paulson's *The Noise of Culture*.
2. All translations are my own, unless otherwise noted.
3. It is difficult to find single volumes of Martí's work; unlike the poetry of such modernists as Rubén Darío, whose *poemarios* are regularly published (with prologues and the poems in their planned order), Martí's poetry most frequently appears in editions of his complete works, or in collections with a particular focus (*poesía mayor*, etc.). An early Cuban edition of *Versos sencillos* (published by El ciervo herido, Havana, 1939) is notable for its simplicity: it is small, the paper cover has only the title, and the poems are in plain type on standard grade paper; the volume itself

suggests the simplicity of the title and indicates that the book is meant to be bought and used by ordinary readers.

4. In several of his books (most notably, *Culturas híbridas*), García Canclini has become a major theorist of the multiple, changing inflections of the term in a Mexican–Latin American context. Hartman also provides a useful overview of shifts in the relation between the terms *culture* and *civilization* in Europe from the eighteenth century to the Second World War.
5. The term "geosocial" comes from Damon's fascinating study of an alternative vanguard in United States poetry, *The Dark End of the Street* (6).
6. The term "no-lugar" is used by García Canclini in *Culturas híbridas*. Rice, in her essay "Trafficking in Philosophy," links the expression to the corporate city in the information age.
7. For an exploration of the multiple inflections of "subject" in relation to power and autonomy, see Smith's *Discerning the Subject*.
8. "Tricolor" could refer to the Mexican flag, giving this section another political significance.
9. The appendix to this article includes a study guide for an extended reading of Huerta's and Berenguer's metro poems.

APPENDIX:
TEACHING URBAN POETRY

Guidelines for a comparative reading of two poems on an urban theme, in an advanced undergraduate or graduate course.

Poems

"Santiago metro," by Carmen Berenguer
"Meditación y delirio en el metro," by Efraín Huerta

Prereading Exercises

After briefly introducing the authors, you might ask students to explore the following Internet sites: chile.com, metrosantiago.cl, www.mapcity.cl (for Berenguer); www. metropla.net/am/mexi/mexico, www.mexicocity.com (for Huerta). These sites display scenes and maps of the metros in Santiago and Mexico City. Students can also look for population statistics and other information about urban life, and mass transport in particular. Or you might bring maps of the metro systems to class (they can be downloaded). Examining the maps (or parts of them) in conjunction with reading the poems may encourage students to think about the experience of living in a megacity.

Study Questions

1. Look at the map of the metro and then at the poems. What differences do you notice in the formats without even reading the words on the page?
2. Our reading of a poem is controlled, in part, by its formal properties. How do the following features control our reading of these poems: rhythm, line breaks, punctuation, rhyme, alliteration, assonance? How are the poems different in this respect?
3. How does Berenguer bring the metro stops to life in the poem? How does Huerta? How does the difference in treatment affect our reading of the poems?

4. Do you imagine the speakers in the poems to be looking out the window? Why or why not? What is the speaker thinking about in each poem? Do the speaker's thoughts change in the poem? Explain. For example, does the speaker arrive at a destination?
5. Both poems raise several questions. How do these questions differ in each case? Who hears the questions? Are they answered? Explain.
6. In what way is each poem *about* the metro? What is the relation of the poem to the metro (what does the metro *do*)? What information about the setting would affect our understanding of the poems?
7. Subways, like much mass transport, have been described as "in-between" places. How does each poem express this idea? How is a poem itself a kind of "in-between" place?
8. The Argentine anthropologist Néstor García Canclini says the following about metro travel in Mexico City:

> En la vida de muchos habitantes de la capital mexicana los viajes ocupan entre dos y cuatro horas de su tiempo diario. Por tanto, los medios de transporte son también lugares donde se vive. Al viajar en ellos los habitantes se apropian del espacio urbano, atraviesan zonas que no conocen sino desde la distancia y la fugacidad del vehículo que los traslada. En ese movimiento, van imaginando cómo viven "los otros". Los viajes metropolitanos nos lanzan más allá de la ciudad física, del espacio construido y visible a lo que suponemos detrás de la material de los signos. Nos confrontan con seres diferentes y anónimos que nos acompañan en el transporte público o viven en zonas diversas de nuestro entorno habitual. Por eso interesa estudiar tanto la realidad de los viajes como los imaginarios que suscita en los viajeros.   (*La ciudad de los viajeros* 24)

> In the lives of many inhabitants of Mexico City, travel occupies between two and four hours of their time daily. For this reason, their means of transport are also places where they live. When they travel on them, inhabitants appropriate urban space and cross zones that they know only from the distance and speed of the vehicle that carries them. In this movement they imagine how "the others" live. Metropolitan trips carry us farther than the physical city, from the visible and constructed space to what we suppose is behind the material signs. We confront different and anonymous beings that accompany us on public transport or live in zones that are different from our usual surroundings. That is why it is intriguing to study the reality of the trips as much as the imaginary worlds of the travelers.

Do the poems participate in the project outlined by García Canclini? Are the poems anthropological? Does the fact that these are *poems* make us see familiar experiences differently?
9. Michel de Certeau has compared reading to walking through the grid of a city and explains that, when we create our own paths through a text (or a map or any set of references), we are making "pedestrian speech-acts." How is riding (on public transportation or by car) different from walking through the city? How do the poems suggest the differences?
10. In each poem, what is the relation of the title to the text? How does the title set the tone and indicate (or not) what happens in the poem?
11. What do you think is left out of the poems? What does this excising or cutting away have to do with the experiences they present?

12. Do the poems challenge your ideas about what a poem should be? How and why?

Follow-Up Possibilities

Ask students to contrast their experiences on public transportation with those described in the poems. Have the class discuss which kinds of communities are created in big cities and how, where urban dwellers get their sense of space, and what the boundaries are between public and private places. You can also discuss other urban issues in contemporary Latin America, or compare these poems with poetry about the city from the beginning of the twentieth century, with poetry about other cities, or with pictures of the city (García Canclini's *La ciudad de los viajeros* offers good examples for Mexico City).

Cultural Studies and Business Spanish: A Critique of Imperialism

Danny J. Anderson

I never expected that one day I would teach a class in business Spanish. With graduate training as a literary scholar, I held a view that grouped together all international business interests and dismissed them as ugly-American imperialism. And of course, by my account, my international education, travel, and cultural expertise were only minimally contaminated by exposure to imperialism. The purity of my position as a literary scholar was so clear to me that I would test my allegiances, observing my personal reactions to current events as indications of my real commitments. For example, in December 1999, while reading journalistic accounts of the protests in Seattle, Washington, during the World Trade Organization's summit, I found myself thinking about my course in business Spanish. Rather than teach this course, should I have been alongside the protesters? These days I watch with interest the publicity, debates, and demonstrations that surround international conferences on globalization. Rather than reject teaching business Spanish, I have discovered that this course allows me to participate in debates on globalization locally, in a way that invites my students to engage in critical reflection.

Today, *globalization* has become a buzzword—the demon that protesters in Seattle were seeking to exorcise. On the one hand, the term signals economic integration—a phenomenon usually discussed as global or postindustrial capitalism, neoliberalism, or free trade, rhetorical labels that are applied according to our ideological position. On the other hand, globalization has created worldwide environmental consciousness; advocates of international human rights not only question events in political hot spots but also strive to organize labor across national borders. Like business itself, globalization, neither all good nor all bad, is far more complicated than the one-dimensional evil it is sometimes made out to be.

The complex effects of globalization reach into the university in numerous ways, and especially into classrooms where students seek expertise in modern languages and cultures in order to gain a competitive edge in the job market. In Spanish, in particular, enrollments are rising dramatically. Many of today's students participate in the electoral process, and most are preparing for careers shaped by globalization; they belong to a generation that may determine how free or fair international trade will be. As teachers and scholars in colleges and universities in the United States, we do not provide a neutral, or disinterested, form of knowledge about Latin America. From the language classroom to the doctoral seminar, we create and disseminate knowledge that advances certain interests. Teaching business Spanish from a cultural studies perspective makes language learning relevant to our students and enables me to make explicit, in the classroom, the complex and contradictory interests that affect everyone who studies or teaches Spanish in the United States.

Recent pedagogical emphases have established that effective language learning cannot be separated from the acquisition of cultural information. In business, where the success of a commercial transaction often depends on a keen sense of the unspoken codes of propriety and protocol, this finding is certainly apt. A cultural studies approach goes a step further than a cultural approach in analyzing these cultural codes. Besides teaching the vocabulary and forms of business communication, a cultural studies approach to commercial Spanish permits an analysis of national stereotypes associated with international business, an examination of national cultures, and a questioning about the ethics of United States and Latin American business relations. Cultural studies can turn the business Spanish class into a course on cultural sensitivity, cross-cultural understanding, and a critique of imperialism.[1]

Conceptually, I organize my syllabus and the introduction to the course around the implications of certain terms (see app., syllabus 5). In the introduction to my syllabus and on the first day of class, students explore the connotations attached to the terms *business, negocios, to negotiate,* and *negociar. Negocios* generally refers to business in a commercial sense (although it has interesting, relevant slang meanings as well). Similarly, *to negotiate* and *nego-*

ciar refer to the process of determining the parameters of commercial, political, and legal interaction.

Most important for this class, *to negotiate* and *negociar* have become key words in the cultural studies understanding of identity (I avoid the term *subjectivity* and try to defamiliarize students' sense of the word *identity*). In cultural studies, *to negotiate* refers to the ways individuals respond to the multiple forces that define their identity and strive to make sense of the contradictions in their lives. *Culture* refers to the everyday arena for carrying out the ongoing negotiation of identity; the meaning is not limited to the collection of elite or popular artifacts typically discussed in a literature class or a culture class. To bring the phenomenon into focus, I emphasize, throughout the course, that negotiations of identity that are based on stereotypes of nationality, race or ethnicity, social class, gender, and, especially, profession affect intercultural perception and communication. I also stress the stereotypes that will have the most impact on students who may someday work in Latin America. Students confront the stereotypes they hold about Latin America; they also examine the images Latin Americans have of the foreigner who has arrived to conduct business—most often, the representations of the United States businessman (traditionally there have been few women business leaders, although the situation has changed in recent decades).[2]

In the first days of the course, the terms *globalization* and *neoliberalism* also merit special attention. Most of my students have a working sense of *globalization*, and, through class discussion, I make certain that they not only grasp the concept of economic integration but can comprehend the significance of conceptualizing issues on a planetary scale. Global thinking on issues like nuclear weapons and environmental contamination is familiar to most students, but we also discuss worldwide health concerns (AIDS, for example) and efforts toward international labor organization. Moreover, in an era of rapid communication, local cultures absorb global influences and, at the same time, export their customs and traditions: "world music," available at a local bookstore, is an excellent example. Noting that *culture* often refers to consumer products and the lifestyle their consumption evokes, we discuss why many people equate globalization with "Americanization"—after all, trademarked products like Coca-Cola and McDonald's have become available internationally. These examples broaden students' understanding of globalization as a diverse, complex phenomenon and simultaneously link economic, social, and cultural concepts.[3]

Neoliberalism is intimately related to globalization yet usually needs clarification. Students in the United States tend to associate conservatism and liberalism with the major political parties. In economic terms, however, *liberalism*—a word students may associate with nineteenth-century trade policies—refers to the belief that the state should not intervene in market forces—a notion closely linked to conservative politics in the United States. As Daniel Yergin and Joseph Stanislaw explain, the terminology is vexing:

> For Americans, the global battle between the state and market can be puzzling, for it appears to pit "liberalism" against "liberalism." . . . In the rest of the world, *liberalism* means almost exactly the opposite—what an American liberal would, in fact, describe as *conservatism*.   (xv)

In economic terms, once again, *trade liberalization* refers to the decrease in the government's role in markets.

In historical practice, conditions in the early twentieth century prompted a great deal of state involvement in national economies throughout the world. The welfare state emerged, and nationalistic governments stepped in to protect domestic economies from international competition. Toward the end of the century, the profound economic crises of the 1980s gave rise to neoliberalism, because the earlier policies were no longer effective. The gasoline shortage of the 1970s and the drop in the price of crude oil in the early 1980s revealed how interdependent national economies had become. With the fall in prices, oil-producing countries experienced a significant loss of revenue—an upheaval that affected Venezuela and Mexico dramatically. At the same time, as a result of economic stagnation and severe inflation, many Latin American countries struggled with a tremendous international debt, owed mainly to United States banks. Some Latin American nations debated publicly the possibility of defaulting on loan repayment; doing so would have had profound ripple effects in both the United States and Europe. Capital flight—the removal of savings and investments from domestic economies because of expected currency devaluation—further complicated the ability of Latin American governments to prevent default.

By the late 1980s, strategic solutions to the dilemmas emerged throughout Latin America in the conjunction of practices we today call neoliberalism. In brief, neoliberalism involved (1) converting state-owned or state-subsidized corporations, which were often highly inefficient monopolies (railroads, electricity, telephones, for example), into privately owned companies that would improve efficiency in order to compete in a market economy; (2) eliminating barriers to international trade and deregulating key industries in order to promote competition (lifting tariffs, rewriting trade laws); and (3) promoting the concept of free trade and participating in free-trade agreements. (Mercosur [Mercado Común del Sur] and NAFTA are the best known, but others exist, such as the Comunidad Andina and the Caribbean Community. There are efforts to create a Free Trade Area of the Americas that would link all the treaties for hemispheric economic integration.) In addition to the economic strategies of neoliberalism, however, I encourage students to think about its social and cultural implications. In a nutshell, neoliberalism sees the free market as an arena of competition in which important decisions are made about the allocation of a nation's resources. In highly stratified societies in which access to education has been unequal, what does it mean to allow the market to be the arbiter? Will the market provide opportunities for education and social mobility? Or will the market exacerbate social hierarchies, as those who already have access to resources become the only ones able to afford education and professional training? Given recent debates in the United States on public education versus vouchers for private education, students often discover that they have strong beliefs (that may differ from their classmates') about what is "free" and what is "fair" when the market becomes the determining factor.

To bring this wide-ranging material together in a cultural studies course, I divide the course into five conceptual units (fig. 1). The first unit examines a cultural studies model of negotiation that supports subsequent analytic tasks. The next four units discuss three national case studies and a current topic, NAFTA. The case studies I've selected allow for an in-depth look at such subjects as globalization, neoliberalism, foreign business interests in Latin America, regional free-trade agreements, and the interplay between these developments and Latin America's strong sense of national tradition. Chile provides an opportunity to explore the complex interaction of economic development and close political and economic ties to the United States; Salvador Allende, Augusto Pinochet, and the democratic transition; and Chile's entry into the regional free-trade accord known as Mercosur. In the next case study, on Argentina, we examine its economic and political experiences and consider Argentina's own path to Mercosur. The third case study brings the issues closer to my students. Mexican labor has had a recognizable presence in

Figure 1
COURSE OUTLINE

	Monday	Wednesday	Friday
Unit 1: Weeks 1–3	Cultural studies paradigm and overview of Spanish America		
Unit 2: Weeks 4–6	Business language; weekly vocabulary quiz	Case study: contemporary Chile; writing assignments due on Fridays; exam 1 at end of week 6	
Unit 3: Weeks 7–9	Business language; weekly vocabulary quiz	Case study: contemporary Argentina; writing assignments due on Fridays	
Unit 4: Weeks 10–12	Business language; weekly vocabulary quiz	Case study: contemporary Mexico; writing assignments due on Fridays; exam 2 at end of week 12	
Unit 5: Weeks 13–15	Business language; weekly vocabulary quiz	Case study: NAFTA, United States–Mexico trade, local impact in Kansas City and the Midwest; writing assignments due on Fridays; exam 3 during finals	

Kansas—both historically, in the construction of the Atchison–Topeka–Santa Fe Railway, and recently, in the growth of agriculture, especially the meatpacking industry in Garden City. The fourth case study extends the discussion of Mexico by examining the North American Free Trade Agreement (NAFTA)—Tratado de Libre Comercio (TLC) in Spanish. Each semester I update this section to reflect recent developments. I include material on both sides of the NAFTA debate.[4]

Ideally, I teach this class on a Monday, Wednesday, and Friday schedule. In the last four units, I also work through a textbook and the business language component of the course.[5] Textbooks for commercial language usually follow the divisions associated with functional areas in a school of business; chapters are devoted to such topics as macroeconomics, microeconomics, management, finance, marketing, international trade, business law, and human resources. Each chapter presents a coherent vocabulary group, short readings, and sample business letters. As an instructor juggling the dual goals of teaching business Spanish and teaching cultural studies, I use the vocabulary and business topics from Mondays in the analytic discussions on Wednesdays and Fridays—an approach that requires the careful selection of materials.

Selection is crucial not only for connecting the units but for increasing student motivation to read literature. As Spanish enrollments have risen, the undergraduate interest in reading Spanish-language literature seems to have plummeted. With reactions that range from disinterest to adamant resistance, students often rank literature low on a scale of utilitarian value yet place language and culture high on the scale. A cultural studies approach can help change such attitudes, however—it gives students new strategies for reading literature and makes explicit the inseparable ties, in literary texts, between language and culture. In the course, I use the cultural studies component to work extensively with literature as an entry to the language and cultural elements that attract students. Throughout the semester, I identify literary readings that provide images of the business world and of foreigners doing business in or with Latin America. To round out and contextualize the literary core, I introduce fragments from films and a wide range of journalistic materials.

My cultural studies paradigm for understanding negotiation is modest. Although a sophisticated body of theoretical writings and practical analyses exists for introducing the methodology of cultural studies, I develop only a basic model. Sometimes I have asked students to read short passages from theoretical works by Roman Jakobson, Emile Benveniste, Louis Althusser, and Stuart Hall, but I find that the class responds best to a guided presentation of ideas, with a handout rich in quotations and definitions of key concepts. The purpose of unit 1 is to outline Althusser's concept of interpellation and to help students consider its implications for understanding identity in a social context.[6] I begin with Jakobson's standard model of the communication act, organized around six elements: a sender employs a context, a message, a contact, and a code, in order to communicate with a receiver (see fig. 2). Although this model is open to critique from many perspectives, it establishes elements that students can distinguish in communication.

The second step, based on the writings of Benveniste, is to point out the unique role of subject pronouns in language (see 195–203, 217–22, 223–30). The first-person pronoun *yo* indicates the person speaking, the sender. The *usted* or *tú* addressed by *yo* is the receiver. In communication, however, the roles are constantly shifting; an individual who occupies the role of sender may later become the receiver of messages from other senders.

Not only are sender and receiver components of a communicative act, as Jakobson's model asserts; they are also positions that individuals take as they organize their roles in social interactions. That is, individuals recognize or misrecognize their identities in the various ways they assume the position of receiver, offered in a wide range of communicative exchanges. To develop this notion, in the third step, the class explores Jakobson's and Benveniste's concepts in terms of Althusser's explanation of ideology and the notion of interpellation. For Althusser, ideology works through the mechanism of interpellation, or hailing, which transforms individuals into the subjects of ideology. He describes a "theoretical theatre" in which "the most commonplace everyday police officer" hails an individual by saying: "Hey, you there!"

> Assuming that the theoretical scene I have imagined takes place in the street, the hailed individual will turn round. By this mere one-hundred-and-eighty-degree physical conversion, he becomes a *subject*. Why? Because he has recognized that the hail was "really" addressed to him, and that "it was *really him* who was hailed" (and not someone else).   (163)

Students readily relate the communication model developed from Jakobson and Beneviste to Althusser's example of the individual who recognizes his identity in the interpellation. As a group, we explore the implications of the model and, intuitively, discover some of the limitations to it that become apparent in the skillful work of Stuart Hall ("Encoding"). Mainly, we make the leap from direct verbal communication to larger symbolic systems that create social roles for individuals.

Whereas I present the basic model in terms of verbal communication and emphasize the role of subject pronouns, I point out that these pronouns are representations in which we recognize our identity. We then explore how everyday life is made up of multiple forms of representation in which we find different aspects of our identity. Television, films, the mass media, and popular music immediately come to mind, as well as literature, but students usually broaden the discussion to include political campaigns, marketing, consumerism, and other examples of signifiers, or coded messages, that are used in constructing and representing our sense of identity. Indeed, the quick realization by some of the brightest students that the textbook's organization creates a specific role for students leads to a critique of the ideas implicit in the messages about Latin America sent to them as receivers. With this wide array of representation under discussion, the group usually notes how individuals do not respond to a single, monolithic interpellation but, rather, to a constellation of often contradictory interpellations. And finally, we consider

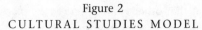

Figure 2
CULTURAL STUDIES MODEL

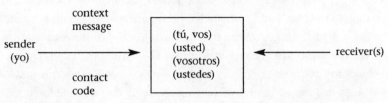

interpellation: sender	*representation*	*interpellation:* receiver(s)
hailing	second-person pronouns as linguistic representations of receiver's identity	(self)-recognition in pronouns offered through hailing; possibilities of acceptance, resistance, negotiation, etc.

whether individuals are forced to accede to interpellations or have some form of "agency" that allows them to resist, subvert, or recast the social role that some interpellations offer. I bring this basic model to bear on all the representations we analyze in the cultural components of the course (fig. 2).

In relating this model to the business content of the course, I provide, in the introductory unit, a series of exercises highlighting the range of United States stereotypes about Latin Americans, international stereotypes about those of us from the United States (and from other countries—often my class includes students from Europe, Africa, and Asia, who add unique dimensions to these discussions), and the use of stereotypes in scholarship on international business managers and cross-cultural communication. On the second or third day, we watch a documentary on the history of United States stereotypes about Latin America. DeeDee Halleck's film *Gringo in Mañanaland* is a collage of images and sounds, from feature films, documentaries, textbooks, popular music, and ordinary speech. Punctuated by words periodically appearing on the screen—"arrival," "the past," "paradise," "ambition," and "thrift"—the documentary reveals the coded messages these stereotypes convey. In the introductory image, from the early days of filmmaking, photographers manually crank their cameras as a voice-over narrator says that the Cuba of Hollywood movies was not the Cuba where she lived, in 1952:

"This film is a look at that other Latin America, the place in the movies. It's still there . . . at the movies, in our schoolrooms, on our TV sets, in our head." According to the film, Latin America has been portrayed as an empty territory with the potential for generating immense wealth; the continent's "natives," however, are depicted as being too corrupt to be trusted with such wealth or too backward to tap the resources without foreign know-how. This juxtaposition suggests how adventure stories in many early movies were intended to justify United States and other foreign business intervention in Latin America by denigrating Latin American autonomy, intelligence, and identity. As the image of the filmmaking inside the narrator's head emphasizes, the perception of Latin America promoted by the entertainment industry and in the schools may exist in the minds of spectators and students; such representations also provide the conceptual frame for reimagining and understanding life abroad.

To discuss this film in terms of negotiation, we identify who played the roles of sender and of receiver in these old movies, and we examine how the documentary, by pointing out the flaws in the representations, challenges viewers to reconsider these communicative roles. The international students in the class often energize the analysis as we explore why audiences in the United States identified with many of the representations without guilt or an awareness of contradictions, whereas Latin Americans and other groups who have been stereotyped find these images deeply offensive.

After this first exercise, which serves to put students in touch with United States representations of Latin America and to raise the question of dilemmas of negotiating recognition and resistance to representations, the class reads a chapter from Phillip Harris and Robert Moran's *Managing Cultural Differences*, "Doing Business with North Americans—U.S.A./Canada" (335–70). The reading provokes frustration and at times anger. Although Harris and Moran keep their language generally positive, students feel resentment when they see a list of cultural traits that, according to others' stereotypes of them, define them as competitive, superficial in their approach to friendships, unemotional and unexpressive, sloppy in dress and potentially immoral in behavior, and probably quite dangerous (this conception results from publicity about alcoholism, drug addiction, and crime). Working with this material leads back to the discussion of representations—how they interpellate us and how we recognize or resist our identity in such images. Class discussion usually tempers the collective reaction as students ask where these stereotypes come from—

even if we do not see ourselves in this way, what behavior has led others to make such interpretations?

To round out the introduction, students review the cultural studies model of identity negotiation and read a chapter from Nancy J. Adler's *International Dimensions*, "Communicating across Cultures." Rather than condemn all use of stereotypes, Adler advocates thinking of the stereotypes we have acquired as merely "best first guesses"; when they do not coincide with experience, we can reconsider the experience and reformulate our stereotypes as models of perception. Although many students are uneasy about Adler's unwillingness to disqualify stereotypes altogether as illegitimate forms of perception, they accept the responsibility her model places on the individual for his or her patterns of perception and response.

These experiments in analytic and experiential responses to the negotiation and construction of identity prepare students for the cultural studies component developed around Chile, Argentina, Mexico, and NAFTA. In these units, students confront the often-negative stereotypes of United States citizens conducting business in Latin America; in addition, they respond to a series of questions about the historical events that led to the creation of these representations. And, given their own goals of working with or in Latin America, they consider how they might negotiate their identity in Latin America in the face of any lingering stereotypes and how they can display the kind of behavior that may improve the images of North Americans abroad.

In the remaining weeks, as noted earlier, I link the business topic and vocabulary covered on Monday with complementary readings that lend themselves to the cultural studies analysis of negotiated identity. To illustrate how this analytic component works, I will describe a week of assignments that pair up a language-textbook chapter on importation and exportation with a Mexican short story, "Canastitas en serie" ("Assembly Line"), by Bruno Traven.[7] On Monday, after students have prepared the textbook chapter, we brainstorm about the range of imported products we can buy locally. Knowing that someone will mention Mexican beers or Chilean wines, I use the chapter vocabulary by talking through the series of documents required in exporting a product from Latin Ameica and importing it all the way to Lawrence, Kansas. I end the discussion with a brief preview of the language used in the short story assigned for Wednesday.

On Wednesday, students have read the first half of "Canastitas en serie" (consisting of five sections). The title suggests business terminology learned in an earlier week: *la producción en serie* for "mass production." In class, we look at the language of the story, identifying the business-related words students have already learned, and summarize the events and the business situation in the story. Briefly, in the first half of the story, the narrator describes a United States tourist, Mr. E. L. Winthrop, who travels to Mexico for a rest. Like other tourists, after only a few days in Mexico, Mr. Winthrop "ya tenía bien forjada su opinión y, en su concepto, este extraño país salvaje no había sido todavía bien explorado, misión gloriosa sobre la tierra reservada a gente como él" ("had already thoroughly formed his opinion and, in his view, this strange, untamed country had not yet been explored, a glorious mission on this earth reserved for people like him"). He travels to Oaxaca, where he meets "un indio" ("an Indian") who is making "canastitas de paja y otras fibras recogidas en los campos tropicales que rodean el pueblo" ("baskets from straw and other fibers gathered in the tropical fields that surround the village") (9). The narrator characterizes the "pequeña industria" ("small business") of the indigenous artisan, with its low "rendimientos" ("returns") but high artistic worth because of the artisan's aesthetic investment in each creation. As portrayed by the narrator, the indigenous basket maker is a victim of Mexico's middle-class mestizo society that does not recognize the value of his labor or the beauty of his craft. The narrator ironically contrasts the modern preference for "los objetos que se fabrican en serie por millones y que son idénticos entre sí" ("objects mass-manufactured by the millions, each one just alike") with the small-scale production of handmade baskets, each one a "pieza de arte único" ("unique work of art") (12).

In the second section of the story, Mr. Winthrop sees the basket maker and "en su mal español" ("in his bad Spanish") decides to purchase a basket: "Muy bien, yo comprar" ("Very well, me buy"). The narrator makes the stereotype of the United States entrepreneur ironic by having Mr. Winthrop pronounce these words with the same tone and gesture he would have used "al comprar toda una empresa ferrocarrilera" ("when buying a complete railroad company") (13). Given the low price for the basket, Mr. Winthrop immediately begins to think about "las grandes posibilidades para hacer negocio" ("the great opportunities for doing business"). He negotiates a price reduction and purchases sixteen baskets, but he drops the entrepreneurial idea at this point. In the third section, Mr. Winthrop is convinced that he knows Mexico thoroughly after three weeks and returns to New York, "un lugar civilizado" ("a civilized place") (14). He remembers the baskets he purchased and tells a candy manufacturer, Mr. Kemple, that he can provide them as imported packages for selling fine candies—"envoltura de fantasía para nuestro mejor praliné francés" ("luxury packaging for our best French candy"), in the words of Mr. Kemple (16). In the fourth section, after a scene of negotiating over the price, they settle on terms, decide who will pay "los derechos" ("customs taxes") and the "embarque" ("shipping fees"), as well as the minimal number of baskets.

The fifth and final section of Wednesday's reading assignment explores the machinations that run through Mr. Winthrop's mind on his return flight to Mexico. He develops a business plan for mass production, packaging, shipping, and exporting, aware that he will dramatically increase the basket maker's earnings while making a cool profit for himself. The narrator concludes with an interior monologue expressing Mr. Winthrop's jubilation over his coming fortune:

> ¡Magnífico! Me quedan alredor de veinte mil dólares limpiecitos. Veinte mil del alma para el bolsillo de un humilde servidor. ¡Caramba, sería capaz de besarlos! Después de todo, esta república no está tan atrasada como parece. En realidad es un gran país. Admirable. Se puede hacer dinero en esta tierra. Montones de dinero, siempre que se trate de tipos tan listos como yo. (19)

> Wonderful! I still have a profit of twenty thousand dollars in the clear. Twenty thousand soul-filled dollars for the pocket of a humble servant. Hell, I could even kiss them! After all, this country is not as backward as it seems. As a matter of fact, it's a great country. Impressive. You can make real money here. Mountains of money, as long as you're smart like me.

Discussion of the first half of the story centers on characterization. I divide the class into small groups and assign each the task of explaining the details that make up the narrator's characterization of Mr. Winthrop, of the basket maker, and of the middle-class Mexican housewives who haggle over prices with the artisan. After the groups compare their findings, we return to our cultural studies model and examine the various negotiations of identity at work and what the text encourages readers to imagine about the United States entrepreneur in Mexico. We speculate about experiences in Mexico that may have given Traven the basis for his representation of Mr. Winthrop and debate whether the story simply uses the basket maker as a foil in the process of ridiculing Mr. Winthrop or whether Traven is providing insight into indigenous mentality. For the next class, students finish the story and consider how they would turn the story into a movie—the actors they would cast and the scenes that would dramatize the conflict.

On Friday, we briefly review the vocabulary in and plot of the second half of the story. Mr. Winthrop fails because the basket maker is not interested in mass production. The two characters, the artisan and the entrepreneur, are unable to make sense of or to each other. I then show a clip from the movie *Canasta de cuentos mexicanos*, an adaptation of several of Traven's stories, including "Canastitas en serie." The movie version, with its faded colors and 1950s fashions, adds a twist to the story. Mr. Winthrop has gone to Mexico with his wife. Mrs. Winthrop, a beautiful but manipulative social climber, can get her husband to do anything to satisfy her ambitions. With his business connections and her drive, they negotiate a contract in New York for importing baskets, use the advance money to buy a mink coat that she wears on the plane back to Mexico, and meet their defeat in Oaxaca when the basket maker staunchly refuses their offer. The film version not only makes the negotiated identities visual but, with the addition of Mrs. Winthrop, adds a layer of class, race, and gender to the national and ethnic identities at play in "Canastitas en serie."

To focus the analysis and raise it to a higher level, the class wrestles with two sets of questions. First, is it accurate to say that there is a failure to achieve cross-cultural communication between the basket maker and Mr. Winthrop? Or is it more precise to say that there is communication but the two characters have irreconcilable attitudes toward "mass production"? What strategies does each character use to "interpellate" the other, and how does the other character "negotiate" this interpellation? These questions are crucial because the story, with its obviously "loaded" representation of Mr. Winthrop, should be read with skepticism regarding the narrators characterization of the basket maker. Even if he is indeed the victim of economic injustice, as described in the story, the narrator represents the "humilde campesino" ("humble peasant") (10) idealistically, almost as a Gramscian "organic intellectual." Although we may sympathize with the narrator's desire to represent the indigenous basket maker, the storyteller's strategies are as "othering" and exoticizing as Mr. Winthrop's opinions about Mexico.

The second question is more speculative: Is it possible for someone like Mr. Winthrop to establish an import-export business in handmade baskets that would not be exploitative? This question, which the week has prepared students to address, brings up the ethical issue of what students hope to accomplish by taking business Spanish. As students use their newly learned commercial vocabulary to discuss, in Spanish, the differences in labor costs in the United States and in Mexico, we are also paving the way for later class discussions. In the following weeks, we examine the *maquiladoras*, located throughout Mexico and concentrated on the United States border; students discuss their reactions to free trade as promoted by NAFTA, and fair trade as promoted by nongovernmental organizations seeking to form international alliances in the era of globalization.[8]

The unit on importation-exportation and the short story "Canastitas en serie" embodies the basic procedure I follow throughout the semester, connecting vocabulary and culture with a cultural studies approach to representations of international business. Students often react with resentment to many of the images that the texts offer as representations of their identity as United States citizens. They become more understanding of these images as they take into account the history of United States relations that may explain, if not justify, why writers, scholars, journalists, and filmmakers from Latin America would construct such representations of Americans abroad. At the same time, students confront the stereotypes with which they may have to contend if they live and work in Latin America, and they think about how they might be able to dispel some of these stereotypes as they negotiate roles for themselves in commercial relations, as well as ways of promoting mutually advantageous practices in international business.

Students who take this course have responded with enthusiasm. Most of them begin with utilitarian motives, but, by the end, they are aware of how profoundly relevant the cultural studies approach to business Spanish is. One of the great dilemmas for literary scholars today is how to respond to students who complain that literature holds no purpose and therefore is of no interest. For those of us who work in Spanish, with its burgeoning enrollments, the complaint is growing louder as students demand a curriculum that they perceive as immediately practical, especially in terms of their career plans. Teaching business Spanish from a cultural studies perspective has allowed me to struggle against the utilitarian trend by pushing my students to discover the significance of understanding other points of view, of examining stereotypes that may limit their room to maneuver in international business, and especially, of reading literature as a way to gain insight into other societies, other people, and even oneself.

However, the students come away from the class with a different sense of relevance, a change that I believe Sylvia Molloy accurately describes. She has critiqued the reductive understanding of linguistic and cultural competency that posits "prepackaged communication" as "information, not relation." Instead, she calls for notions of competency that include an acceptance of the impossibilities of cross-cultural translation and a thorough engagement with the dilemma: "Surrender your cultural authority, if only for a moment, and try to relate" ("Presidential Address 2001" 409). The cultural studies approach to business Spanish constantly foregrounds the struggle with one's "native" linguistic and cultural expectations and stereotypes, the dilemmas of translation and cross-cultural communication, and, above all else, the willingness to "surrender . . . cultural authority" in order to create important human relationships.

In addition, the course is relevant for teachers because it lays bare the interested nature of our work, the investments we all have as we create and teach knowledge about Latin America. When I teach a language and culture class that focuses on competency in linguistic skills, I am providing students a tool they may go on to use in ways that I might never condone. But when I teach a language and culture class that focuses on linguistic and cultural competency and, through cultural studies, makes it clear that we must negotiate international relations in the wake of other, more problematic relations, I have the opportunity to make my field relevant to students. I can invite them not simply to use knowledge about Latin America but to analyze their very identities in the process of forging better relations with Latin America.

Finally, all these considerations reveal my personal strategy for negotiating the multiple forces that pull on me as an instructor. By teaching business Spanish with a cultural studies approach, I negotiate my multiple commitments as a literary scholar with aesthetic interests, a Latin Americanist with ethical concerns, a member of an institution that promotes collaboration across units (a language department and the School of Business), and a teacher who helps students acquire a knowledge of Latin American languages and cultures and helps them prepare for competitive job searches. In this course I strive to challenge the unspoken assumptions that have produced dead ends in the past; I encourage students to think differently about their own identities and responsibilities in the future, the choices they have as they engage in commerce in Latin America, and the profound knowledge of language and culture that can emerge from reading literature with a cultural studies approach. After a semester of wrestling with the images of United States business executives in which they do not recognize themselves or else see a self they want to change, students have new ideas about the kinds of businesspeople they want to become, the future stereotypes—in Adler's conception of the term—they hope to create, and the business relations they wish to establish and maintain.

Occasionally I wonder how I came to teach business Spanish. I discuss quite heatedly with students the debates over free trade and fair trade, as well as the events that promote or protest globalization. We agonize together as we examine the economic benefits of *maquiladoras* and question the human, social, and ecological costs often excluded from the bottom line. At the same time, I am certain that globalization will not disappear if I simply ignore it. Globalization, whether I like it or not, is the context in which I must negotiate my commitments, choices, identity, and profession. By teaching business Spanish as a response to globalization, in all its complexity and contradictions, I create a role for myself. I also help students prepare to negotiate their identities as global citizens who seek not merely to profit but to build lasting relations of respect throughout the world.

NOTES

1. I use the term *Latin America* rather than *Spanish America* because, in my course, I address the implications of this proper noun. However, because I teach Spanish and not Portuguese, the linguistic emphasis is on Spanish America. Latin Americanist literary scholars interested in broadening their knowledge of economics in order to teach business Spanish can begin with two basic works. *Modern Latin America* (Skidmore and Smith) provides an overview of nineteenth- and twentieth-century economic and political development and then focuses on selected countries and regions for case studies. The chapters on Mexico, Argentina, and Chile in *Politics of Latin America* (Vanden and Prevost) cogently examine the relations between politics and economics. A third text, *Latin America's Economy* (Cardoso and Helwege), is the standard introduction to regional economic issues.
2. I make clear, from the start, that I am providing a cultural studies class in Spanish. My goals—to teach language and culture and to offer a set of analytic tools called "cultural studies"—are consistent with the principle that Business Spanish is not a course in which students gain specialized business knowledge. Articles by Evans, by Parle, and by Ulrich establish both the breadth of areas that can be covered in a business language class and the limits on what teachers can properly address. Fryer and Guntermann's *Spanish and Portuguese for Business and the Professions* gathers excellent essays on conceptualizing Spanish for business.
3. For the literary scholar preparing to teach a course on business Spanish, excellent starting points are Anthony King's *Culture, Globalization, and the World-System* and the special issue of *PMLA*, edited by Gunn. Anthologies compiled by Jameson and

Miyoshi and by Appadurai provide useful background on globalization. Yergin and Stanislaw's *The Commanding Heights* traces the emergence of economic integration and places shifts in the Latin American economy in an international perspective (see chs. 9, 13, and 14). The book has a Web site: www.pbs.org/wgbh/commanding heights/lo/.

Students can explore the Internet, where major players in globalization maintain multilingual Web sites and where opposition groups form alliances and publicize their efforts. The following list includes key Web sites:

Major institutions for globalization
  Organización Mundial del Comercio (World Trade Organization), www.wto.org/
    indexsp
  Banco Mundial (World Bank), www.bancomundial.org

Critiques of globalization
  Global Issues That Affect Everyone, www.globalissues.org
  International Forum on Globalization, www.ifg.org/index
  People for Fair Trade, home.att.net/~sally.pfft/index
  Seattle Times, Seattletimes.nwsource.com/wto

4. Orme's *Understanding NAFTA* is an invaluable guide. For the growing scholarship on the relation between national identity and negotiating styles in business, see Fisher's *International Negotiation* and Novinger's *Intercultural Communication*, which use Mexico as a case study for contrast with the United States.

5. College textbook publishers have promoted the development of materials for teaching business Spanish. The most popular textbook is Doyle, Fryer, and Cere's *Exito comercial*. Pascal and Rojas's *Relaciones comerciales*, more limited in scope, allows the instructor greater freedom in using supplementary material. A textbook suitable to a wide range of intermediate levels is Galloway, Labarca, and Rodríguez's *Saldo a favor*.

6. Paul Smith, in *Discerning the Subject*, surveys the critiques of Althusser's initial formulation of interpellation, which emerges as a monolithic phenomenon. Interpellation is perhaps best understood as an ongoing process in which multiple forces act simultaneously on individuals. Individuals—and Smith explains this loaded concept well—"negotiate" among the varied, often contradictory interpellations.

7. I cite the published translation of this story, but in order to be clear about the points I am emphasizing and the use of language, the translations in the text are my own. The published translation does not include some of the lines that I translate from the Spanish version.

8. Four trading organizations based in England have created alternative import-export agreements to benefit local producers: Equal Exchange Trading, Oxfam Trading, Traidcraft Plc, and Twin Trading. Examples of their success are the coffees sold under the label "Cafédirect" and the chocolate sold as "Divine" with the slogan "Heavenly milk chocolate with a heart." For information on fair trade, see Zadek and Tiffen. The Project on Business Environment and Social Responsibility Resource Center at the University of Colorado maintains a Web page that includes teaching modules on fair trade. Students can conduct Internet searches using the key phrase *comercio justo* or *comercio alternativo* to discover groups in Spanish-speaking countries promoting fair trade. The following list includes selected addresses for sites that I have recommended to students:

Fair trade—Comercio justo—Comercio alternativo
International Federation for Alternative Trade (IFAT), www.ifat.org/dwr/home
Comercio alternativo, sponsored by Central Interregional de Artesanos del Perú
  (CIAP), www.ciap.org/comalt
Alianza Chilena por un Comercio Justo y Responsible, www.comerciojusto.terra
  .cl
Asociación Europea de Comercio Justo (European Fair Trade Association—
  EFTA), www.eurosur.org/EFTA/
Comercio Justo México Asociación Civil, www.comerciojusto.com.mx

PART THREE   *Cultural Identities*

Drums of Resistance: Hybridization, Cultural Imperialism, and Caribbean Popular Culture in the Classroom

Kirwin R. Shaffer

An increasing number of students in North American colleges have traveled abroad by the time they begin their freshman or sophomore year. Because of the growth and affordability of Caribbean cruises, coupled with economic good times in the United States in the late 1990s, many of these students traveled to the islands. International travel often broadens our understanding of regions outside the United States. Too frequently, however, students traveling to the Caribbean come away with the very tourist images offered in the cruise line's advertisements. Even students who have not traveled to the region have probably seen and appropriated prettified views of the islands. North American popular culture, especially Hollywood movies, re-creates scenes of a visitor's paradise, where natives constantly smile and serve gringos, who lounge about looking for fun, sex, and a little adventure. In short, both the cruise industry and Hollywood have been instrumental in shaping the idea of the Caribbean as an exotic and erotic locale. Consequently, whether they have cruised the region or simply watched films set there, students generally enter a course on Caribbean popular culture with the same unrealistic impressions. When asked, on the first day of class, "What comes to mind when I mention the Caribbean?," most students mention sun, water, and beaches.

The study of Caribbean popular culture is an appropriate venue for chipping away at these impressions and highlighting the political, religious, and cultural forces that shape and reflect the region. One way to teach the course is to take the "cultural imperialist" approach. According to this view, local and national cultures and their productions have been dominated, if not obliterated, by outside forces. The Coca-Cola-ization effect, as it is sometimes called, occurs when multinational corporations and imperialist governments impose their products, values, and cultures on a region—and, in the process, may destroy what was deemed natural or authentic to the local society (see Guback and Varis; Mattelart; Schiller; Varis).

The approach taken in this article veers significantly from the cultural imperialist model. That paradigm tends to see culture, and thus popular culture, as static—as existing relatively unchanged from an earlier, ambiguous era, waiting to be manipulated and shaped by outside forces. I believe we must, however, understand that popular culture is not static. It constantly borrows, adapts, and evolves. Therefore, looking for authentic expressions of culture before international influences made their presence is fruitless. Rather, utilizing the concepts of hybridization and deterritorialization, this essay moves beyond the simplistic notions of cultural imperialism to illustrate how forms of popular culture throughout the Caribbean have been socially and historically constructed—and continue to evolve. Caribbean popular culture may at times follow or look like Western versions, but the Caribbean manifestations frequently serve to resist outside domination. The distinctive racial, ethnic, and class features evident in popular religious expression, film, music, and sport all reveal vibrant Caribbean cultures of resistance, which themselves reflect and contribute to ethnic and national identities.

FINDING THE "POPULAR" IN POPULAR CULTURE

What is popular culture? Let's just say that there is little agreement on a definition. Is popular culture a market-defined term—that is, does the commercial appeal of a culture determine how popular it is? Raúl Leis rejects this capitalist definition, choosing, instead, to understand popular culture as "emancipatory and revolutionary in contrast to oppressive mass culture," which is often considered to be the expression of a society's dominant ideology. To Leis, the "alternative" and "impugning dimension" of popular culture emanates from the people. In Leis's view, popular culture, while offering a vision of reality different from the "hegemonic culture," provides a way to challenge, complain, and wish for changes (64). Ray Browne believes that a definition of popular culture must encompass the complexity of daily life, not just popular entertainment. Adding an important sociopolitical ingredient to understanding popular culture, he argues that "popular culture democratizes society and makes democracy truly democratic. It is the everyday world around us: the mass media, entertainments, diversions; it is our heroes, icons, rituals, everyday actions, psychology, politics, and religion—our total life picture" (26). Jean Franco's ideas merge those of Leis and Browne. Franco has noted the multitude of terms frequently used to discuss popular culture, such as "mass culture," "popular culture," "folk culture," and "media." The term "popular culture" is ambiguous itself, as it refers "both to what belongs to and what comes from the people." She concludes that her "preferred definition would be the broadest possible" and should focus on all arenas of " 'everyday life' in which new policies of control and discipline have been exercised and which has now become crucial as an arena of struggle and resistance" ("What's in a Name?" 6). Thus popular culture is not a reflection of the marketplace but a concept that includes the whole array of a people's cultural artifacts and productions that themselves reflect the society's sociopolitical values and conflicts.

While we have now begun to define popular culture, we should remember that the artifacts and productions, as well as the societal values and conflicts they express, do not remain static. Rather, the outward displays of popular culture evolve, as do the values and messages conveyed. It is useful, then, to understand how popular culture arises and develops. William Rowe and Vivian Schelling's *Memory and Modernity,* the classic theoretical work on popular culture, shows that no cultural impulse can be lifted as a whole from one context and relocated unchanged. Instead, when cultural elements are separated from their original purpose and combined with other elements to represent new practices, hybridization takes place. When the new cultural forms are transported and established elsewhere, deterritorialization occurs. Thus cultural forms that superficially resemble each other from place to place, or over time, are in fact hybrids adapting to different environments. Rowe and Schelling urge us to see popular culture not as an "object" but as a "site" where various cultural forms interact in new settings. Popular culture, then, is a mix of the old and the new. It includes traditions from the past and present and from different countries that intermingle at a new site (2–3).[1]

Ultimately, the hybridization approach to popular culture enables us to unravel the transnational and transcultural dimensions of the Caribbean. While not rejecting the role of colonial and neocolonial influences, the hybridization approach explores the way local and national forces have responded to, sometimes adopted, and constantly adapted these global forces to reflect local conditions. A cultural imperialist approach to the region diminishes the role of the Caribbean peoples as actors and instead posits them as victims. Hybridization recognizes that the Caribbean has been victimized by international forces but has reacted by shaping the terms of international-local contact. When we view the situation this way, we see that Caribbean writers, religious practitioners, movie makers, musicians, athletes, and other creators of the region's popular culture are agents of resistance to foreign domination and developers of the islands' cultural, ethnic, and national identities.

BON VOYAGE! SEPARATING TOURIST CULTURE
FROM POPULAR CULTURE

As noted, most students arrive in the Caribbean popular culture course with notions of a society that are largely based on tourist or "video-tourist" images. The class spends a few days examining the sources of these preconceived ideas. During the semester the class will view three movies *from* the Caribbean, but we begin by observing how Hollywood has portrayed the region, in order to understand where many false impressions come from. Several genres of film are available, and watching clips from an array of movies allows students to see the celluloid images and compare them with their own preconceived ideas about the islands.

Students see the region as a site for romance in pre-1959 Cuba in *Week-End in Havana, Havana* (with Robert Redford), and DeeDee Hayden's documentary *Gringo in Mañanaland*. The notion of the Caribbean as a land of sex and tropical enchantment is reinforced in *How Stella Got Her Groove Back* (starring Angela Bassett). In the movie version of Jean Rhys's novel *Wide Sargasso Sea*, set in the nineteenth century, the Caribbean is depicted as erotic and dangerous; a central figure in the film is the obeah woman Cristafina, who is skilled in the arts of black magic. Moreover, magic and other unusual practices found expression over the years in horror films, such as the 1940s-era *I Walked with a Zombie* and Wes Craven's adaptation of Wade Davis's *The Serpent and the Rainbow*, supposedly about Vodou and zombies during the dictatorship of Baby Doc Duvalier in Haiti. Finally, the Caribbean has been portrayed as a place for fun and comedy, especially in films like *Captain Ron*; the Disney take on the Jamaican bobsled team, *Cool Runnings*; and *Holiday in the Sun*, starring the teenage franchise Mary-Kate and Ashley Olsen. Other movies may come up in class discussion.

While viewing clips from these films, students notice several interlocked themes in the way popular culture from the United States has characterized the Caribbean. Most of the movies focus on an outsider (often a tourist or an expatriate) who has escaped his or her world to arrive in the sunshine. As with *Stella*, the visitors need not always be white. On arrival, they experience the Caribbean as mysterious and frequently uninhibited: pre-Revolution Havana is a site for intrigue and sex, Jamaicans are oversexed (*How Stella Got Her Groove Back* and *Wide Sargasso Sea*), and these exotic locales become the backdrop for eroticism. Even the horror classics are rooted in exoticism, with a little romance on the side (*Serpent*). "Fun-loving" movies like *Captain Ron*, *Runnings*, and *Holiday* appeal to tourists' interest in having a good time.

To overcome the notion of tourist culture as synonymous with Caribbean culture, students take a critical look at island tourism, especially from the differing viewpoints of Caribbean residents themselves. Students read Jamaica Kincaid's brief but powerful exposé *A Small Place*, in which the author reveals what visitors *won't see* when they arrive in her native Antigua: the crumbling library, the crumbling hospital, the crumbling streets, the crumbling houses, the drought-prone island. Much of her attack focuses on the Antiguan government, which she believes has sold the country into a new kind of slavery: poor blacks function as servants to wealthy international whites. The government's promotion of tourism has turned Antigua into a spectacle to be consumed by outsiders while the needs of the masses are ignored.

In some ways, Kincaid's book exemplifies a cultural imperialist critique of tourism: Antiguans, victimized by national and international bourgeois forces, have developed few if any strategies to oppose this imperialist juggernaut. A more nuanced critique of tourism's effects and the local responses to it is offered in the video *The Toured: The Other Side of Tourism in Barbados*, which portrays the arrival of tourists en masse in Barbados in the 1950s and tourism's subsequent consequences for the residents. Students hear from Barbadians employed in the tourist sector and see local television commercials extolling Barbadians to "always wear a smile." Perhaps most eye-opening are interviews with Barbadians who are "freelancers," selling trinkets on the beach and picking up white women tourists who have come looking for sex. In contrast to the cultural imperialist model, the video shows some Barbadians using the presence of tourists to earn much-needed foreign exchange, which some then invest in their own businesses. Certainly, tourism has had an impact on peoples' lives and culture, but Barbadians are not slaves or purely victims. They respond, adopt, and adapt.

The course returns to a focus on tourist culture at the end of the semester, with a look at Cuba. With the collapse of the socialist bloc in the late 1980s and early 1990s, Cuba's economy rapidly disintegrated. By 1994, the Cuban government, desperate to revive the economy, began to develop its tourist industry. Almost at once, multinational corporations entered into joint partnerships with the government to build hotels and create a hospitality infrastructure. In 1993, Cubans were allowed to possess United States dollars as a means of stimulating microenterprises and of filling the gaps in the state-run, shortage-plagued ration system. How did average Cubans get the dollars? The growing flood of Western tourists found that everything they wanted (private restaurants, rooms in private homes, legal and illegal taxis, hotels, sex . . . you name it) required payment in dollars. Quickly, aspects of popular culture were reoriented to meet tourist demands. Tourists could hear traditional and modern music played on street corners in a restored Old Havana; they could absorb commodified Afro-Cuban culture in Havana, Matanzas, and elsewhere (paying $5 to record and photograph the performers); they could even watch Santería ceremonies.

In *Ay, Cuba!* Andrei Codrescu takes readers on an outsider's trip through Cuba to illustrate how "dollarization" has reshaped the island and how Cubans have responded. An educated United States tourist whose roots are in Romania, Codrescu brings his experiences of growing up in an Eastern European country to an analysis of socialist Cuba as it responds to increasing capitalist pressures. But what kind of tourist is Codrescu? Is he the type portrayed by Kincaid? Is the Cuban government's focus on tourism having the effects discussed in *A Small Place* and *The Toured*? As their final writing assignment, students are challenged to compare Kincaid, Codrescu, and other writers who explore the merging of tourist and popular culture, to come to their own conclusions on the interaction and its effects on Caribbean popular culture. In the same vein, through the tourism–popular culture filter, students reflect on the two theories discussed in class—cultural imperialism and hybridization—and consider which applies to their own experiences and to those of Caribbean peoples.

REBEL SPIRIT: POPULAR RELIGIOUS
EXPRESSION AND HYBRIDIZATION

In the Caribbean, religious expression is important not only in people's everyday lives but also in its contributions to other forms of popular culture, especially music. Religious expression is also significant in the role popular culture plays as an agent of ethnic and national identity. While numerous religions are practiced in the region,[2] three (the most hybrid ones, as it were) best illustrate this role: Rastafari, Santería, and Vodou.

Most students enter the Caribbean popular culture course knowing a little about Rastafari, mostly from images of the reggae musician Bob Marley. Laying out the religious tenets and history of the movement enables students to follow the emergence of Rastafari in the Caribbean in the 1930s—in particular, how it developed from nineteenth-century religious traditions like Myal and Revivalism, hybrid religious expressions that emerged out of the Jamaican slave and peasant traditions. These expressions, when merged with Christianity, focused on spirit possession and controlling the evil, harmful spirits associated with sorcery (known as obeah). Rastas add a fascinating international and hybrid twist to old-time Protestantism. They reject the New Testament except the Book of Revelation and posit themselves as the true Jews and the Ethiopian emperor Haile Selassie I (overthrown and killed in a Marxist coup in 1974) as the biblical God living on earth. Students see how certain Jamaicans in a postslavery colony adopted Christianity but added political and religious beliefs derived from their own experiences, in a racist society, as descendants of slaves. Students then observe how, from the 1930s to the 1960s, Rastafari's early adherents—who themselves faced the full weight of colonial repression—used this hybrid movement to challenge the Jamaican colonial government. Independence from colonial rule strengthened support for Rastafari, especially after the 1966 visit of Haile Selassie I to the island (see Barrett; Campbell; Chevannes's *Roots* and *Worldviews*; Waters; Savishinsky).

A useful way to illustrate the political and identity aspects of Rastafari is to show how Rasta messages of resistance and identity are reflected in music and film. The oldest and most fundamental wing of Rastafari is the House of Nyabingi. Through their "churchical chants," the Nyabingi present Rastafari in its purest form: as an emancipatory theology advocating freedom from "Babylonian oppression," including capitalism, Western politics, and materialism. The Nyabingi served as the basis for later branches of Rastafari and the reggae music that emerged from the movement. Reggae evolved from Ny-abingi drumming adapted to Western musical instruments through the ska and rock steady beats. The hybrid musical creation became a vehicle for promoting issues central to Rasta identity and Rasta as a resistance movement: anti-imperialism, pan-Africanism, anti-Babylonianism, and reaction to regular harassment for smoking ganja (marijuana). In class, musical selections from the more politically conscious reggae artists can bring these messages home to students. In particular, the music of Bob Marley, Jimmy Cliff, Burning Spear, Peter Tosh, and Mutabaruka is widely available in the United States. *World Music*, edited by Simon Broughton, provides overviews of musical styles, along with recommended passages. It is an invaluable guide to music throughout the Caribbean, not just reggae.

Two Jamaican movies help contextualize Rastafari as a movement of resistance and identity. *The Harder They Come* and *Countryman* show Rastas, marginalized in Jamaican society, as representative of a kind, sharing, and peaceful alternative to the corruption of that society, which is under the influence of "Babylonian captivity." *The Emperor's Birthday* takes this alternative identity, born in Jamaica, back to Ethiopia. The video, which stresses the importance of Haile Selassie in African and world history, examines the problems that Rastas from around the world experience when they bring their reverence for Selassie to the country that assassinated him.

A combination of popular cultural forms (movie, music, and documentary) illustrates the hybrid origins and evolution of Rastafari, as well as its role in positing an alternative identity for its adherents. Students come to understand, first, how this form of religious expression has generated and been reflected in popular culture and, second, what happens when this belief system goes abroad in what Rowe and Schelling label deterritorialization. On going abroad, Rastafarian culture is adopted and adapted to fit local realities, in England, the United States, and throughout the Caribbean; or it is rejected by local realities, as in Ethiopia.

While students may approach Rastafari with a certain air of comfort thanks to their earlier encounters with Bob Marley, they are likely to approach Santería and Vodou with trepidation. To many, Santéria and Vodou conjure images of animal sacrifice, zombies, and black magic. To understand Santería, students might examine brief introductions to the religion: they can log onto OrishaNet.com or read "The Religion" from Joseph M. Murphy's *Santería*. Murphy's book also provides a useful two-page chart of the main orishas (Santería saints), their Catholic equivalents, dancing postures and foods appropriate to worshiping each, and so on. Students' frequent confusion when they hear that believers in Santería also see themselves as Catholic opens the door for an explanation of the hybrid nature of Santería. In the eighteenth century, slaves from west Africa brought with them the memory of orishas. Early attempts by the Catholic Church to convert the slaves resulted in a dual worship in which slaves openly prayed to Catholic saints but ascribed one orisha to each saint so that open worship of the saint was also a private worship of the orisha. The merging of the two religions can be vividly illustrated through video, including a section from *Portrait of Castro's Cuba*; a presentation from CNN on 18 January 1998, just before the historic visit of Pope John Paul II to Cuba; and *Voices of the Orishas*. All three allow practitioners to speak for themselves and provide footage of Santería ceremonies.

No discussion of Santería can exclude the role of the religion as a form of resistance and its relation to the Cuban revolution (1959). Throughout slavery, Santería posited itself as a form of resistance to European domination. Over the years this spirit of resistance became linked to the quest for Cuban national identity. When Castro first addressed audiences in 1959, newsreel cameras captured the landing of white doves on his shoulders—to some Santería worshipers, a symbol that the orishas had blessed Castro (this scene appears in the videos mentioned above). Castro is associated, as well, with Eleggua, the trickster orisha who also guards and directs the pathways of Santería, and thus the course of the Cuban revolution. The rise of first-rate filmmaking in Cuba after the revolution captured the spirit of liberation associated with Santería and increasingly ascribed to the revolution. In Tomás Gutiérrez Alea's *The Last Supper*, a slave uprising pits Santería followers against Spanish imperialism. Likewise, in his final film, *Guantanamera*, Gutiérrez Alea includes a Santería-inspired legend to challenge Cuba's leaders to remain true to their revolutionary principles for the sake of the youth. Through history, its use by the revolution, and its incorporation into Cuban popular culture, Santería has come to embody a central aspect of Cuban national identity, especially as a form of cultural resistance linked to the island's revolution.

Haitian Vodou is similar to Cuban Santería. The same process of hybridization occurred, as slaves carried the knowledge of "loas" or "lwas" (spirits), whose teachings helped Africans in the Americas live and worship. The notion of a practical religion is important to stress, for Vodou and for Santería. Both religions focus on the here and now, offering believers advice on such daily concerns as health and relationships. A useful starting point is "Introduction to Voodoo in Haiti" at www.uhhp.com/voodoo. Students should also see at least parts of two videos: *Haitian Pilgrimage*, about a Vodou priest in exile who returns to Haiti, and the classic documentary *Divine Horsemen*, set in the 1950s. The films go far in demystifying Vodou for North Americans by explaining some of the intricate ceremonies and by showing average people incorporating Vodou into their everyday lives.

Like Santería, Vodou served as a force of resistance to slavery. The narrative of the Haitian revolution—which began with a Vodou ceremony—has been captured by the Cuban novelist Alejo Carpentier in *The Kingdom of This World*. Vodou continued to play important roles in Haitian cultural politics. The dictator François "Papa Doc" Duvalier came to power in the 1950s as a supporter of *noirisme*, a movement celebrating Haiti's long-suppressed black culture, championing pan-Africanism, and promoting Vodou. Papa Doc quickly came to employ the symbolism of Vodou, however, to achieve his political ambitions and to maintain an iron-fisted rule.

By the 1970s, a countercultural movement arose on the island and in the Haitian exile communities in Paris, Quebec, and New York. The *kilti libète* (freedom culture) used Afro-Haitian symbols directly linked to Vodou ceremonies and music to challenge the dictatorship now headed by Jean-Claude "Baby Doc" Duvalier. Musicians played songs with Afro-Haitian roots and openly practiced Vodou; music became a means of promoting freedom and of highlighting, to the world, the liberating aspects of Vodou. As Lolo Beaubrun of the band Boukman Eksperyans noted, "When I heard Bob Marley sometime around 1976, I decided that if he could do something like that in Jamaica, we could do that with Vodou in Haiti" (Averill 133). In 1992, Haitians were poised for the return of Jean-Bertrand Aristide, the island's first democratically elected president, who had been overthrown by a military coup the year before. The Boukman Eksperyans's song "Kalfou Danjere," filled with Vodou phrases and symbolism, warned the military that it was at a "dangerous crossroads" (an explicit Vodou reference) and not to ignore the will of the people. The song soared to the top of World Music charts,[3] helping to bring international attention to the island, while the band's concerts around the island were teargassed. (Part of a performance by the Boukman Ersperyans is on the video *Haiti: Killing the Dream*.) Vodou had been incorporated squarely into Haitian popular cultural forms, like music, as a symbol of democracy and resistance to tyranny.

CELLULOID RESISTANCE: CARIBBEAN
CINEMA AND POPULAR CULTURE

No course on Caribbean popular culture would be complete without showing
and interpreting feature films from the region. The course utilizes one film
from each major cultural grouping in the islands: *Sugar Cane Alley* from Martinique (francophone Caribbean), *The Harder They Come* or *Countryman* from
Jamaica (anglophone Caribbean), and *Strawberry and Chocolate* (Hispanic Caribbean). While each film represents a particular region, students analyze how
it addresses the specific issues of race, ethnicity, gender relations, and identity.[4]

Sugar Cane Alley, set in Depression-era Martinique, focuses on a young
boy, José, who lives with his grandmother in the sugarcane fields. Through
sacrifice and determination, the grandmother enables the boy to receive an
education so that he can escape the misery of the fields. Students are asked
to look for the underlying cultural struggles at work in the film. For instance,
what possibilities do the black-shack alley residents have for social advancement? What does the boy's old friend Medouze, who teaches him about Africa
and the history of Martinique from a slave's perspective, contribute to the
boy's knowledge? How does such traditional, oral learning balance the formal
French schooling José receives? What role does *noirisme* play, especially regarding relationships among whites, mulattos, and blacks? By coupling the
film with Maryse Condé's novel *Crossing the Mangrove*, set in contemporary
Guadeloupe, or Edwidge Danticat's short-story collection *Krik? Krak!*, students
analyze the intersections of race, class, ethnicity, and gender in the francophone Caribbean. Because Martinique and Guadeloupe are still part of France
and not independent countries, students can use their knowledge of the interactions among these social factors to critique the role of popular culture in
shaping and reflecting national identity. In particular, students should note
that the movie is dedicated to people still living in black-shack alleys. The class
can discuss what message those residents would take from this film, and why.

Of the two films from the anglophone region, *Countryman* and *The Harder
They Come*, by far the better and historically more important is the latter.[5]
Harder is generally recognized as the first truly Jamaican film, coming at a
time when reggae music exploded onto the world stage. Reggae artist Jimmy
Cliff stars as Ivan. Set in the slums of Kingston, the film is based on the
exploits of the Jamaican folk hero Rhygin, the first and most dramatic of the
great ghetto gunmen. Using Rhygin's career as characteristic of working-class

life and culture in postindependence Jamaica, the movie recounts the last months of his journey from the countryside to the predatory slums of Kingston. Rebelling against the poverty and corruption of postcolonial Jamaica, Ivan kills police, hunts down drug dealers, and leads a Robin Hood–like existence, while his record soars up the charts. Students can analyze the film in conjunction with Earl Lovelace's novel *The Dragon Can't Dance*, about ghetto life and carnival in Trinidad, or with Lovelace's award-winning novel *Salt*, which examines class, ethnicity, and popular culture in the context of Trinidad's history from slavery through independence. Linking film and novel gives students insight into the way popular culture emerges from and reflects the broader dimensions of urban working-class life in the two countries. As in the case of *Sugar Cane Alley*, students are asked what opportunities exist for social mobility among ghetto populations. Students can also consider the effects, on Caribbean society and popular culture, of the increasing commercialization of island life in the 1970s, when *Harder* and *Dragon* appeared. The class can examine, in particular, the impact of commercialization on music lyrics and music sales, ganja trafficking, movies (characters in both the film and the novel are dazzled by Hollywood shoot-'em-up Westerns), and carnival. Such a study brings students back to the question of cultural imperialism. Does the growth of European-style capitalism and the commercialization and commodification of society reflect a form of imperialism? Or is hybridization at work, especially in the way the island peoples respond to outside influences by adapting them into their own cultural productions?

Cuban cinema has a recognized place at the top of the Caribbean movie industry. Students need to grasp the difference between what Cubans call "mass art" and "popular art." The former is intended for mass consumption; the works are created by a cultural elite for the sole purpose of profiting from an audience that is reduced to the role of spectator—in short, mass art is like Hollywood-style production. Popular art, in contrast, is designed for average people to both produce and consume. As the filmmaker Julio García Espinosa put it in 1969, "The essential lesson of popular art is that it is carried out as a life activity; man must not fulfill himself as an artist but fully; the artist must not seek fulfillment as an artist but as a human being" (171). For instance, average Cubans received cameras to film their lives and what they deemed important. The aim was for Cubans to film Cubans, developing a common understanding and purpose in order to construct a popular revolution in which people felt a direct intimacy and responsibility. This is not to say that stars have not been born in Cuba. Directors like Sara Gómez, Humberto Solás, and Tomás Gutiérrez Alea received national and international honors for their provocative films.

Since the 1960s, the best Cuban movies are those that criticize aspects of society or of the revolution that are thought to hinder advancement toward a better life. Gutiérrez Alea's international hit *Strawberry and Chocolate* was the first Cuban movie nominated for an Academy Award in the United States— reflecting the movie's high production values as well as the growing acceptance of controversial Third World cinema. The movie's most sympathetic character is a dissident homosexual artist, Diego, while the most despised character is an overzealous Young Communist university student. Through comedy and romance, Gutiérrez Alea calls on Cuban audiences to examine societal shortcomings and bureaucratic inefficiency. In *Strawberry*, he urges Cubans to be more tolerant not only of homosexuals but also of viewpoints different from their own. Students can read two interesting interviews from the director and one of the film's stars, Jorge Perugorría, who plays Diego ("Tomás Gutiérrez Alea"; Birringer). Because the Cuban film industry is a state-run system, students are challenged to think of this film as "art," "propaganda," or both. Similarly, students can be asked what they can learn about Cuban society from *Strawberry*: How can a film critical of the revolution be made in Cuba? Does the film serve the purpose of expanding the revolution by criticizing it? Although Cuban film utilizes the latest in Western technology (films are being made digitally), one would be hard pressed to see cultural imperialism here (Mireya Castañeda 3). Rather, Cubans create films as an expression of popular culture that serves the revolution and thus Cuban national identity, then export the images and sense of identity abroad.

REVERSE IMPERIALISM? MUSIC AND
SPORT CONQUER THE WORLD

Caribbean music has been discussed as a form of resistance, especially music intimately linked to movements for social change, such as Rastafari and the *kilti libète*. Not all Caribbean musical styles have such political dimensions, yet the process of hybridization at work in their formation speaks to issues of ethnic and national identity. Francophone zouk is a classic World Beat music. In the 1980s, zouk was one of the most frequently copied rhythms in World Beat music, but the rhythms developed over decades. To understand the history, students can hear selections of *gwo ka,* a traditional drum and vocal music performed, with up to ten drums, in the hills of Guadeloupe and elsewhere. Students can trace the evolution through the beguine (1920s–1930s) to cadence music, which by the 1970s had adapted North American–style funk into its rhythms; performers included such groups as Exile One and the Guadeloupian Vikings. A decade later, full-fledged zouk, originating in Paris among Caribbean expatriates like the group Kassav, had arrived. While zouk is dance music (the word itself is Creole slang for "party") and generally lacks a political edge, its hybrid nature illustrates the ongoing evolution of Caribbean music and the ability to merge First and Third World styles and technologies to create a genuine Caribbean product (see Guilbault; Behague; Broughton; Berrian).

Students will probably know more about music from the anglophone Caribbean, and many students may have selections of reggae and dancehall in their CD collections. Because students tend to think of Bob Marley and Jamaica when they hear of reggae, they are frequently surprised to learn that it has sprung up around the world and has become as hybridized as it has been deterritorialized. For instance, reggae has been adapted in Martinique by Kreyol Syndikat and in Brazil by Zeca Baleiro. American reggae bands may be familiar to students, who might enjoy listening to reggae classics set to different musical styles, like jazz and bluegrass. You can also illustrate how this music from the colonies has returned to the imperial seat of England, as a result of Antillean immigration, and has taken on a life and an influence of its own. Students listen to Afro-English bands like Steel Pulse, Aswad, and Desmond Dekker and white bands like the punk group the Clash, UB40, and the Police. Finally, internationalized reggae, combining reggae beats with local styles, has emerged out of Africa: Majek Fashek's blend of reggae and pangolo in Nigeria, Rocky Dawuni's odes to Ghanian independence, and Lucky Dube's mix of reggae and "zulu jive" in South Africa. In Jamaica, dancehall reggae began to replace the traditional sounds associated with Marley and others (see Cooper; Stolzoff; Chang and Chen; Jahn and Weber). The dancehall became the center of innovation in reggae music, with DJs speaking over tracks, adding commentary, and mixing songs that increasingly took on the influences of hip-hop. Thus dancehall became a hybrid of island reggae and North American hip-hop and rap music—a hybrid that found global acceptance in the 1990s with artists like Beenie Man, Buju Banton, Ini Kamoze, Patra, Shabba Ranks, and Shaggy. Labeled "ghetto music" in 1960s Jamaica, reggae overcame the stigma by going international (hybridizing and deterritorializing) and, in the process, becoming a highly successful form of Caribbean popular culture.

Carnival music in Trinidad and Tobago provides an excellent example of hybridized popular music that brings to mind the important issues of ethnic and national identity. Students are introduced to carnival with a discussion of its history and pageantry. The film *Mas Fever* takes viewers on a whirlwind tour that ends with the judging of floats and the crowning of the carnival queen. Lovelace's novel *The Dragon Can't Dance*, as noted earlier, illustrates the meaning of carnival for Trinidad's lower classes; it also examines the commercialization of the celebration. Students can learn about the evolution of carnival music by listening to the classic steel band and calypso—two forms discussed at length in Lovelace's novel. Modern carnival music in Trinidad is linked to the broader popular music scene, which revolves around soca and chutney soca. In the 1960s and 1970s, calypso evolved into soca with the introduction of the electric guitar and bass. Soca is more up-tempo, free-flowing, and louder than calypso.[6]

Increasingly, traditional East Indian chutney music influenced soca rhythms. Nearly half the population of Trinidad and Tobago is of East Indian descent; their ancestors were brought to the island after the abolition of slavery in the 1830s. Through the 1990s, the East Indian community gained social and political influence on the island, partly by creating a hybrid musical style known as chutney soca, played on the traditional Indian sitar. The short film *Chutney in Yuh Soca* includes chutney soca videos and live performances at carnival. One commentator in the video explains that the blending of black and Indian music is a sign of growing ethnic harmony on the island. Students might examine soca and chutney lyrics, characters in Lovelace's novel, and the rise to power in Trinidad, in 1996, of the first prime minister of East Indian descent, to find clues to the development of ethnic harmony and national identity. Unfortunately, the political milestone was followed by the growth of anti-Indian soca songs in carnival 1997. In response, the new attorney general introduced legislation to prevent racist lyrics in carnival. While the government may have promoted the slogan "All o' we is one" as a wishful call to national identity after independence from England, East Indian–black rivalries threatened this ideal. Thus, both dimensions of identity (national and ethnic-racial) are exemplified in Trini popular culture.[7]

Until 1959, Cuba was one of the most influential sources of popular musical styles in the world. Cuban dance crazes like the rumba, cha-cha-cha, and mambo swept the Americas and Europe, and Cuban music profoundly affected American jazz. Most students have seen old episodes of Ricky Ricardo's band in *I Love Lucy*, and some have read Oscar Hijuelos's Pulitzer Prize–winning *The Mambo Kings Play Songs of Love* or seen Antonio Banderas in the movie *Mambo Kings*, based on Hijuelos's novel. After the Triumph of the Revolution, though, Cuban music virtually disappeared from the United States; Cuban music continued to grow and thrive on the island, however. Pablo Milanés and Silvio Rodríguez, with their warm and sometimes political ballads in the Nueva Trova style, were welcomed throughout Latin America. One Cuban group to find success at home and abroad was Los Van Van, notable for its infectious salsa dance beat. The big-band salsa sound of bands like Cubanismo ripples throughout Cuba to this day and still finds export audiences. Also, Cuban jazz riffs are heard from Chuco Valdés and Irakere.

By the late 1990s, Cuban popular music felt the impact of two important international influences. On the one hand, the award-winning *Buena Vista Social Club* CD of classic 1930s-style music, played by survivors of the era, was not only a commercial success in Europe and the United States but also affected the Cuban scene—especially in conjunction with the rise of tourism on the island. Throughout Cuba, street-corner bands played their own versions of tracks from *Buena Vista Social Club*. Some people complained that the music was intended mainly for tourists who felt nostalgia for prerevolutionary days. To have a better chance at gaining recording-studio time or obtaining permits to play locally—and to get tips from appreciative tourists—bands increasingly played this evocative music. On the other hand, Cuban music has incorporated international genres, infused them with a modern consciousness, and exported the results. Along these lines, Cuban hip-hop and rock groups, like SBS and Moneda Dura, blended traditional Cuban sounds and instruments with modern rock formats. Similarly, the group Orishas added the sounds of rap to Cuban music.[8] We may be tempted to say that the *Buena Vista* phenomenon was a form of cultural imperialism, but that seems too strong a condemnation. Cuban musicians who played this music were performing for tourists, but . . . the music sounded great, and after all, this was Cuban music played by Cubans (a parallel phenomenon is the swing craze that hit the United States in the 1990s). Cuban rock and rap groups likewise dispelled the notion of cultural imperialism. By incorporating these international genres but injecting them with Cuban instrumentation and commentary on Cuban social reality, SBS, Moneda Dura, and Orishas highlighted the hybridization of popular music for both national and international audiences. Orishas reflected this when the group sampled the Buena Vista Social Club's "Chan Chan" in the song "537 C.U.B.A." (works on Cuban music include Díaz Ayala; Daniel; Peter Manuel's two collections; and Pacini Hernández).

Two sports are synonymous with the Caribbean: baseball and cricket (we'll skip the Jamaican bobsled team, as well as the 2002 Winter Olympics bobsled team from the United States Virgin Islands—about which no movie has been made, yet). While imported from abroad, and thus vulnerable to characterization as agents of cultural imperialism, the games in fact have been refashioned to reflect and shape Caribbean identities. Like Caribbean musical groups, the region's athletic teams have achieved international success. Just as Caribbean popular music has evolved, hybridized, and gone on to conquer the world, baseball and cricket challenge and even dominate international competition. As a result, they have become sources of nationalist pride in the region—especially Cuban baseball. Students need to understand how baseball evolved in Cuba, beginning in the 1860s and developing alongside of, and closely linked to, baseball in the United States. After 1959, baseball was thoroughly incorporated into the revolution.[9]

As noted earlier, Cuban film, intended for popular participation, still saw the rise of superstars as symbols of socialist success; baseball too played both dimensions. Students can read about this mass-elite phenomenon in Paula Pettavino and Geralyn Pye's *Sport in Cuba* and see it at work in the CNN documentary *Cuba's Boys of Summer*. The prowess of Cuban baseball players on the international stage led to numerous Pan-American Games titles, gold medals in the 1992 and 1996 Olympics, and a silver medal in the 2000 Olympics. The defeat of the Baltimore Orioles in 1999 reinforced the notion that Cuban baseball (and thus Cuban socialism) would resist becoming prey to United States imperialist might.[10]

The story of West Indian cricket mirrors the history of the region in the 1900s.[11] Over the years, black players from the lower classes replaced wealthy whites, as black consciousness movements and political independence grew during the first two-thirds of the twentieth century. The international success of the teams composed of players from different islands both reflected and stimulated the rise of a West Indian nationalist consciousness—though inter-island rivalries remained. National pride escalated whenever the West Indies defeated the formerly imperial England. Island cricket also took on a life of its own, both in the more aggressive play of its teams and in the rise of mass participation by bands, drums, and shouting fans—a far cry from the more tranquil game in England. In a sense, cricket was Caribbeanized, or hybridized, and the process led to international success that, in turn, boosted the feelings of national identity.

Caribbean music and sport reflect well the hybrid quality of Caribbean popular culture. Fusing international and local dimensions, the two activities highlight not only the creativity of the islands' peoples but also their ability to adapt and evolve. The success of athletics and music illustrate, as well, the peoples' capacity to resist cultural imperialism. Such resistance and adaptation reflect aspects of ethnic and national identity emerging from these cultural endeavors. Like Cuban film and Caribbean fiction, Caribbean music and sport have achieved world-class status. Ultimately, Caribbean popular culture is an important ingredient in the cultures of other societies, yet we are not witnesses to a cultural imperialism in reverse. Rather, by recognizing the hybrid, international dimensions of Caribbean popular culture, we can better understand the free exchange of energy and ideas that exemplifies humanity's complexity and creativity.

NOTES ON COURSE CONSTRUCTION

The course can be structured in at least two ways: topically and regionally. A topically constructed course would have an organization similar to that of this chapter: an examination of popular and tourist cultures transitioning to an introduction to nineteenth-century cultures followed by a focus on the twentieth century, which can be divided into subtopics like Race, Ethnicity, and National Identity; Religion and Popular Expression; Popular Culture, Resistance, and Social Change; and Music, Sport, and Globalization. While such an approach allows the instructor to delve into a specific topic in depth for a couple of weeks, it also runs the risk of offering examples from three completely different areas of the Caribbean (such as Haiti, Cuba, and Trinidad) and not adequately setting these in their historical contexts—contexts that are crucial in understanding how popular culture evolves.

Instead, after experimenting with both the topical and the regional formats, I have adopted and promote the latter. In the regional format, we first look at tourist and Hollywood images, then break the course down into the francophone, anglophone, and Hispanic Caribbean. Such a division is itself not perfect, and some might argue that the division actually mirrors colonial divisions of the islands. By organizing the course this way, however, I can explore the evolution, during more than 150 years in each region, of popular cultural forms like music and religion. After examining the issues of race and ethnicity, religion and popular expression, popular resistance and social change, and music, sport, and globalization in one region, the class considers these elements in the context of the next region and then the third. Thus by halfway through the course, students can draw connections to earlier segments and understand the historical evolution of popular culture in a comparative framework.

One final note on course construction: rather than use historical, ethnographic, and sociological studies of Caribbean popular culture, I prefer that students read actual works of popular culture, like novels and travel accounts, listen to music, and watch movies. The course is aimed at freshmen and sophomores, and experience has taught me that students understand more from the course by being immersed in the popular culture itself. Secondary source materials cannot by their nature provide immersion. Instead, the instructor takes on the role that secondary source reading would. Of course, this stance could be modified if the course is taught as an honors section or as an upper-level course. Still, even here, it seems that immersion is a more authentic approach to helping students experience Caribbean popular culture, its hybrid character, and its reflection and shaping of identity.

Secondary school teachers might consider developing the popular culture of one island or a linguistic set of islands in a world culture class or even a foreign language course. Any one of the three regions discussed here can be covered in a two- or three-week unit. The novels and travel accounts are brief enough to be covered in this span. A movie might easily be shown and discussed in three forty- to fifty-minute class periods, and music can be interspersed throughout. A French course could include a unit on the French Caribbean and read Maryse Condé in French, or a Spanish course could substitute a Spanish-language novel from Cuba, Puerto Rico, or the Dominican Republic. Again, it is important to present works of popular culture to the students.

Since I first imagined it, the course has taken on a life of its own. Students fill sections early in their preenrollments, for it is a course that builds on their love of popular culture. Instructors can turn this interest into a study of popular culture elsewhere in the hemisphere. By using a historical, up-to-date, and comparative approach, instructors can interject analysis of hybridization-deterritorialization theory that can inspire students to interpret global issues beyond movies and sport. Not least, instructors can illustrate how adaptive and creative the world's peoples are, with their own culture and that of others.

NOTES

1. For further useful theories on the hybrid nature of culture, see García Canclini, *Hybrid Cultures*, and Hall, "The Local and the Global." For a look at how hybridity can be viewed in the Caribbean, see Lent. A useful academic journal that frequently includes articles from a resistance standpoint is the *New West Indian Guide*.
2. Some other religions are American Methodist Episcopal in Jamaica, Islam in Jamaica and Trinidad, and Hinduism in Trinidad (see the useful video *Worlds Apart* for Hinduism).
3. World Music is an umbrella term referring to all forms other than Western classical music. World Beat emerged as a subset of World Music to include more modern, dance-oriented music that was the product of First and Third World blendings—a kind of hybrid form of modern music.
4. Several books provide useful information on Caribbean, especially Cuban, film. They include the essays collected by Cham and the books by Chanan and by Paul Julian Smith.
5. If it is available, the recent hit movie in Jamaica *Dancehall Queen* can be used. The problem with it and with *Countryman* is that they are in Jamaican Creole and usually difficult to understand. In *The Harder They Come*, the Creole is subtitled in standard English—a fact that Jamaicans have found amusing.
6. Students might read selections from Donald Hill's *Calypso Calaloo* or Louis Regis's *The Political Calypso* to understand the evolution and political context of calypso lyrics.
7. Two works that provide useful background on the emergence of chutney soca in Trini popular music are Manuel's *East Indian Music in the West Indies* and Myers's *Music of Hindu Trinidad*.
8. The impact of rock, rap, and techno music on Cuba's youth culture is illustrated in the video *¡Cuba Va!*.
9. Students can read selections from González Echevarría's *The Pride of Havana* or from Rucker and Bjarkman, *Smoke: The Romance and Lore of Cuban Baseball*, which has numerous illustrations.
10. Of course, a discussion of Cuban baseball should include the issue of defections and the roles of Cuban players in the United States. A useful introduction for students is Codrescu's *Ay, Cuba!*, especially the last chapter and the epilogue on Orlando "El Duque" Hernández. Codrescu was the last foreign journalist to visit Hernández in December 1997, just days before he left Cuba in a boat.
11. Students might read selections on the political context of cricket in Beckles and Stodart, *Liberation Cricket* or in James, *Beyond a Boundary*.

Surfing the Oblique: Latino / Latin American Cultural Studies in Hawai'i

Joy Logan

SURFBOARDS

Longboard: 8–10 feet long, with a rounded tip for small to medium waves

Shortboard: 5–7 feet long, with a pointed tip, more maneuverable in bigger waves

Gun: 7–9 feet long—a longboard, but pointed at the end like a shortboard; often used for big waves

Using a surfing analogy and labeling cultural studies as the *gun* of cultural critique is an easy way in Hawai'i to get students to visualize how cultural studies blends disciplines and redefines fields of study. Just as the *gun* combines features from two board types to surf bigger waves with greater speed and precision, cultural studies can be seen as a tool of criticism that links practices from multiple disciplines to traverse the ever-more-complex slopes of society and culture.

The hybrid and open nature of the mise-en-scène of cultural studies projected in the surfing analogy cuts across the wake of the cultural anthropologist Néstor García Canclini's questioning of the efficacy of separate, parallel disciplines to represent culture. Certainly García Canclini's pronouncement, in the early 1990s, that the "opposition between cultured and popular is unsustainable" (*Hybrid* 273) evokes the kind of cross-disciplinary, or synthetic, work on which cultural studies is based. The union of popular and elite expressions, however, is only one current flowing from the cultural studies watershed. More important, cultural studies was evolved from the contextualized and multidisciplinary examination of the ways "text and discourses . . . are produced within, inserted into, and operate in everyday life of human beings and social formations, so as to reproduce, struggle against, and perhaps transform the existing structures of power" (Grossberg, "Circulation" 180). This kind of purview breaches the traditional boundaries that, García Canclini believes, are problematic in separating disciplinary representations of sociocultural life. Certainly, Lawrence Grossberg, Cary Nelson, and Paula Treichler consider cultural studies, as practiced in the United States today, to be an "interdisciplinary, transdisciplinary, and sometimes counterdisciplinary field that operates in the tension between its tendencies to embrace both a broad, anthropological and a more narrowly humanistic conception of culture" (qtd. in Saldívar 11).

Because of its multiple, hybrid, unstable character, though, many theorists view cultural studies as an interpretive tool of uncertain use. In addition, cultural studies creates a thorny methodological problem for educators seeking to implement it in the classroom. At the crux of the matter, paradoxically, is García Canclini's assertion that, despite the impossibility of maintaining distinct spaces of academic pursuit, the "opening of each discipline into the others leads to an uncomfortable insecurity in studies on popular culture" (*Hybrid* 204). Such uneasiness, which has spurred heated debates about the validity of cultural studies as a medium of inquiry, is essentially what challenges the cultural studies educator. If we think of cultural studies both as an amalgam of nontraditional, transdisciplinary approaches and as a locus from which to frame new fields of study, then the teaching and implementing of it into the curriculum surely require preparation. In particular, we must create or adapt teaching strategies that are broad-based and malleable. Yet reconciling divergent disciplinary paths may lead us away from other possible pedagogies for introducing cultural studies into the classroom. Instead, by recognizing the tensions intrinsic to cultural studies, educators can both traverse and highlight the contested spaces between disciplinary fields rather than try to conflate them.

In the cultural studies I envision, instructors would use transdisciplinary methodologies to articulate and interrogate the concerns inherent in its practice. But beyond such theoretical, self-critical observations, the linking of methodology and discipline requires instructors to look, obliquely, not only at pedagogical objectives but also at the economic and political exigencies of institutional support, as well as at the geohistorical content of the course, or the politics of location that construct the learning environment. Opening up the field of interests and power supports the ideological or critical framing of cultural studies as a discipline; the broad scope of the enterprise, however, creates a multiplaned, unstable situation that makes course planning seem overwhelming and chaotic.

These are the concerns I faced in an undergraduate-class project on the representation of culture. Using this experiment as a point of departure, I will discuss here my experiences in developing flexible and tangential pedagogical methods to teach Latino/Latin American cultural studies at the University of Hawai'i, at Manoa (UH). I was confronted with the question of how to teach and practice Latino / Latin American cultural studies in an environment in which cultural hybridity, multi- and interculturalism, bilingualism, colonial and postcolonial relations, international tourism, and indigenous rights are more than sensitive issues—they are everyday factors in the dynamics of a Hawaiian Islander–Asian American–North American sociocultural context. I sought to implement exercises and activities that would bring to the foreground the theoretical underpinnings of the course; I was also concerned about curriculum development in a university that had suffered from severe budget cuts and was in the process of changing its core education courses. Moreover, my home department was under both budgetary and academic attack, and I was the only Latin Americanist on campus.

WHY CULTURAL STUDIES?

The need for malleable and oblique methodologies became obvious to me in two sections of a Latin American literature-in-translation course that I taught in fall 1997 and in which I incorporated a cultural studies component. The course, which fulfilled a UH core humanities requirement at the junior level, was taken by students from a wide range of majors. My decision to include a cultural studies component was based, in particular, on my desire to make the study of Latin America more interesting and to provide a more broadly based Latin American curriculum. The University of Hawai'i clearly defines its mission as having an Asian–Pacific Basin focus; the school has largely been indifferent to Latin America's relation to this region.[1] There is no Latin American anthropologist or sociologist on campus, and the only historian focusing on Latin America recently retired. As a result of budgetary cuts, my department, Languages and Literatures of Europe and the Americas (LLEA), lost two Latin American positions, leaving me as the sole Latin Americanist (the two positions were reinstated in 2002). To expand the limited focus on Latin America that I, as a professor of literature, was able to offer, I incorporated my own research interests and developed a cultural studies component within the Spanish division of our department.

This approach is somewhat at odds with the tendencies of my department as a whole, but within the context of Latin American–based literature classes in the Spanish division, it seemed a natural step to take.[2] Our tradition at the UH reflects Idelber Avelar's view that, in Spanish departments, "literary studies was always 'cultural' and 'political' in a sometimes vague, diffuse, but irreducible sense" (50). Thus, moving into cultural studies from this sort of hybrid, diffuse conjoining of sociopolitical and aesthetic approximations of literature was not an incoherent or radical move. However, my task was not simply to conduct business as usual after giving it a new name. While the project was a natural-enough outgrowth, it entailed refocusing class content and thematics and reformulating teaching strategies so as to include a cultural studies perspective.

Implementing a cultural studies module in an established literature course was the first step in defining cultural studies to meet our departmental needs and in introducing it into our curriculum. Since this initial project, I have proposed, and have had approved, four other courses, for both Spanish majors and nonmajors, that fall under the cultural studies rubric.[3] This change in our curriculum has provided a four-fold benefit to our department. First, it has allowed us to expand the study of Latin America as much as possible within the curriculum that our academic field encompasses. Second, the change brings Spanish more into line with the university curriculum; the move also echoes the English department's much more aggressive incorporation of cultural studies into its undergraduate and graduate programs and allows us to participate in the East-West Center–University of Hawai'i International Cultural Studies Graduate Certificate, which promotes the practice of cultural studies in the state. Third, the step should help us attract more students—an extremely contentious issue recently, since departmental budgets are now tuition-based. Fourth, it should enable us to incorporate more of our classes into the new core education curriculum; doing so will very likely increase our enrollment as well.

CONTEXTS

When we decided to create a cultural studies segment in our program, the question of how to teach such a course was certainly as important as how to articulate our motivation and objectives for doing so. To discuss how I envision the development of methodologies for the cultural studies classroom, I return to the practice and theory of the cultural studies module I tried in my Latin American literature class. In that class I linked the study of literature and anthropology, of narrative and ethnography, by connecting the reading of a novel by Mario Vargas Llosa with participation in a series of out-of-class activities on the Yucatec Maya and Chichén Itzá that included an ethnographic documentary. In coupling these two areas, I was adhering to a well-worn, generalized definition of cultural studies that links anthropology and literary criticism as the foundations on which cultural studies analyses are based. In addition, the literary criticism–anthropology connection paralleled my own interests and background and took advantage of the extracurricular events I had planned and coordinated: to bring a cultural anthropologist, Quetzil Castañeda, whose research is based in Yucatán, to campus for a lecture-presentation on the Yucatec Maya and to premier the documentary he co-produced with Jeff Himpele, *Incidents of Travel in Chichén Itzá*. I programmed into the class schedule this extracurricular, multi-event, multiformat series on Chichén Itzá and cultural anthropology in the Yucatán, which was sponsored by the Hawai'i Committee for the Humanities. The inclusion of this series, which consisted of a video presentation, panel discussion, lecture, and exhibit-reception, was not serendipitous. I myself wrote the grant proposal, did the planning and coordinating, and incorporated the project into the syllabus. Because the university budget and its composition do not offer many economic incentives or collaborative opportunities to generate cross-disciplinary events on Latin America, my interest in expanding dialogue on Latin America at the UH depends on bringing speakers and Latin American–based projects to campus; doing so means looking for funding outside UH institutional channels. The Hawai'i Committee for the Humanities, the state branch of the NEH, has been especially generous in this regard. In some ways the lack of university assistance has been beneficial, since HCH support has taken these Latin

American–based projects out of a strictly academic arena into a more inclusive forum that benefits the general community.[4]

The organization of the Maya series was guided by my dual desire to appeal to the interests of students and to bring to the community, and to the UH, material on Latin America not offered anywhere else on the island. I specifically organized the Maya project because of its resonance for Hawai'i. I hoped that in the execution of the cultural studies module of my class, both the study of the novel and student participation in the Maya series would provide a forum for comparative and interdisciplinary dialogue in which local and Hawaiian discourses were included. I imagined that it would encourage my students to consider how categories and relationships of colonialism-neocolonialism-postcolonialism, ethnic identity, national identity, and the economics of center-periphery are constructed, bounded, and contextualized according to geography and history, immigration patterns, and local, national, and global politics. One benefit of having to go outside Latin American studies or off campus to find collaboration and support is that, paradoxically—despite being isolated in my specific field—I never work, or present Latin American topics, in a vacuum. My very isolation forces me to be in contact with other disciplines and other specialist, and to do research in other areas. By embedding observations on Latin America in the geohistoric specificity that is Hawai'i, our project opened up discussions of global-local dynamics and avoided isolating, ghettoizing, or objectifying Latin America as a topic of study. Rather, the work sought to highlight crossings, links, and relationships in a multidisciplinary, multithematic framework.

CONTENT

The cultural studies module combined a traditional literary criticism class discussion and a nontraditional ethnographic theater to raise basic questions about culture, place, identity categorizations, and the conflicting drives to maintain and to rupture boundaries. The use of a variety of texts, themes, and formats parallels the hybrid configuration of disciplines and subject matter that is cultural studies but strays from the more widespread expectations of cultural studies to focus on popular culture or to juxtapose, in its analyses, the expression of pop culture and what García Canclini calls "cultured" texts and forms. Instead, I designed the course and the exercises to consider the kinds of disciplinary tensions that are present in any examination of the multiple ways culture is represented—be it through history, archaeology, ethnography, literature, oral history, film and other media, or cultural studies.

I moved the class from the literature module into the cultural studies component by easing from class discussion and dialogue into various visual and field activities. I began the module with what could be called a more traditional literary approach, a classroom analysis of Vargas Llosa's novel *El hablador* (*The Storyteller*). Consideration of *The Storyteller* leads to some theoretical and critical questioning about representation that spills over into the ethnographic theater experiment that later accompanied the Maya series.[5] *The Storyteller*'s beginning, with the narrator situated in Florence, provides a basis for discussing the geohistorical construction of subjectivity; postcolonial critiques; the legacies of Occidentalism and post-Occidentalism—themes running through the student activities in the Maya series (see Mignolo's treatment of these issues in *Local Histories*). In the novel the narrator sees an exhibit of photographs of the Peruvian Amazon, documenting the lives of the Machiguenga peoples. In several of the photographs, the narrator views the Machiguengas listening to a storyteller whom he believes to be an old friend he thought had died in Israel in the Six-Day War. From this starting point, he tells the story, in flashback, of his friend, Saúl, or Mascarita, and their differing obsessions about and perspectives on the Machiguengas. As students of history and anthropology, respectively, the two characters debate the study of culture in their native Peru and the consequences of such critical discourse on the material existence of Peru's indigenous peoples. In the story, which spans several decades, the narrator and Saúl meet North American missionaries and relate the history of the rubber boom and its effects on the Amazon, both socioculturally and economically.

The novel allows for classroom discussion of a variety of themes and issues that will lay the groundwork for the later exercises. The novel itself debates Western categories of cultural study: history, literature, linguistics, and anthropology. As the narrator, in self-reflection, outlines the process of putting the novel together, other topics—such as Western research methodology (bibliographic and ethnographic work), photography, oral history, magic realism, marginality, documentary making, and the ethics of storytelling—also are brought up. I supplemented class discussion with a documentary, *Travels: Iquitos*, in which Vargas Llosa himself appears. The documentary focuses on the history of Iquitos, a city on the Amazon—its European settlement and the history of the rubber boom, the creation of a contemporary tourist industry, and the effects of economic globalization. A traditionally filmed documentary, with an offscreen narrator providing background information, it contrasts with the narrative style and structure of the later video, *Incidents of Travel in Chichén Itzá*. From both the novel and the video on Iquitos, tangential discussions can be initiated. Here I would suggest visiting Renato Rosaldo's essay "Imperialist Nostalgia," about the effects of democratization, neoliberalism, and globalization on native peoples and provincial regions. I introduced the novel in relation to these critical purviews in order to prepare the class for a consideration of these topics from a different perspective when we started the Maya segment.

By reading the novel first, the class was able to examine the variety of issues it presents; the explorations also provided a comfort zone for students who had had experience with small-group and whole-class discussions. Their familiarity with these topics facilitated their moving on or into other kinds of exercises that would approximate and link anthropological practices in the second part of the cultural studies component. In shifting the first part of the module from a primarily aesthetic discussion of the novel to a sociocultural examination of its themes—in preparation for the second part of the module—I sought to confront the criticism cultural studies has received for maintaining, according to some anthropologists, a too-close association with literary criticism's textual focus. Sherry Ortner, for instance, has stated that "American versions of cultural studies have been largely focused on media or 'public culture' analysis and, despite some partially answered calls for ethnographic work on 'reception,' have tended to maintain a primarily textual focus" (2). Our project tried to go beyond the purely textual. It crossed into the area of postmodern ethnographic practices to reflect on questions previously brought up in connection with the novel, such as framing, perspective, reception, ideologies, exchange of information, and the ethics of ethnography.

THEORY

In creating a methodological frame for the cultural studies module of this class, I was faced with the lack of any real guidelines for such academic exercises. The absence of a model is a principal difficulty in teaching cultural studies, whose hybrid and dynamic nature hinders the prescription of a stable pedagogy. As Richard Johnson has clearly proclaimed, "a codification of methods of knowledges (instituting them, for example, in formal curricula or in courses on 'methodology') runs against some main features of cultural studies as a tradition." Yet Johnson, in disavowing the viability of a definitive methodology, allows for pedagogical-theoretical parameters that I *did* invoke. Johnson states that cultural studies is a tradition based on

> openness and theoretical versatility, its reflexive even self-conscious mood, and especially, the importance of critique . . . not criticism merely, nor even polemic, but procedures by which other traditions are approached both for what they may yield and for what they inhibit. Critique involves stealing away the more useful elements and rejecting the rest. From this point of view cultural studies is a process, a kind of alchemy for producing useful knowledge; codify it and you might halt its reactions. (75)

In following Johnson's idea of cultural studies as alchemy, I sought to borrow—or, as Johnson puts it, steal—from several disciplines the pedagogical strategies and exercises that in their combination might prove problematic for strict adherents to disciplinary-bounded perspectives.

The theoretical framework of the second part of the module, in both its thematics and its execution, was intended to evoke the connections between anthropology and literary criticism in other than just a textual manner. The linking of these two disciplines traced the legacy of cultural studies from Clifford Geertz's fundamental work in redefining, pushing, crossing, and blurring disciplinary lines in his interpretive-empiricist reading of culture through thick description; it also presupposed James Clifford's textual notions of "writing culture" that reworked such connections.[6] Our class experiment, in linking the study of literary texts, video documentary, and ethnographic practices, moved beyond critical discourses in anthropology to engage the theatricality, performativity, and postmodernist aspects of culture as articulated by Abdel Hernández and Castañeda, who speak of experimental ethnography and the ethnography of evocation.[7] Derived from these theoretical underpinnings, our theater encouraged student ethnographers to experience the multiple flows of discourses that compose the ethnographic exchange of information. In this way we were able to examine how representations of self and other were exchanged, reworked, and doubled back on themselves.

We created the ethnographic theater to focus on the issues we had discussed in the novel, as well as to provide a medium from which we could examine ethnography as a cultural tool. The theater as a participatory act highlighted the performativity of ethnography and enabled students to become aware of the ethnographer's and informant's positionings, to discern underlying ideologies in the construction of the ethnographic mise-en-scène, and to question the exchange and reception of knowledge.

PRACTICE

As a class, we configured a series of open mise-en-scènes by fashioning a community made up of students and of people attending, or in the vicinity of, the four events in the Maya component. Initially we outlined a loosely bound field in which we would question the ways self and other were conceptualized—specifically, to elicit how categories of identity of local and Maya were used. Although we had geographic and temporal limitations, there were no critical, ethnic, racial, class, gender, age, linguistic, or academic categories that narrowed our frame(s). Establishing the mise-en-scène was in itself problematic, because, other than the logistics of time and the location of the events, no parameters were fixed or stable. As each event took place, we reworked the parameters to include previous and subsequent events. We ended up expanding the original frame, at the same time that we developed successive mise-en-scènes that evoked multiple, superimposed, open, and self-consciously artificial frames.

The first of the four events (see app., Schedule) serving as vertices of the frames of our fieldwork was the anthropological-historical lecture "On How to Be Maya: Living in the Shadows of Chichén Itzá," in which Castañeda described the archaeological reconstruction of the ruins at Chichén Itzá—and his ethnographic project in Pisté, the Maya village four kilometers from Chichén. The second was the reception-exhibit immediately following the talk. The third was the premier of the video *Incidents of Travel in Chichén Itzá.* The topics the film treats—archaeology, history, the creation of a "heritage industry," and the impact of international tourism at Chichén—are all categories of interest or concern in Hawai'i today. The fourth was the interdisciplinary panel discussion by a group of UH professors. While these four events were the general focus of the project, issues of identity formation, cultural critique, and representation were juxtaposed in a variety of other ways.

Thus there was a layering, or building up, of frames, discourses, critiques, and representations that our ethnographic theater sought to dramatize. The theater was in two acts: "doing" and "presenting" ethnographies. The class divided itself into eight ethnographic-video teams of at least three students

Students unknowingly interview anthropology
professor about ethnography. Photo courtesy of LLEA
362 classes.

each. (We had eight teams because the university made only eight camcorders available to us.) Four of the teams documented the knowledge about the Mayas that the "community" we had established possessed. The other four teams interviewed the "community" about sociocultural constructions of identity in Hawai'i. There were also two groups of photographers who documented the interaction between the ethnographic groups and the "community" and the presentation of the theater's ethnographies at the reception.

From their discussion of *The Storyteller*, students had more than enough information to reflect on basic issues of representation, identity construction, postcolonial politics, ethnicity, gender. To prepare for the interviews, each group of student ethnographers created a list of questions, and as a class we discussed interview techniques, guidelines, and filming strategies (see app., Ethnographic Theater Guide). The students did not preview the Chichén Itzá video, nor were they briefed on what the lecture on the Yucatec Maya would deal with. They had no information about either presentation other than the titles and the publicity blurbs. Each member of the eight teams of ethnographic-video groups had to participate in three different categories: as the camera operator, as the ethnographer, and as an informant. Real interviews were then intermixed with staged ones on every video. In this way we highlighted the fact that students are aware of their own prejudices, experiences, and knowledge; we observed students projecting images of what they expected tourists to know and of the stereotypes they expected tourists to have. We learned how nonclass members might react to students' questions and how informants could also project "othered" images and reflect back what they assumed to be expected of them. Students' understanding of roles and of the positioning of subjectivity allowed them to challenge notions of objectivity in cultural critique, as the participants realized that projecting, or stereotyping to fit expectations, is not a unidirectional process but one that goes back and forth between ethnographer and informer.

The video documenting took place both before and after the lecture by Castañeda. Student teams asked questions of onlookers, passersby, students waiting at the bus stop, and members of the general public heading to the talk on the Mayas. All students wore name tags identifying themselves as student ethnographer, informant-tourist, informant-student, informant-Hawaiian, informant-professor, and so on, depending on the role they were playing. Four teams asked informants what they knew about the Maya—as noted, students had developed the questions themselves (see app., Student Questions). The questions asked for definitions, descriptions, or any other information interviewees had about the Maya. The other four teams asked questions about island categories of identity, such as "What does it mean to be Hawaiian?" "What is 'local'?" "Can a haole be local?"[8] All interviews ended with the question "Do you know what ethnography is?" and an invitation to the reception for viewing and discussing the interviews. Several of the ethnographic teams also interviewed spectators leaving the auditorium after the talk on their way to the reception. The two teams of photographers filmed the ethnographic experiences and the reception.

At the reception we presented the video ethnographies that the students had made just two hours earlier. We set up four video stations—where two Maya tapes and two local–Hawaiian tapes continuously played—so that students and the public could review and discuss the films. In other words, the "community" under study received immediate information and offered feedback and participated in the analysis of the "ethnography." The video stations were coupled with the five poster boards, created by Castañeda's field school in Pisté, that discussed postmodern ethnography, art, economics, and archaeotourism in Pisté; the town of Pisté; the art exhibit of Pisteleño wood carvings of traditional Maya figures; and the teaching of English in Pisté. By using the room in which the reception was held, we could discuss, in a relaxed environment, the audience's thoughts about the lecture

Students role-play in ethnographic theater. Photo
courtesy of LLEA 362 classes.

and about new ideas elicited by the videos and posters—we thus created a
space for dialogue to flow, bounce back, and cross on the transversal. The
juxtaposition of topics, voices, and visions that brought Hawaiian issues
into contact with those from the Yucatán enabled us to see connections, between one area and another, that had not been explicitly articulated in the
lecture or by the video groups. The layout of the reception erased boundaries between geographic areas, between teacher and student, between disciplines, and between identity categories. It generated a blending of dialogues
and a plurality of voices. In contrast to the earlier exercises, in which students role-played and specifically labeled their roles as a way to set clear de-
marcations, here boundaries were minimized, crossed, and transgressed. The
event was a reception, yet it was not just about social chitchat and food. It
was an exhibit with sociability; at the same time, it was an ethnography of
the moment in the moment.

    It was an ethnography that combined the visual (videos) and the textual
(the posters) and that highlighted participation, collaboration, multiplicity,
and inclusivity. The photographs of the reception-ethnography formed an
ethnographic document that was later used for class commentary and as a
display. All the video and photographic documentation was made available
to the audience and to the class, the very "community" members represented

Viewing station at reception. Photo courtesy of LLEA
362 classes.

in the ethnographic theater. The materials became a focal point in our discussion of the ethics of representation and the politics of the transmission
of knowledge. We used the documentation, as well, to consider to whom most
ethnographies are directed, how the objects of study or the cultures of study
are commodified, and how indigenous traditions of orality and nontextual
cultural expressions figure into ethnographic representation. From the discussion of these topics, the class decided to create another public forum for
critique and feedback, by setting up a photo display (done by the student photographers) of the events for reception by the "community" it was
documenting.

On the second evening of the Maya series, two video stations were set up
for viewing before and after the documentary and panel discussion. One
played ethnographic-theater tapes, alternating the Hawaiian and the Maya
videos. The other played tapes of Castañeda's field school; they showed scenes
representing topics similar to those that the poster boards had displayed at
the reception. We framed the evening's presentations, once again, within the
politics of location that constituted our three focal points: discussions of identity at the local level, local definitions of who the Maya are, and film of Pis-
teleños and North American students in the field school in the Yucatán. In
other words, the public attending the Chichén video and panel discussion
encountered a visual representation of the theoretical framework of the evening's events. My students' videos evoked local notions of self and others,

while the tapes of Castañeda's field school offered a North American academic-ethnographic point of departure.

Castañeda and Himpele's work is a self-reflective critique on ethnographic documentary making. The film opens with a list of ten questions about the Maya (see app., Questions from the Video Incidents), nine of which were similar to those my students had prepared without having seen the video. (The answers my students received were what was being played in the video outside the doors.) However, the documentary goes on not to answer those questions but to focus on the tenth question, on representation—or as the documentary makers say, on the invention of Chichén and the Maya by a variety of groups: New Age tourists, the Instituto Nacional de Antropología e Historia, the people of Pisté, a Catholic priest, the federal (Mexican) government, and the two filmmakers. The video provides a nontraditional, or unexpected, perspective; it is not a historical, social view of the "lost Maya" but a look at the way the Maya are represented and constructed in a variety of discourses.

In setting up the panel to discuss the documentary, I was aware that there were no Latin American specialists at the UH to invite, as had been done in discussions of the film at the University of Houston.[9] Again I was forced to work tangentially. Taking into consideration how this film might resonate in the geohistoric specificity of Hawai'i, I invited an archaeologist, Terry Hunt (who focuses on the Pacific Islands), who stressed, in his commentaries, the ethics of doing archaeology; a cultural anthropologist, Geoff White (who also works on the Pacific Islands), who addressed the making of the film and the video's ironic tone in representing ethnography; a professor of cultural studies, Constance Sherak (French), who explained the discourse of museums, collections, archaeotourism, the Louvre, and Chichén; and a native Hawaiian professor of Hawaiian culture and language, Naomi Losch, who commented on the tensions between expanding tourist markets and indigenous rights and traditions. The panel members' individual readings and commentaries were interdisciplinary, but the subsequent discussion became transdisciplinary, in that the audience and Castañeda questioned and commented on their reactions to the video by blending information and insights. Students were encouraged to participate in the discussion. In the panel discussion we configured a broader interdisciplinary and transdisciplinary space that encompassed the Pacific Islands, Hawai'i, Europe, and the Yucatán. Within a global frame of crossings and connections, the discussion also traversed academic issues, as well as the concerns and interests of the general public and of students and educators in Hawai'i.

REVIEWS AND REVISIONS

After the event, in discussing the ethnographic theater, we added a layer of dialogue and feedback in returning to the traditional classroom structure. As we reviewed student videos, we talked about the dynamics of the reception-ethnography (the social forces, discourses, and information exchange at play). We critiqued the documentary and the panel discussion and viewed the photographs. At each step there was a layering of review upon review, documentation upon documentation. Feedback on feedback was incorporated, and students viewed themselves creating the ethnographies, participating in the reception-exposition, being represented by the photographers, and recounting the issues of the panel discussion and video. In focusing on the process of ethnography, students commented that a major aim of the project, for them, was to make visible the unseen, "natural" assumptions that filter our representations of identity, self and other, and culture. However, the exercises were not just about the process of cultural critique; they also highlighted the difficulty in defining identity categories and the social and political ramifications of such categories. Other topics students raised were the information gleaned from their informants and speculation about how such ideas came into being, were circulated, and ended up supporting specific ideological positions. The final essay assignment, or reaction paper, functioned as another medium of feedback, or documentation, in a kind of mini-autoethnography. Thus, in the variety of forms and forums for both discussion and evaluation, the coursework reflected the hybrid quality of cultural studies itself.

As I consider how I constructed the methodology of this class module, I find that I strongly agree with Leslie Deveraux's assessment that

> cultural studies is a cultural anthropology of ourselves, and at the same time the radical, formal, critical theories of which it takes part lay bare, from historical and philosophical points of view, the conditions of anthropology and all other social sciences' knowledge production. (17)

This was indeed the kind of understanding of cultural studies that I wanted to manifest in the activities I created. The exercises were developed with three goals in mind: to introduce students to different disciplinary approaches to cultural critique, to provide a forum to examine such approaches, and to contextualize these exercises in course work on Latin America and within the sociocultural setting of the University of Hawai'i. If I undertook this project again, I would set aside more time for reviewing disciplinary tensions as seen in the current debates about cultural studies. I might ask students to consider García Canclini's depiction of an encounter between an anthropologist, a cultural studies professor, and a sociologist and to think about his criticism of cultural studies' short-sightedness in not being more "scientific" in its analyses and in not dealing more energetically with economics (*Globalización* 134). I might also have the class consider Lila Abu-Lughod's statement describing "popular culture studies" as "disappointing" because they "do not seem to be trying to offer profound insights into the human condition, or even into the social, cultural and political dynamics of particular communities . . . goals anthropology has set for itself . . ." (111). These are provocative follow-up themes that should stimulate interesting debates.

In addressing these concerns, I would like to point out that in the project I have described, my students—from their island- and cultural studies–based perspectives—did not shy away from discussing the material consequences of the representation of ethnic, national, and racial identity categories. Aware of the political and economic overtones of such categorization in Hawai'i, students can imagine similar distinctions being made in Latin America. As we wrapped up the module, class discussion turned to issues of Hawaiian sovereignty, the role of OHA (Office of Hawaiian Affairs) and voting privileges on Hawaiian issues, the Bishop trust, determination of Hawaiian bloodlines with respect to Kamehameha schools and land grants, colonization, land use and the construction of the H-3 highway through sacred areas, stereotypes and tourism, bilingualism, oral history, and nontextual methods of narration such as dance and sculpture. At this juncture I would have liked to have a detailed study of corresponding issues in Latin America that might incorporate more overtly economic, sociological, or political analyses. While cultural studies creates a locus for such discussions, other disciplinary approaches might offer greater depth and complexity to the consideration of these topics. Introducing a multidisciplinary Latin American focus in response to discussion of the local issues is another addition I would include in the module were I teaching it today. The final revision would be to return, or double back, to working through a definition of cultural studies. While critique and self-reflection form an essential part of cultural studies, the nagging suspicion remains that cultural studies has become the scapegoat for other disciplines' need to find an absolute way of looking at culture, a universal of cultural critique.

Recognizing the impossibility of a disciplinary absolute leads me back to the surfing analogy. Like the handy, multipurpose gun, cultural studies allows us to surf the transversal, the oblique, the tangential of cultural critique. Just as a gun may not be the best ride for both the Pipeline and Waikiki, cultural studies is not the end-all of social sciences and humanities, but it does allow us to participate in both as it slides across disciplines, reframes fields of study, and links global and local issues in a way that separate disciplines do not. As I see it, teaching cultural studies is always surfing the oblique. It is about moving laterally and tangentially outside the classroom to contextualize theory and practice within geohistorical, institutional, and community concerns and issues;[10] it is about recombining class exercises to encourage critique and self-reflection; and it is about breaching disciplinary boundaries to reflect the hybrid nature of itself. When all these elements come together, teaching cultural studies is, as they say in surfer jargon, "toes on the nose."

NOTES

1. The mission statement in the university catalog reads: "The system's special distinction is found in its Hawaiian, Asian, Pacific orientation and international leadership role" (*University of Hawai'i*).
2. My department consists of five divisions: Classics (Greek and Latin), Russian, German, French, and Spanish. Spanish is the only division to explicitly name cultural studies as part of its curriculum. (Our unusual name stems from the makeup of the department and parallels the geographic denominations of other language departments: Hawaiian and Indo-Pacific, East Asian.)
3. LLEA 372, Indigenous Peoples of Latin America; LLEA 683, Hispanic Cultural Studies; SPAN 495C, Literature and Society; SPAN 495D, Literature and Film.
4. The program described here is the third one HCH has supported for the Spanish division since 1993. One of the stipulations of these grants is that all activities must be geared toward the general public.
5. Debra A. Castillo's treatment of this novel provides a provocative point of departure for this kind of analysis. See her "Tropics."
6. Ortner specifically decides not to include any cultural studies articles in her collection on Geertz, *The Fate of "Culture."* Her need to address this lack, however, points to the obvious connections that can be made. See Clifford and Marcus, *Writing Culture*, a seminal work in positing the intersections between ethnographic and literary critical discourses.
7. These ideas are developed by Castañeda, in "Installing" and in "Paradigms of Fieldwork"; by Hernández"; and by Hernández and Angelini.

8. *Haole*, a term applied to outsiders, also denotes a racial category, white. Its pejorative connotations are contextual and often contested.
9. Film Screening and Panel Sponsored by the American Cultures Program and Anthropology Student Forum, University of Houston, 19 Sept. 1997. Moderator: Steve Mintz, history and American cultures, University of Houston. Commentators: George Marcus, anthropology, Rice University; Susan Rasmusen, anthropology, University of Houston; Abdel Hernández, curator, Contemporary Museum of Art, Caracas; Quetzil Castañeda, anthropology, University of Houston.
10. This is perhaps the key point I have tried to make in this essay and the reason that I have not included a more detailed and specific syllabus. The activities I discussed are not offered as a course plan that can be plugged into any cultural studies syllabus. Rather, I have given readers a perspective from which to think about how they would teach cultural studies, to consider in what ways Latino / Latin American cultural studies might have resonance for their own communities, and to question their interpretation of cultural studies as a tool of cultural critique. It is from these personalized, local considerations that I expect educators would create activities, events, readings, discussions, exhibits, and forums in which to explore both the theory and the content of cultural studies.

APPENDIX

Schedule of Events

Weeks 1–2   Discussion of *The Storyteller* and *Travels: Iquitos*
Week 3   Day 1: Ethnographic Theater (interviews and filming—students were instructed in filming techniques by Quetzil Castañeda and an LLEA 362 student who worked at a local TV station)
Presentation–Lecture "On How to Be Maya: Living in the Shadows of Chichén Itzá"
Reception–Ethnographic Theater (video viewing and discussion)
Day 2: Ethnographic Theater (videos before and after documentary and panel discussion)
Viewing *Incidents of Travel in Chichén Itzá*
Panel Discussion
Week 4   Class Critique of Ethnographic Theater, Documentary, and Panel Discussion
Discussion and Setting Up of Photo Displays

Ethnographic Theater Guide —Last-Minute Instructions

1. Remember to wear your name tag: "Student Ethnographer."
2. First Point. Always ask your interviewee if s/he would be willing to answer some questions for a class project.
3. Start with general questions—let the conversation take you to more specific points.
4. Be flexible. Not every interviewee will be able to answer all your questions. If someone really opens up to a specific topic and gives a good, lengthy answer, don't cut him/her short just to get to all your remaining points. You don't have to ask everyone everything. Listen to where the conversation is going and go with it!
5. Last question of every interview: "Do you know what ethnography is?"

6. Remind interviewees that we will be previewing the interviews at the reception, and they are invited to come and comment.
7. Change roles. Everyone in each group should have an opportunity to film, interview, and be interviewed. Remember to choose a character and put on a name tag: "Tourist," "Student Athlete," "Uninformed Student," "Informed Student," "Hawaiian," "Local," "Maya," "Here for Extra Credit," "North Shore Resident," "Once Traveled through Guatemala." "Saw the *Popol Vuh* video," "Haole," etc. (Be inventive—this is ethnographic theater!)

Students' Questions about the Maya

Why are you here?
What do you know about the Maya culture?
Is the Maya culture extinct, or is it still alive?
What language do the Maya speak?
Where are the Mayas?
What is distinctly Maya?
What do you think of when you hear "Maya"?
What does Maya mean to you?
What do you know about the Maya culture? What would you like to learn?
What do the Maya eat?
What do the typical Maya look like?
How do the Maya dress?
Do you know the differences between Maya and Inca?
What religion do the Maya practice?
What do you know about Hernán Cortés and Maya history?
Where do the Maya people live?
Are the Maya and the Hawaiians related?
What have the Maya given to our culture?
How do the Maya live? Where do they dwell? Work?
Do you know what ethnography is?

Questions from the Video Incident of Travel in Chichén Itzá

Where did they come from?
How did they adapt to the harsh environment of the jungle?
Did they build true cities? or sacred pilgrimage centers?
Why did they abandon their civilizations?
When will they return?
Do they still exist?
How did Maya culture develop advanced sciences like astronomy?
Why the need for precise calendars that calculate celestial events thousands of years into the past and future?
What is the meaning of the serpent that appears on the day of the equinox?
What is the origin of these questions?

An Approach to Gender and Sexuality Studies in the Undergraduate Curriculum

Robert McKee Irwin

LATIN AMERICANISM AND CULTURAL STUDIES PEDAGOGY

What is a cultural studies pedagogy? How can it be applied to teach undergraduates about gender and sexuality in Latin America? This article addresses how to introduce the study of gender and sexuality in Latin America in the upper-level Spanish or Portuguese classroom in the United States.[1]

Traditional programs of Spanish and Portuguese encompassed the study of language and literature. Once students became sufficiently advanced in language, they moved on to literature courses focusing on literary movements (*modernismo*, the Boom), periods (the colonial era, the nineteenth century), literary forms (poetry, the essay), national or regional literatures (Mexican literature, literature of the Andes), or authors (Machado de Assis, Borges). Recent critical debate has made clear the shortcomings of such a program's exclusively literary focus.

First, as the Uruguayan cultural studies scholar Abril Trigo has pointed out, "the Latin American literary canon has been built with and from extra-literary and non-literary texts since its early beginnings" (79). For example, much of the material studied as colonial literature—the letters of Hernán Cortés, the diaries of Cristóbal Colón, the protoethnography of Bernardino de Sahagún, the historiography of El Inca Garcilaso de la Vega, the hyperbolic rhetoric of Bartolomé de las Casas—would hardly conform to traditional definitions of literature.

Likewise, it has been common to look at Latin American (and all Third World) literature less as aesthetic object than as sociological artifact. For example, the study of Argentine *gauchesca* literature, novels of the Mexican revolution, or the poetry of José Martí and Pablo Neruda has frequently treated such material principally as social commentary. Thus Beatriz Sarlo charges:

> Everything seems to indicate that as Latin Americans we should produce objects suited to cultural analysis, whilst others (basically Europeans) have the right to produce objects suited to art criticism. The same could be said of women or of the working class: they are expected to produce cultural objects while White males produce art. . . . It is our duty to claim the right to the "theory of art," to its methods of analysis.   ("Cultural Studies and Literary Criticism" 123)

Still, the focus on a limited range of texts, those sanctioned as literary, produced a field of study that was essentially elitist and far from representative of the diversity of Latin American culture. As Angel Rama demonstrates forcefully in a classic study of literature and power in Latin America, the "priestly caste" of "the lettered city" historically exercised enormous power through its mastery of the written word (*Lettered City* 16). However, the cultural production of this small minority of men, too often as white as Sarlo's Europeans, represents quite a narrow view of Latin America.

For a deeper understanding of Latin American culture, Néstor García Canclini suggests that

> it is necessary to deconstruct . . . that layered concept of the world of culture, and find out whether its hybridization can be read with the tools of the disciplines that study them separately: art history and literature, concerned with "high culture"; folklore and anthropology, dedicated to popular culture; communications, specialized in mass culture. We need nomadic [disciplines], capable of circulating among all layers of culture.   (*Culturas híbridas* 15)[2]

Literary studies, which in many ways has been bursting at the seams for Latin Americanists, needs to give way to cultural studies. And while the term *cultural studies* has been used in different ways and often seems to resist definition, we might usefully reiterate a list of characteristics generally shared by texts classifying themselves under the rubric of Latin American cultural studies:

> First, work in cultural studies questions disciplinary boundaries. Second, such scholarship displaces "literary" texts as the traditional or sole objects of study and opens the way to academic consideration of other cultural expressions. Third, a cultural studies approach contends that all forms of cultural production have a political dimension. . . . And fourth, cultural studies makes a claim for political participation. (D. Anderson 5–6)

Such a rubric calls for a reconfiguration of upper-level Spanish and Portuguese courses to legitimize the incorporation of nonliterary objects of study, including film, music, and popular legend, as well as to introduce a critical stance more explicitly conscious of ideology and difference.

GENDER AND SEXUALITY IN LATIN AMERICA

The issues of gender and sexuality, basic elements of contemporary identity constructs, provide the foundation for the kind of inquiry that a cultural studies pedagogy encourages. Approaches to teaching gender and sexuality in Latin America are multiple and go well beyond such mainstays as traditional analysis of literary history, aesthetics and stylistics, and authorial biography (though all these elements may be included). The overarching goal would be to bring into focus a broad and diverse perspective on Latin American culture. Students would likewise confront a range of linguistic registers, not just those of literary language, to encompass other, more popular or specialized styles of discourse. The linguistic element would be addressed through both text and film (or other visual media) and supported by speaking and writing exercises.

The core of the course, however, would be the analysis of gender and sexuality, concepts often taken for granted as natural. The analysis would apply specifically to Latin America, but it might also be extrapolated to other contexts, including students' everyday life. A cultural studies approach that takes into account feminist and queer theory reveals the distinctive cultural and historical features of both gender and sexuality and challenges the rhetorical strategies that foment popular beliefs regarding femininity, machismo, homosexuality, promiscuity, homosocial bonding, and similar issues. The cultural studies perspective also brings to light the ways in which constructions of gender and sexuality have been linked to other social building blocks, such as nation, race, and class.

In this essay I describe a course focusing on nineteenth- and early-twentieth-century Mexico. Similar courses might look at another country or region, or at Latin America as a whole, or at other time periods, although the topic should be sufficiently diverse to show that constructs of gender and sexuality are not fixed, either by time or by place. For example, a course on contemporary Cuba might not demonstrate the way gender constructs shift over time; likewise, a course that presented attitudes toward homosexuality similar to those that students in the United States regard as natural would falsely imply that culturally defined notions of sexuality are irrelevant.

The politics of pedagogy is another important consideration in configuring a course. While I would not advocate any particular point of view nor stifle diversity of opinion, I would present a perspective that includes recent developments in feminist and queer theory for students to consider. And while it is interesting to teach students already knowledgeable about such theory, especially if they have studied it in a context other than Latin America, reaching students who know little or nothing about feminist and queer theory, and perhaps harbor prejudices that they have never been forced to question, is even more rewarding. Moreover, an adamantly feminist course (e.g., Women's Resistance in Latin America) or an openly gay-studies–focused course (e.g., Latin American Homosexualities) might explore its subject in greater depth than a course with a less transparent political agenda. One non-Latin Americanist colleague recently made headlines by offering a course provocatively titled How to Be Gay.[3]

Such courses can be popular and productive, especially in large urban universities with strong liberal arts programs and in certain fields. However, as Sylvia Molloy and I have indicated,

> Hispanism has traditionally conceived itself in monolithic terms, as an oddly defensive family whose members supposedly share basic cultural values and engage in common cultural practices. Hispanism . . . has not usually taken kindly to the practice of rereading and revising and has not in general appreciated critical inquiry.   (x–xi)[4]

More specifically, departments of Spanish and Portuguese have not often been centers of cutting-edge pedagogy in queer studies. Homophobic tradition is not necessarily the only force at work, however. Many undergraduates in our programs are preparing for careers in business, medicine, engineering, law, and other professions, and are less interested in reading the canon than in mastering the language and getting a feel for cultures with which they may need to deal. Professors of gender and sexuality studies in departments of Spanish and Portuguese may not always be able to design courses that mimic those by offered by departments in which classes are in English and therefore open to a larger pool of students. Nonetheless, a more subtle approach to gender and sexuality studies than "Cómo ser gay" ("How to Be Gay") might attract a broader range of students—in particular, students interested in Latin American culture who might be turned off by what they might perceive as militant feminist or gay-rights rhetoric.

The approach I'm outlining is intended to inspire reflection on the habitus of gender and sexuality, as Pierre Bourdieu would put it—that is, the things we take for granted regarding gender and sexuality—in all kinds of students: male, female, queer, straight, bisexual, undecided, Latin American, Latino/a, gringo/a.[5] It introduces gender theory and queer theory to a wide variety of students without intimidating them by getting bogged down in questions of identity politics, while at the same time encouraging them to confront their own assumptions about gender and sexuality.

In the early 1990s, such courses were nonexistent, but the fact that they have been institutionalized into the curriculum of many Spanish and Portuguese departments attests to their relevance for undergraduates. Similarly, culture-specific pedagogical tools—almost nonexistent a decade ago—abound. A number of first-rate critical anthologies are available, any of which can be used alone or in combination as the basis of an undergraduate course. Of particular interest are Emilie Bergmann and Paul Julian Smith's *¿Entiendes? Queer Readings, Hispanic Writings*; Daniel Balderston and Donna Guy's *Sex and Sexuality in Latin America*; David William Foster and Roberto Reis's *Bodies and Biases*; Susana Chávez-Silverman and Librada Hernández's *Reading and Writing the Ambiente*; the special issue of *Revista iberoamericana*, edited by Daniel Balderston, entitled *Erotismo y escritura*; and Sylvia Molloy's and my *Hispanisms and Homosexualities*. Also of interest are Lucía Guerra Cunningham's *Splintering Darkness*; Balderston's *El deseo*; José Quiroga's *Tropics of Desire*; David William Foster's *Gay and Lesbian Themes in Latin American Writing* and *Sexual Textualities*; and Elena Martínez's *Lesbian Voices from Latin America*, to name a few examples. Again, the model course outlined here takes advantage of the shift from literary to cultural studies to introduce an interrogation of gender and sexuality into the curriculum—in Spanish (or Portuguese).[6] Materials like those I have listed might help shape a course whose cultural focus is not that of nineteenth- and early-twentieth-century Mexico.

When giving this course to undergraduates, I generally introduce gender and sexuality theory in small doses, and in my brief introductory lectures to each text. The syllabus to this course, therefore, has no theoretical readings. The inclusion of select theoretical texts might be appropriate, especially in higher-level courses. Naturally, there are many to choose from, particularly for instructors working from English-language sources. The useful publications in this field are too numerous to mention here; however, if I included only one introductory text in Spanish, it would be Marta Lamas's *Cuerpo: Diferencia sexual y género*. A social scientist, Lamas is also longtime editor of *Debate Feminista*, the journal responsible for, among other things, introducing the Mexican academy to queer theory and transforming *estudios de la mujer* ("women's studies") into *estudios de género* ("gender studies"). The book presents a number of contemporary debates on gender and sexuality. While challenging to intermediate-level undergraduates, it is by no means above their heads.

A MODEL COURSE: BEFORE MACHISMO

Before Machismo, a course I gave for the first time in 1999, has generated strong positive feedback from students (see app., syllabus 6). It is offered at the 400 level, which, at my university (Tulane), targets high-intermediate-level students who have normally taken three to six courses beyond the basic language requirement. Naturally, the course could be adapted to another level— even to graduate study—by adjusting the quantity and difficulty of the readings and other assignments, as well as by introducing more rigorous theoretical material.

Its title, Before Machismo, is meant to be provocative. The course looks at the constructions of masculinity before the term *machismo* came into use; it also examines notions of femininity and sexuality (male and female) from a historical perspective. In short, it highlights the cultural and temporal specificities of constructions of gender and sexuality.

The course opens with a look at mid- and late-twentieth-century stereotypes of gender and sexuality in Mexico, to provide a basis for comparison with the views presented in the nineteenth- and early-twentieth-century texts.

Octavio Paz's landmark work on Mexican national identity, "Los hijos de la Malinche" (1950; "The Sons of la Malinche"), explicitly defines masculine identity in men as heterosexual and opposed to effeminate homosexuality. Heterosexuality is defined as the rape of the indigenous woman by the Spanish conqueror; thus mestizos are the sons (and daughters) of an alliance based on hatred and violence. Masculinity, essentially machismo, is based on a pose of invulnerability and a will to dominate. Femininity, including male homosexuality (assumed invariably to be effeminate), is linked to passivity and subjugation.

An article by the Mexican feminist Lilia Granillo Vázquez, "La abnegación maternal" (1993), further explores gender stereotypes as it offers a critique of Paz—a critique that brings to light the power of canonical texts to shape assumptions about culture; at the same time, Granillo Vázquez highlights the ideological importance of the mother figure and proposes that Mexico is in some ways more matriarchy than patriarchy.

Initial class discussion compares the notions of gender and sexuality as elaborated by Paz and Granillo Vázquez, on the one hand, with contemporary concepts of gender and sexuality as understood and experienced by students in the United States, on the other hand. At this point, students are not asked to absorb feminist or queer theory but to become aware of their own beliefs, to explain how their ideas compare with those they consider to be mainstream or traditional perspectives in the United States, and to voice their doubts about the ideas they encounter. As they bring their conclusions into dialogue with those of the two authors, students keep in mind that Paz's essay was meant to articulate stereotypes and that Granillo Vázquez's article is a contemporary, feminist response to such stereotypes.

This discussion undergirds the readings assigned throughout the semester, all from nineteenth- and early-twentieth-century Mexico. During the discussion, instructors might review key terms of gender and sexuality theory that arise (*gender* and *sex*; *constructionism* and *essentialism*; *intersexuality*; *performance*; *homosocial bonding*). If the class seems uncomfortable with the material at this time, the instructor may prefer to deal with terminology later, as it becomes pertinent to the discussion of specific texts. To engage students fully from the start, I may assign a short (3-page) essay asking them to summarize main ideas of one of the readings, such as Paz's notions of masculinity and (homo)social relations between men, or to list the ways in which Granillo Vázquez's treatment of femininity goes beyond the simple stereotypes presented by Paz.

The body of the course begins with a look at José Joaquín Fernández de Lizardi's *El periquillo sarniento* (*The Itching Parrot*) (1816). Like many nineteenth-century novels, it is excessively long, more than five hundred pages, and is often dismissed as unwieldy for the university classroom. However, as is true for many texts initially published in installments, key episodes—including those of greatest relevance to the course—can be read on their own. Furthermore, because the language is difficult—informal, regional, and sometimes archaic—instructors might provide vocabulary lists, particularly of Mexicanisms, such as *arrastraderito* ("seedy dive") or *lobo* ("person of mixed African and indigenous descent"), that students are unlikely to find in their dictionaries. Such preparation facilitates student comprehension and allows the class to advance more quickly beyond comprehension questions. The rest of the texts assigned in the course are easier to read and require less hand-holding.

Mexico's first novel is widely recognized as a foundational text in the construction of commonly held notions of a national character.[7] Moreover, it is a text in which nation is constructed through a series of relations between the novel's *pícaro* protagonist and a string of father figures who represent different vocations, social classes, regions, and races and who together sketch out an early nationalist vision of Mexicanness. It is a text, also, in which nation is allegorized as patriarchy through a matrix of homosocial bonding, male bonding that is not without a homoerotic component. In the absence of discourses on machismo and homosexuality, neither of which took form in Mexico until after the revolution of 1910–20, Paz's scheme of gender relations does not seem to apply.

In general, I would structure such clusters of classes (for example, there are four sessions on Lizardi) as follows: the first session would include a brief lecture introducing the text(s) at hand; I would then elicit, from students, profiles of main characters and a summary of key events; finally, I would raise a question or a series of questions on the treatment of gender and sexuality in the text(s). Subsequent sessions would follow this format except that additional background information may be unnecessary.

In class discussions on Lizardi, students would explore issues of manliness and of male bonding, of homoeroticism, and of heterosexuality, to identify how Lizardi's representations of these ideas differ from the mid-twentieth-century stereotypes laid out by Paz. Here might be a good time to present background information and/or theories regarding male homosocial bonding, the invention of homo/heterosexuality, and other topics, before discussion begins. I find it most productive, in classes at this level, to assign different questions to small groups (of about four students each) and then have each group report its findings to the class for discussion. This student-centered approach keeps everyone involved and gives students the opportunity to speak in the target language more frequently.

Another foundational fiction is Ignacio Altamirano's *El Zarco* (published 1901, written several decades earlier). Recognized for its place in the national literary canon, this popular novel by Mexico's leading promoter of literary nationalism in the nineteenth century also raises issues of race and class (see Blanco; Sommer 220–32). The handsome blond bandit, el Zarco, seduces the middle-class beauty Manuela, who rejects her less glamorous but more noble, swarthy, working-class neighbor Nicolás, whom she describes as "ese indio horrible" ("that horrid Indian") (9). The mestizo author Altamirano reverses the allegory of the rape of Mexico by casting his male hero (Nicolás) as indigenous and his heroine as Spanish-looking (white), although Manuela quickly becomes an antiheroine as her darker-skinned foster sister Pilar comes to take her place.[8] Pilar eventually marries Nicolás, and the evil but ever-alluring Zarco is executed. The allegory of mestizo nation in Altamirano is constructed quite differently from the way in which it appears in Paz, and any number of questions regarding race, sexuality, and nation can be raised. For example, since the steamy affair between Manuela and el Zarco fails and the platonic bonding of mutual moral admiration between Pilar and Nicolás succeeds, has Altamirano characterized the nation as sterile and asexual? Or, does Altamirano's insistence on el Zarco's physical beauty, as compared with Nicolás's moral beauty (and physical repulsiveness), imply that an aesthetic hierarchy of race remains in Altamirano's idealized Mexico? And does an independent spirit and an unchecked libido on the part of Mexican woman as represented by Manuela imply national catastrophe?

Noncanonical texts such as Refugio Barragán de Toscano's *La hija del bandido* (1880; *The Bandit's Daughter*)) offer a different perspective that challenges many gender stereotypes put forward by mainstream male authors such as Lizardi and Altamirano. Few and far between are Mexican women writers before the latter half of the twentieth century, and those who did publish their work have often fallen into obscurity. Barragán de Toscano's novel has recently been rescued from oblivion by Mexican critics (Domanella and Pasternac). Her strong female protagonist challenges stereotypes by being a woman of action and principle, by rejecting her father's banditry and her assigned role—in the absence of a mother figure—of *ama de casa*, and by refusing to live happily ever after with her middle-class boyfriend. At the novel's end, she rejects romantic convention and leaves her devoted suitor to become a nun. Here students might brainstorm the differences in notions of gender and sexuality in Barragán de Toscano, on the one hand, and in Lizardi and Altamirano, on the other, and then debate the possible effects of the author's gender on her writing.

Interestingly, although the constructions of gender and sexuality that Paz delineates appear to be rooted in Mexican history—specifically, in the sixteenth-century Spanish conquest of the Aztec empire—numerous differences are apparent in the nineteenth-century texts. Photos of nineteenth-century Mexican men and women invite further speculation regarding the appropriateness of imposing twentieth-century stereotypes on the nineteenth century. The image opposite might contribute to a discussion on the nature of male homosocial bonding before the advent of discourse on homosexuality, at the turn of the century, or on the effect of race and social class on the way the men pictured identify as men and perform masculinity.[9] Additional photos might show an indigenous-looking woman ironing, a smartly dressed dandy, or newlyweds in which the husband looks a good twenty-five years older than his adolescent wife.

Students might be divided into groups, with each group assigned a photograph and asked to interpret it. The photographs are not meant to introduce questions into the discussion, although they might. Instead, they should provide a platform for students to synthesize and articulate what they have learned about gender and sexuality in the nineteenth century.

Such materials can be put to excellent use in written work as well. I have assigned students to write a three- to five-page (invented) biography of one of the Mexicans represented in a photo. The biography, of course, must be set in the nineteenth century and reflect Mexican notions of gender and sexuality of the age. To involve them more deeply in the material, I encourage students to apply new vocabulary from the texts they have read and to mimic the style of the authors. These assignments are then graded based on two criteria (50% each): form—organization, vocabulary, grammar, and spelling; and content—completeness of the portrait, appropriateness to the context (nineteenth-century Mexican), and understanding of gender and sexuality in the given context.

A look at the *fin de siglo* brings out a range of historical shifts occurring in notions of gender and sexuality by the century's end. Ciro Ceballos's short

Photograph, c. 1900. Courtesy of Archivo Fotográfico
Pedro Guerra, Universidad Autónoma de Yucatán,
contact print copy from the Latin American Library,
Tulane University.

novella "Un adulterio" (1903) describes the convalescence of the upper-class
narrator, whose lack of sexual restraint—that is, his moral decline—has
brought on his physical decline. While resting in the country, he falls in love
with his neighbor, a virgin widow, who spends most of her free time with her
pet gorilla. Without going into any of the extravagant details of the very
modernista plot, I will highlight its source of sexual tension: the apparent competition between the delicate narrator and the burly gorilla for the heroine's
attentions. Geraldina becomes the active sexual agent of the story, with the
narrator and the gorilla as her passive objects of desire. Ceballos raises provocative questions about the masculinity of indolent upper-class men and the
sexual autonomy and agency of women. Specifically, students might be asked
to define how masculinity relates to social class—to compare how upper- and

lower-class masculinities are represented in the epoch. They might also evaluate how notions of female sexuality have evolved; here a comparison between Manuela of *El Zarco* and Geraldina of "Un adulterio" might be particularly interesting.

The popular artist José Guadalupe Posada's broadsheets (1901) celebrating the scandal of the Famous 41 transvestite ball, along with the sometimes over-the-top Mexico City press coverage of the incident and its aftermath, show themes of sexual subversion to be fashionable among the less-literate classes of turn-of-the-century Mexico as well.[10] These early representations of a very Mexican-style homosexuality seem both to give rise to the twentieth-century stereotype equating male effeminacy with homosexuality and to refute it; they clearly treat transvestites as homosexuals but are ambiguous in dealing with their more masculine sexual partners. Students can probe the definitions of Mexican homosexuality by looking at whether all forty-one men arrested were categorized as *maricones* or only half of them (the transvestites); the class can also discuss the kinds of homosexual relationships that appear to exist among the Famous 41, and the attitudes of the popular press (reproof, curiosity, or delight?) toward male homosexuality in 1901. How did gender and male homosexuality interact at the turn of the century? How stable were national constructions of gender and sexuality at that moment?

Once again, the images themselves provide a platform for further discussion. Small groups might be given a Posada representation of the forty-one and then asked to list the apparent assumptions it makes about male sexuality. Additionally, students can consider how the introduction of explicit notions of male sexuality into Mexican culture would likely affect evolving notions of masculinity and male homosocial bonding.

A homework assignment might involve other Posada images of sex crimes.[11] In writing a three-page newspaper article describing the crime pictured, students would imitate the sensationalistic journalism used in reports of the scandal. Students would again be expected to pay careful attention to turn-of-the-century attitudes about and interest in sexuality and would be encouraged to engage more closely with the newspaper texts whose style they mimic.

"Las inseparables" (1916), by Heriberto Frías, provides one of the first and most detailed accounts of female homosexuality in Mexico. A little-known short story written in the personal style of a *crónica*, a gossipy depiction of everyday life, it clearly presents itself as class critique (the lesbians are wealthy) in the context of the Mexican revolution. The students would first identify the story's characterization of Mexican lesbianism and then evaluate its accuracy—determine how much the author actually knew about the topic, and how much of his information is presented as gossip or speculation. A similar questioning of the author's knowledge might then be pursued regarding the 41. Further discussion can focus on the public-private dichotomy: What does public appearance have to do with private sexual practice? In early-twentieth-century Mexico, how did nonhomosexuals (artists and writers) represent homosexuality? Can homosexuality be discussed objectively in a social context in which it is considered an abomination?

These questions might lead to an examination of textual authority. What makes a reader believe in a text? Is it the erudition of its author? the author's claims to firsthand experience? the appearance of verisimilitude? a book's canonization as a classic of national literature? the moral authority of religion? The class can explore the issue in small groups, with each group addressing a different text from the reading list. Such a discussion, moreover, provides a lead-in to the next cluster of texts, Luis Lara y Pardo's *La prostitución en México* (1908) and Carlos Roumagnac's *Los criminales en México* (1904) and *Crímenes sexuales y pasionales* (1906), positivist studies in the new science of criminology.

Lara y Pardo's report on prostitution in Mexico City is based on his analysis of public registers. He assembled and interpreted a range of data, including birthplace, age, social class, education level, and even the women's degree of ugliness.[12] Students can evaluate the author's text-based methodology, identify his rhetorical strategies in representing prostitution, and discuss the limitations of scientific discourse in general.

Roumagnac's more eclectic methodology, in his studies on a broad range of criminals—the excerpts chosen for this course all reflect sex crimes—involved reading case files, interviewing inmates about their personal and sexual history, examining mug shots of convicts, and observing the measurements of key body parts believed, at the time, to indicate criminal disposition.[13] According to Roumagnac, crime had three possible root causes: innate inclination, stemming from degeneration; acquired proclivity, resulting from bad influences, poor education, and improper upbringing; and external circumstances, such as the effects of alcohol or random occurrences that might, at any given moment, provoke a "normal" person to commit a crime. His case studies of pedophile rapists, lesbian kidnappers, prostitute murderers,

hermaphrodite imposters, deranged necrophiliacs, and exhibitionists in bes-
tiality are often shocking and always compelling. Like other materials in the
syllabus, they raise interesting questions about science, sensationalism, and
morality. Here students work in groups on particular case studies. What methods did Roumagnac employ? What conclusions did he draw? What is the
nature of the crime? What relations did he find between sexuality and criminal proclivity? To what extent did he allow his prejudices to interfere with
his science? In what ways did his biases manifest themselves?

Another turn-of-the-century novel, Federico Gamboa's best-selling *Santa*
(1903)—the tale of a prostitute who confronts the sexual desires of men, her
own lust, and even that of a lesbian colleague—both reinforces traditional
notions of fallen femininity and challenges stereotypes of heterosexual love
that had developed in nineteenth-century novels such as *El Zarco*. The character Santa elaborates on the fallen-woman image hinted at in Altamirano's
Manuela by sexualizing it. Students explore what it means for Santa to be
neither Paz's sexually passive matron nor his raped Indian maiden but a
woman whose libido is so strong that she loses control of her life.

Santa is not to be read, however, but seen on film. The silent version
(1918) is nearly impossible to obtain, but the 1931 version—Mexico's first
sound film—introduces a range of issues that the novel does not.[14] The ability
of film to bring works of fiction, and public dramas chronicled in newspapers,
to a mass audience, literate and illiterate alike, gives the cinema greater cultural influence than the written word. García Canclini writes, "In our America,
where illiterates became a minority only a few years ago and not in all countries, it is not strange that culture has been predominantly visual" ("Epica"
151–52).

Discussion of the film might begin by examining the protagonists: Santa,
the fallen woman; her possibly single mother; her manipulative first lover, a
military man; el Jarameño, the dashing Spanish bullfighter who rescues her
from the brothel; doña Elvira, the brothel madame; and Hipólito, the blind
bordello pianist who chastely loves Santa and cares for her at the end of her
life when she is stricken with cancer of the uterus. Students can create profiles
of the characters, emphasizing questions of gender and sexuality. They might
also compare the characters with protagonists of earlier works, including the
prostitutes of Lara y Pardo and the sex criminals of Roumagnac.

A final project would be a three- to five-page profile of Santa, written in
the scientific register of Roumagnac. Students would present Santa's case his-

tory, recount an interview in which she discusses her personal experiences, give a physical description, and conclude with an analysis of the case.

The subtlety of my own politics has worked well as I taught the course. Most of the students who have taken it would probably not have identified themselves as queer or admitted to a personal interest in homosexuality, although a number might have called themselves feminists despite their unfamiliarity with feminist theory. Most of the students, Spanish majors and minors preparing for professional careers, would probably never have considered taking a gay studies or even a gender studies course; they were most likely attracted to the course by an interest in Latin American culture. Yet, almost from the beginning of the course, they were debating gender constructions, applying queer theory, deconstructing national gender stereotypes, and learning to view gender and sexuality not only in Mexico but in their own lives, in a critical way.

It is much less important to present literary canons to undergraduates than to introduce them to broad representations of Latin American culture. The work of cultural studies scholars such as García Canclini has been instrumental in persuading Latin Americanists to restructure the undergraduate curriculum to move beyond narrowly defined literary analysis. Furthermore, recent work in gender and queer studies demonstrates that the male *letrados* have manipulated notions of gender and sexuality in constructions of national culture and that, therefore, we need to go beyond literary canons (without eliminating canonical works from our syllabi) for a more comprehensive picture of the complexities of Latin American cultures.[15] A cultural studies approach permits students a deeper understanding of these complexities.

NOTES

I would like to thank Idelber Avelar, Licia Fiol-Matta, and the editors of this volume for their generous and insightful comments and suggestions.

1. Here I refer to courses in which the primary focus is no longer language acquisition. In most university Spanish programs, this category would encompass most courses beginning around the fifth semester of study. I use the term *Latinamericanism* to refer to the study of Latin America in the United States as a gesture to the need to recognize the problems in the structure of the transnational discursive community of Latin Americanists that has been raised in recent debates, whose contents are beyond the scope of this essay. See, for example, de la Campa.
2. Note that this and all other translations, unless otherwise indicated, are my own.
3. This was the title of an English course taught by David Halperin at the University of Michigan, Ann Arbor, in 2000 (Willdorf).

4. Certain cultural specificities that ought to be addressed here are beyond the scope of this essay. I am oversimplifying when I apparently equate what a queer critical approach would be to Hispanic culture in general, to Mexican culture in particular, and to Latin American culture (which includes Brazil). However, in the context of my arguments on the reluctance of such fields of critical inquiry as Hispanism, Mexican studies, and Latin Americanism to address questions of sexuality until recently, these epistemological slippages seem inconsequential.

5. For a fruitful application of Bourdieu to Mexican cultural studies, see Lamas.

6. While such a course could also be taught in English, instructors might have difficulties locating a diverse range of primary texts in English translation. Canonical literature is often available in translation, but less-literary texts (newspaper articles, ads, television programs, scientific works, and so on) usually are not. Likewise, historically marginalized texts such as writings by women are often hard to get even in the original. Thus this course is presented as a model to be taught in Spanish or in Portuguese.

7. See, for example, Benedict Anderson (29–30). On questions of masculinity and sexuality, see Irwin.

8. Altamirano was actually of mixed blood, born to an indigenous father and a mestiza mother, although he is often thought of as having been indigenous himself because he was raised as such and learned Spanish only as an adolescent; see Campuzano (12).

9. While any photographs from the relevant place and time period will do, I have been fortunate enough to draw from the marvelous Photographic Archives of Tulane University's Latin American Library. A sampling of its materials can be found online (www.tulane.edu/~latinlib/lalphoto); for this course, the Cruces y Campo and Guerra collections are of greatest interest.

10. For a detailed analysis of the Famous 41 scandal and its broader implications with respect to notions of gender and sexuality in Mexican culture, see the essays collected in Irwin, McCaughan, and Nasser. This volume also includes highlights of newspaper coverage of the scandal (in bilingual form) and reproductions of the famous Posada engravings of the 41.

11. Since the work is in the public domain, Posada's images are easy to find on the Internet. For example, see the University of Hawai'i's Art Gallery at www.hawaii.edu/artgallery/posada. Of special interest are the images archived under "Sensational Crimes."

12. On Lara y Pardo (and Gamboa's *Santa*) as models for representations of prostitution in Mexico, see Castillo, *Easy Women*.

13. The definitive study on Roumagnac, to date, is Buffington's.

14. Antonio Moreno's classic film can be obtained from the Latin American Video Archives (www.lavavideo.org/). This is usually cited as the best film version of *Santa*; unfortunately, for the purposes of this class, it leaves out one minor character, la Gaditana, a prostitute with lesbian inclinations.

15. Regarding Mexican women writers from a historical perspective, see, for example, Franco, *Plotting Women*; Domenella and Pasternac. For sketches of how sexuality has been treated in Mexico over the past century or so, see Monsiváis, "Ortodoxia"; González Rodríguez.

APPENDIX: SAMPLE
COURSE SYLLABI

his appendix includes six sample course syllabi, including courses designed
or the undergraduate and graduate levels as well as reading schedules orga-
ized for semesters, trimesters, and summer sessions. The course texts and
eadings identified throughout are referenced in the list of works cited. The
st at the end of the appendix, after syllabus 6, includes information on ob-
aining copies of many of the films and videos mentioned in this book.

SYLLABUS 1

ourse   The Incas and Other Andean Peoples

nstructor   Gustavo Verdesio

bjective   This course focuses on ancient Andean civilizations and the early
olonial period in Peru. The course provides an overview of the cultural dis-
nctiveness of the Inca civilization, with special attention paid to its institu-
ons and religion.

escription   We read two authors whose native language was Spanish (Pedro
`ieza de León and El Inca Garcilaso de la Vega) and whose cultural back-
round was mostly European. The latter, the son of a Spanish captain and an
ıca princess, was familiar with Quechua, the most important indigenous lan-
uage of the Inca empire. We study the writers' descriptions of Inca social,
olitical, and economic organization, as well as of Inca religion. We read a

scholarly work on religious issues (by Sabine MacCormack) and compare he
treatment of the topic with that of the earlier authors. Next, we study th
texts of two Quechua native speakers—Titu Cusi Yupanqui (the penultimat
Inca) and Santa Cruz Pachacuti (whose Spanish was strongly contaminate
by his native tongue)—that provide substantially different views on Inca cul
ture. Two other contemporary works offer an additional perspective. Stev
Stern deals with the various ways in which indigenous peoples from the Ande
adapted to European colonization. Finally, the compilation by Michae
Malpass sheds light on research that combines the study of colonial chronicle
with archaeological investigations.

Evaluation   The midterm (35%) and the second exam (45%) follow the sam
structure: four identifications (of which students must answer only three) an
two essay questions (students answer only one). Throughout the course, eacl
student presents an article in class (20%). The primary texts must be rea
carefully, to grasp the differences among them and to draw conclusions abou
the cultural clash that gave rise to them.

Schedule

Week 1	Introduction
Week 2	Cieza de León, *El señorío de los Incas*
Week 3	Film: *Inca: Secrets of the Ancestors*; conclude Cieza de León
Week 4	Inca Garcilaso, *Comentarios reales;* presentations
Week 5	Film: *In the Shadow of the Incas*; El Inca Garcilaso continue; presentations
Week 6	Film: *The Incas*; Inca Garcilaso concluded
Week 7	Midterm exam; MacCormack, *Religion in the Andes*
Week 8	MacCormack concluded; presentations
Week 9	Santa Cruz Pachacuti, *Relación de antigüedades*
Week 10	Titu Cusi Yupanqui; begin Spalding, *Huarochirí*
Week 11	Spalding concluded; begin Stern, *Peru's Indian Peoples;* presentations
Week 12	Conclude Stern; presentations
Week 13	Begin Malpass, *Provincial Inca*
Week 14	Conclude Malpass; second exam

SYLLABUS 2

Course   Mexican American Literature

Instructor   Jesse Alemán

Objective   This introductory course examines the process and problems of representing Chicano/a culture.

Description   Too often, we assume that there is one authentic Mexican American identity, but by focusing on issues such as race, class, gender, religion, family, education, and language, however, students discover that Chicano/a culture works through a series of complex contradictions that make the task of singling out an essential Chicano/a identity a difficult one. In fact, Chicano/a literature represents multiple Chicano/a cultural identities. Once the class understands this idea, we examine how other Chicano/a practices, such as folk traditions, films, street art, and even family stories, invent their own sense of cultural identity.

Evaluations   Students are asked to write two analytical essays (4 pp.; 20% each) and a final research project (15 pp.; 60%). The four-page essays focus primarily on close analysis of texts covered in class. The final project develops a cultural analysis of Chicano/a film, music, art, local history, family *testimonios*, photography, graffiti, car clubs, or representations of Mexican Americans in the media.

Schedule

Week 1	Introduction to course and syllabus; the problems of representation: ethnography and ethnocentrism
Week 2	The new ethnography: Rosaldo, "The Erosion of Classical Norms," in *Culture and Truth* (25–45). Chicano/a studies and ethnography: Vaca, "Mexican-American,1912–1935"
Week 3	Vaca, "Mexican-American, 1936–1970"
Week 4	Paredes, "On Ethnographic Work; Paredes, begin *George Washington Gómez*
Week 5	Paredes, conclude *George Washington Gómez*
Week 6	Paredes, *With His Pistol in His Hand* (part 1)
Week 7	First essay due; Cabeza de Baca, *We Fed Them Cactus*
Week 8	José Antonio Villarreal, *Pocho*
Week 9	Ponce, *Hoyt Street*
Week 10	Ana Castillo, *So Far from God*
Week 11	Second essay due; Cantú, *Canícula*
Week 12	Pat Mora, *House of Houses*
Week 13	Anaya, *Zia Summer*
Week 14	Brainstorm approaches to final project; discuss research and reference guides for Chicano/a studies
Week 15	Conduct workshop for drafts of final project
Examination Period	Final project due

SYLLABUS 3

Course   Brazilian Culture and Civilization

Instructor   Piers Armstrong

Objective   The course introduces students to Brazilian civilization by exam
ining its historical development and by exploring various subjective cultura
issues.

Description   Each week, a historical period is presented in tandem with a pa
ticular theme of ongoing cultural expression. While diverse elements of pop
ular culture are included, literature (fiction) is privileged as a source of cultura
commentary. Students are expected to assimilate the background informatio
but are also encouraged to develop their own perspective and interest
whether in the social sciences, the humanities (including the fine arts), rel
gious studies, or other area.

Evaluation   Active participation is expected (10%). Absorption of the reading
(and other material) is tested through sets of questions on facts and concep
(two quizzes, each for 10%). Students write a paper relating the characters an
events in *Tent of Miracles* (Amado) to what they have learned about Brazil i
the course (20%). Each student gives a seven-minute presentation on an aspe
of Brazilian culture not covered in class—for example, Bahian cuisine, Brazi
ian rock music, or Amazonian basket weaving; this section is graded lenientl
(5%). The midterm exam consists of short essay questions from a list of que
tions distributed in advance (20%). The take-home final consists of longe
essay questions (25%).

Schedule

Week 1

SESSION 1   Introduction, Geography
Core reading: Maps: geographic, demographic, climate
Multimedia: Tolman, "Geographic Overview" and "Ethnicity and
Population" in *Brazil Slide Series*

SESSION 2   Encounter, Indigenous Population, European Arrival
Core reading: Burns, Introduction, ch. 1 (throughout, "Burns,"
refers to *A History of Brazil* unless noted otherwise)
Suggested reading: Staden, chs. 2–5, 19–22, 39–40; Levine and
Crocitti 12–44
Documents: Treaty of Tordesillas; Letter of Pero Vaz de Caminha
Royal Letter Granting Powers, in Burns, *Documentary History*
15–29, 34–39
Multimedia: *How Tasty Was My Little Frenchman*

Week 2

SESSION 1 Colonial Period, Slavery, Race Relations
Core reading: Burns, ch. 2; handouts 1–3, "Things You Need to Know"; "Slavery in the Luso-Brazilian World"; "General Observations," in French, *Sharing the Riches* 27–40
Suggested reading: ch. 4, "The Negro Slave," in Freyre, *Masters* 278–323; Telles, "Ethnic Boundaries."
Multimedia: *Xica* (video); Tolman, "Colonial Legacy," in *Brazil Slide Series*

SESSION 2 Elements of the Afro-Brazilian Cultural Heritage, *Candomblé*, *Capoeira*
Core reading: Omari, *Inside* (12–26); Almeida, *Capoeira* 1–8, 84–93, 143–150
Suggested reading: Lowell, *Ring* 19–50
Multimedia: *Quilombo* (video); Tolman, "*Candomblé*," in *Brazil Slide Series*

Week 3

SESSION 1 Nineteenth-Century Empire, Patriarchal Evolutions
Core reading: Burns, chs. 3–4
Documents: Declaration of Brazilian Independence; Constitution of 1824, in Burns, *Documentary History* 197–200, 206–10

SESSION 2 Inventing National Mythologies, Romantic Indianism, Realism
Core reading: Alencar, *Iracema* 1–11; Machado de Assis, "Alexandrian Tale," "Devil's Church," "Strange Thing," "Final Chapter," and "The Diplomat," in *"Devil's Church"* 19–52, 68–77
Suggested reading: Haberly, *Three Sad Races* 1–17
Multimedia: *Light Memories of Rio* (video) 33

Week 4

SESSION 1 *Mulatos* versus *Mulatas*; Urban Life; *O Malandro*
Core reading: Azevedo, *Brazilian Tenement*, chs. 1, 3, 7; start Amado, *Tent of Miracles* (1–50)

SESSION 2 The Old Republic, European Immigration, Positivism and Ethnic Engineering
Core reading: Burns, chs. 5–6; continue Amado (51–121)

Week 5

SESSION 1 Canudos, Millenarianism, Subalterns, and State
Core reading: da Cunha, from part 1, "The Backlands" and "The Man," in *Rebellion in the Backlands* 82–136
Multimedia: *Canudos Revisited* (video); Tolman, "*Sertão*," in *Brazil Slide Series*

SESSION 2   Midterm exam

Week 6

SESSION 1   Miscegenation, Racial Democracy?
Core reading: Freyre, ch. 12, "Reflections on Miscegination" in
Mansions (400–31); continue Amado, (122–47)
Suggested reading: Skidmore, *Fact and Myth*

SESSION 2   Cultural Sovereignty, Modernism
Core reading: Mário de Andrade, chs. 1, 2, 14, in *Macunaíma*
(3–15, 120–30; Oswald de Andrade, "Cannibalist Manifesto";
continue Amado (148–93)
Multimedia: *Tenda dos Milagres* (video)

Week 7

SESSION 1   Estado Novo (1930–45), Modernization, Rio's Samba and
Carnaval
Core reading: Burns, ch. 7; continue Amado (194–215)
Multimedia: *Black Orpheus* (video)

SESSION 2   *Nordestinos*, Novel of the Northeast
Core reading: Ramos, *Barren Lives* 3–44, 100–30); continue
Amado (216–344)
Multimedia: *Barren Lives* (video)

Week 8

SESSION 1   Postwar: Jet Age, Democratic Experiment (1945–64), Dictatorship
(1964–85), Futurism in Architecture—Brasília, *Bossa Nova*
Core reading: Burns, chs. 8–9
Documents: Suicide Letter of Getúlio Vargas; State of Faith in
Nationalism; Resignation of President Jânio Quadros;
President João Goulart Explains Some Policies of His
Government; Inaugural Speech of President Huberto Castello
Branco, in Burns, *Documentary History* 368–84
Multimedia: *Capital Sins* (video); Tolman, *"Brasília,"* in *Brazil Slide
Series*

SESSION 2   Socioeconomic Realities, Injustice
Core reading: Schepper-Hughes, "Everyday Violence"; Patai,
"Vera"; finish Amado (345–95)
Suggested reading: García and Hall, "Urban Labor"; Levine and
Crocitti 319–36
Multimedia: *Pixote* (video), Tolman, *"Favela,"* in *Brazil Slide Series*

Week 9

SESSION 1   Religion: Catholicism, Umbanda, and Evangelicals
Core reading: Burdick, "What Is the Color of the Holy Spirit?" in
Blessed Anastácia 119–48; Brown, "The Founding of
Umbanda," in *Umbanda* 37–51; Chesnut, "Conversion:
Crisis, Cure, and Affiliation," in *Born Again* 73–91

Suggested reading: Sturm, "Religion"

Multimedia: *Miracles Are Not Enough* (video)

SESSION 2   New Social Movements: Popular Protest; Bahian *Carnaval*

Core reading: Guillermoprieto, "*Baianas* 1" and "Rituals and Celebrations," in *Samba* 44–49, 115–23; Dunn, "Afro-Bahian Carnival"

Suggested reading: Hanchard, "Black Cinderella?" in *Racial Politics* 59–81

Multimedia: music by Paul Simon; Olodum; Caetano Veloso and Gilberto Gil; *Off the Streets* (video)

Week 10

SESSION 1   Amazonian Amerindians: Tropical or Darwinian Jungle?

Core reading: Hemming, "Extermination"

Multimedia: *At Play in the Fields of the Lord* (video)

SESSION 2   Conclusion

Discussion about Brazilian identity: national unity? national identity?

SYLLABUS 4

Course   Cities in Latin America

Instructor   Luis Fernando Restrepo

Objective   This course analyzes the past and the present of cities in Latin America. The approach is interdisciplinary (art history, architecture, literature, cinema, history, and anthropology). The course, which proposes that urban space is a cultural production, deals with a semiotics of the city and asks, "What does the city mean?" Beginning by discussing texts that describe a semiotic approach to the city, the course follows a chronological order, from the pre-Hispanic city, through the utopian city of the Renaissance, the colonial city, the nineteenth-century city, up to the megalopoles of the present. The course is not exhaustive; it focuses on aspects that reveal the complexity of Latin American cities and that, in turn, provide insights into Latin American culture.

Description   The history of the city is much more than its buildings, plazas, and streets. In literature, the arts, cinema, sacred music, and rock, we encounter the city as created, lived, and experienced, from the remarkable Tenochtitlán of the Aztecas and the Maya cities of the Yucatán, to modern-day Mexico City, Rio de Janeiro, Buenos Aires, Havana, and Bogotá. We study selections of Nahuatl and Maya poetry; texts by Borges, Neruda, Cortázar, and Carpentier; essays by historians, art critics, and anthropologists such as José Luis Romero, Angel Rama, and Néstor García Canclini; artistic representations from pre-Columbian societies and postconquest communities, as well as examples from contemporary art; and films such as *Quilombo, Los olvidados,* and *Rodrigo D: No futuro.* This course is open to undergraduates and graduate students.

Internet   Course site: uark.edu/campus-resources/katio

Evaluation   Participation is evaluated on the basis of contributions to class discussions—comments as well as questions (20%). A fifteen- to twenty-minute presentation allows students to explore a topic of personal interest (15%). Each week students turn in a short essay corresponding to a topic under discussion (3-page papers for undergraduates; 5-page papers for graduates). These essays should develop students' reading skills, analytic abilities, and expression. They are not research papers but rather opportunities for students to synthesize their understanding of the materials read for class (50%). In addition, students keep a diary of reactions to the course readings; students write a brief entry for each class session. Undergraduates may write half-page entries and graduate students page-long entries (15%).

Schedule   (Readings with an asterisk are optional for undergraduates; "workshop" identifies group activities in class.)

Week 1

Monday   Introduction, Semiotics of Urban Space, Workshop
Tuesday   Foucault, "Of Other Spaces"; Barthes, "Semiology and
                Urbanism"*; Certeau, "Walking in the City"
Wednesday   The pre-Columbian city: Teotihuacán y Tenochtitlán: Meyer,
                "The City of the Gods," in *Teotihuacan*; Cortés, fragment from
                Segunda Carta; Nahuatl poetry in León Portilla, *El reverso*
Thursday   The Maya city: Schele and Freidel, "Sacred Space," in *Forest of
                Kings*; Fash, "The Copan Mosaic,"* in *Scribes*; video about the
                Maya; The Andean city: Poma de Ayala, selections from *Nueva
                crónica*; Hyslop, "Cuzco,"* in *Inka Settlement; Cuzco, la ciudad y
                su gente* (video); turn in first paper

Week 2

Monday   The utopian city: Manuel and Manuel, "Citta Felice" and
                "Campanella's City of the Sun," in *Utopian Thought; Quilombo*
                (video) and discussion about the *quilombos* of today
Tuesday   The colonial city: Sartor, "Latin American City"; Hardoy and
                Hardoy, "Plaza in Latin America"*; we compare and

contrast the *plaza* with the *plaza comercial* (shopping center); Medina Cano, "El centro comercial"

Wednesday   The Baroque city (17th and 18th centuries): Gutiérrez, "Arquitectura barroca," in *Arquitectura*

Thursday   Activity in laboratory, view images from sixteenth and seventeenth centuries (architecture of Popayán and other cities; *plaza* of Mexico City, by Cristóbal de Villalpando; American Baroque style)

Week 3

Monday   The Enlightenment city: Gutiérrez, "El urbanismo americano en el siglo XVIII," in *Arquitectura*; the nineteenth century: Casimiro Castro, "Vistas, viajes y monumentos en el México del siglo XIX"; activity in laboratory; turn in second paper

Tuesday   The nineteenth-century city: Ramos, "A Citizen Body"; Samper, "La miseria en Bogotá," in *Selección*; Martí, "Amor de ciudad grande"(poem and musical interpretation), in *Ismaelillo*

Wednesday   The twentieth-century city (between the classic, the modern, and the regional): Gutiérrez, *Arquitectura* 532–600; *Los olvidados* (video)

Thursday   Writing the city: selections from Borges, Cortázar and Facio (*Buenos Aires, Buenos Aires*), and Carpentier (*La ciudad de las columnas*); *Graffiti* (video based on a short story by Cortázar)

Week 4

Monday   Caballero Calderón, "Por los caminos de Suramérica"; vanguardist art looks at the city; turn in third paper

Tuesday   García Canclini, "Narrar la multiculturalidad" and "México: La globalización cultural en una ciudad que se desintegra," in *Consumidores*

Wednesday   Shantytowns, *favelas*, and the marginalized: selected readings from Salazar, *No nacimos pa' semilla; Rodrigo D: No futuro* (video); rock music and the city; recommended activities: *Recuerdos de mi barrio* and *Orfeo negro* (videos)

Thursday   Holidays, festivals, carnivals, expos, and the city: Bakhtin, "The Market Place,"* in *Rabelais*; Sudjic, "Walt Disney as City Planner"; second topic: the politicized *plaza*: *Las madres de la Plaza de Mayo* (video); final discussion

Following week

Monday   Turn in fourth paper

SYLLABUS 5

Course   Language and Culture for Business in Spanish America

Instructor   Danny J. Anderson

Objective   This course presents language and culture for students interested in business. Students in journalism, political science, and social welfare may also find the content relevant. A portion of the course introduces the vocabulary and concepts related to business. Most of the course uses a cultural studies approach to explore business customs in, and the cultures of, contemporary Latin American societies. The cultural component of the course examines such topics as how Latin Americans negotiate their sense of identity, how outsiders adapt to Latin American societies to negotiate their place in a new cultural context, and how the various groups in Latin America perceive business (*negocios*).

Description   The course looks at the range of meanings of *negocios* and *negotiate*. *Negocios* usually refers to business in a commercial sense. Cultural studies uses *negotiate* to refer to the ways individuals respond to the multiple forces that define their identity and strive to make sense of the contradictions in their lives; that is, they "negotiate" the complexities of their social roles. *Culture* is the arena for the ongoing negotiation of identity. The course also explores the history and stereotypes of the foreigner conducting business in or with Latin America. Readings include selections from literature, history, journalism, social analysis, and popular culture. Theoretical presentations by the instructor and limited theoretical readings help students develop skills for analyzing cultural texts and dilemmas.

Generally, Mondays focus on language and vocabulary, Wednesdays on language practice and cultural information, and Fridays on the discussion of cultural texts. This is a Spanish course and not a business course; it does not assume an expert knowledge in business, nor does it teach the content provided by courses in the Business School.

Text   Pascal and Rojas, *Relaciones comerciales*.

Evaluation   We complete every chapter in *Relaciones comerciales*. The first day on a new chapter includes a vocabulary quiz; the twelve quizzes account for 10% of the final grade. In addition, homework represents 10% of the final grade; most of the homework consists of exercises, from the textbook, that students correct with a key. Readings and discussions go far beyond the textbook, and students' oral participation grade reflects mastery of the reading materials (15% of the grade). Three exams, covering all components of the course, count 15% each. Preparation of a dossier of six business letters and one résumé accounts for 20% of the grade.

Schedule

Week 1   Cultural studies model and topics (3 weeks): *The Gringo in Mañanaland* (video); reading: Adler, "Communicating across Cultures," in *International Dimensions; Relaciones comerciales,* ch. 1 (vocabulary, cultural reading, and business letter for each chapter); problematize concept of globalization.

Week 2   Presentations and discussion: cultural studies model; overview of Latin American geography and history reading: Harris and Moran, "Doing Business with North Americans—U.S.A./ Canada," in *Managing* 335–70

Week 3   *Relaciones comerciales,* ch. 2; reading: Harris and Moran, "Doing Business with Latin Americans—Mexico, Central and South America," in *Managing* 371–92; short story: Benedetti, "El presupuesto"; turn in business letter 1

Week 4   Chile (3 weeks): *Relaciones comerciales,* ch. 4; over next three weeks, readings on Chile, focusing on recent history, the Pinochet regime, democratic transition, and economic situation; problematize concept of neoliberalism; turn in business letter 2

Week 5   *Relaciones comerciales,* ch. 5; continue readings on Chile and develop understanding of economic strategies; reading: Blount, "Gerencia"

Week 6   Conclude Chile readings; review; first one-hour exam.

Week 7   Argentina (3 weeks): *Relaciones comerciales,* ch. 6, with student presentations on culture and on marketing; over next three weeks, readings on Argentina, focusing on recent history, the "dirty war," Mennem's neoliberal plan, and the economic situation; *Garden of the Forking Paths* (video); turn in business letter 3

Week 8   *Relaciones comerciales,* ch. 7; continue readings on Argentina; have students search Internet for Argentine (and other Spanish-language) reactions to neoliberalism; turn in business letter 4

Week 9   Conclude discussion on Argentina; readings on Mercosur; presentation on history of Mercosur, comparing impact on Chile and on Argentina; short story: Traven, "Canastitas en serie" (cultural studies approach, transition from Southern Cone to Mexico)

Week 10   Mexico (3 weeks): *Relaciones comerciales*, ch. 8; over next three weeks, readings on Mexico, focusing on the debt crisis and devaluation of 1982, the austerity measures under President de la Madrid, the Salinas presidency, the start of NAFTA and the emergence of the *EZLN*, and the election of Vicente Fox

Week 11   *Relaciones comerciales*, ch. 9; *Emerging Powers: Mexico* (video); continue Mexico readings; turn in business letter 5, a job application letter and a résumé; in-class student teams conduct mock job interviews

Week 12   Conclude Mexico readings; review; second one-hour exam

Week 13   NAFTA (3 weeks): *Relaciones comerciales*, ch. 10; over next three weeks, readings on NAFTA, focusing on the nature of the agreement; differences in economies of the United States, Mexico, and Canada; and opinions for and against NAFTA; short story: Fuentes, "Malintzin de las maquilas"

Week 14   *Relaciones comerciales*, ch. 11; readings about *maquiladoras*; debate by students defending or critiquing NAFTA, using materials from readings and other research the teams carry out

Week 15   *Relaciones comerciales*, ch. 12; readings on free trade vs. fair trade; students examine and summarize selected Internet sites and discuss organizations such as the World Trade Organization, the World Bank, and the International Monetary Fund; review for last exam

Final examination period   Third one-hour exam

SYLLABUS 6

Course   Before Machismo: Gender and Sexuality in Nineteenth- and Early-Twentieth-Century Mexico

Instructor   Robert McKee Irwin

Objective   This course provides a diverse perspective on Mexican culture and society by analyzing gender and sexuality in nineteenth- and early-twentieth-century Mexico, before the stereotype of Mexican machismo was institutionalized.

Description   The analysis of essays, novels, short stories, photographs, newspaper reports, broadsheets, and criminological case studies allows students to examine the cultural and historical specificities of gender and sexuality in

Mexico. We consider rhetorical and representational strategies that supported and fomented popular beliefs about femininity, machismo, homosexuality, promiscuity, and homosocial bonding. These explorations bring to light the ways in which gender and sexuality have been linked to other social building blocks, such as nation, race, and class.

Schedule

Week 1

SESSION 1 Introduction
SESSION 2 Octavio Paz: "Los hijos de la Malinche"

Week 2

SESSION 1 Paz continued
SESSION 2 Lilia Granillo Vázquez, "La abnegación maternal," parts 1 and 2

Week 3

SESSION 1 Granillo Vázquez, part 3; written homework: summary of Paz or of Granillo Vázquez
SESSION 2 José Joaquín Fernández de Lizardi, *El Periquillo Sarniento*, book 1, chs. 1–6

Week 4

SESSION 1 Lizardi, book 1, chs. 14, 16, 18, 19, 21
SESSION 2 Lizardi, book 2, chs. 1, 3, 10, and 11

Week 5

SESSION 1 Lizardi, book 3, chs. 9, 19, 14, 15
SESSION 2 Ignacio Altamirano, *El Zarco*, chs. 1–10

Week 6

SESSION 1 Altamirano, chs. 11–18
SESSION 2 Altamirano, chs. 19–25

Week 7

SESSION 1 Refugio Barragán de Toscano, *La hija del bandido*, books 1 and 2
SESSION 2 Barragán de Toscano, books 3 and 4

Week 8

SESSION 1 Barragán de Toscano, books 5 and 6
SESSION 2 Nineteenth-century photographs; written homework: biography based on photograph

Week 9

SESSIONS 1 and 2 Ciro Ceballos, "Un adulterio"

Week 10

SESSION 1   *The Famous 41*, ed. by Irwin, McCaughan, and Nasser: newspaper
reports

SESSION 2   *The Famous 41*: José Guadalupe Posada images; homework:
newspaper report based on Posada image

Week 11

SESSION 1   Heriberto Frías, "Las inseparables"

SESSION 2   Luis Lara y Pardo, *La prostitución en México*, selections: 30–34,
41–43, 48–49, 54–58, 108–10

Week 12

SESSION 1   Carlos Roumagnac, *Los criminales en México*, selections: "María
Villa (a) 'La Chiquita' "; "Ángela R. de P."; "Andrés D."; and
"Casos de hipospadias y de criptorquidia"

SESSION 2   Roumagnac, *Crímenes sexuales y pasionales*, selections: "Francisco
(a) 'El Chalequero' "; "Casos de necrofilia"; and "Bestialidad"

Week 13

SESSIONS 1   and 2 Antonio Moreno, *Santa* (video)

Week 14

SESSION 1   Moreno; written homework: criminology profile of the character
Santa

SESSION 2   Conclusions

FILM AND VIDEO
INFORMATION

The *Internet Movie Database* is a valuable guide for researching international films, and it often includes purchasing information: imdb.com.

For Latin American films as well as films about Latin America, the Latin American Video Archives (LAVA) is the best source for information and purchasing:

Latin American Video Archives
International Media Resource Exchange
124 Washington Place
New York, NY 10014
Phone: 212 463-0108
Fax: 212 243-2007
E-mail: imre@igc.org
www.lavavideo.org/lava/

A source for Mexican videos is:

Agrasánchez Film Archives
2321 Riverside Drive
Harlingen, TX 78550-8245
Fax: 956 412-7142
E-mail: agrasfilms@aol.com
www.agrasfilms.com

Many of the feature films and documentaries mentioned in the essays here are available through several commercial distributors. Especially useful for Latin American videos is Facets:

Facets Multimedia
1517 West Fullerton Avenue
Chicago, IL 60614
www.facets.org/

An excellent source for many videos is the lending libraries hosted by the Title VI Latin American National Resource Centers (NRCs) in the United States. A full list of NRCs is found online at www.uwm.edu/Dept/CLACS/NRC_LRC. htm. Many university libraries and language laboratories also lend films and video materials.

NOTES ON CONTRIBUTORS

JESSE ALEMAN, assistant professor of English at the University of New Mexico, has published articles on narrative, race, and history in collections and in the journals *Aztlán* and *MELUS*. He teaches nineteenth-century American and Chicano/a literatures and is working on a book-length study of the pulp fiction of the Mexican-American War; he is also editing a republication of Loreta Janeta Velázquez's *The Woman in Battle*.

DANNY ANDERSON, professor of Spanish and chair at the University of Kansas, has published articles and chapters on contemporary Mexican novelists, the history of literary taste in Mexico, and the history of the publishing house Joaquín Mortiz. His book *Vicente Leñero: The Novelist as Critic* (Lang, 1989) is a study of the novelist, journalist, and dramatist. Anderson has received an NEH fellowship for university instructors and is completing a book on the social history of literary reading from the late nineteenth century, tentatively titled "Reading, Culture, and Modernity: Literate Imaginings in Mexico."

PIERS ARMSTRONG is an assistant professor of Spanish and Portuguese at Dartmouth College. His first book, *Third World Literary Fortunes* (Bucknell UP, 1999), contrasts the international reception of Brazilian literature with that of Brazilian popular culture. His current work on contemporary popular culture focuses on relations between aesthetics and ethnic identity in Afro-Bahian *carnaval*, cultural tourism, and pragmatic issues in cultural studies. He has published in journals such as the *Luso-Brazilian Review*, *Journal of Iberian and Latin American Studies*, and *Studies in Latin American Popular Culture*.

ROBERT McKEE IRWIN, assistant professor of Spanish at Tulane University, is the author of *Mexican Masculinities* (U of Minnesota P, 2003). He is also the coeditor (with Sylvia Molloy) of *Hispanisms and Homosexualities* (Duke UP, 1998) and (with Edward J. McCaughan and Michelle Rocío Nasser) of *The Famous 41* (Palgrave, 2003). His research and teaching focuses on Mexico, nineteenth- and early-twentieth-century cultural studies, gender and sexuality, and border or intercultural relations in North America. He is working on a book-length manuscript tentatively titled "The Other Borderlands: Border Icons of Northwestern Mexico 1848–1910."

JILL S. KUHNHEIM, associate professor of Spanish and Latin American literature at the University of Kansas, is the author of *Gender, Politics and Poetry in Twentieth Century Argentina* (UP of Florida, 1996). Her research and teaching interests include Spanish American poetry, contemporary literature of the Southern Cone and Mexico, cultural studies, feminist studies, and gender studies. Kuhnheim has published articles in journals such as *Letras femeninas, Hispanic Poetry Review, Revista iberoamericana, Hispamérica, Modern Fiction Studies, Nuevo texto crítico*, and *Siglo XX / Twentieth Century Literature*. She currently has a manuscript under review titled "Textual Disruptions: Spanish American Poetry at the End of the Twentieth Century."

JOY LOGAN is associate professor of Spanish in the Department of Languages and Literatures of Europe and the Americas at the University of Hawai'i. She has published articles on the effects of redemocratization on cultural expression and national identity in Argentine and on gender, feminism, and postmodernism in contemporary Southern Cone literature. Her essays have also dealt with women's collective writing initiatives, creative writing workshops during and after the Argentine military dictatorship, women-authored historical novels in Argentina, and the work of Isabel Allende, Tununa Mercado, and Luisa Valenzuela. Her current project, "Heritage and Display: Developing Cultural Centers in the Andes," focuses on how collective memory and history are evoked by and incorporated into the expansion of tourism in the Mendocino Andes of Argentina.

LUIS FERNANDO RESTREPO, associate professor of Latin American literature at the University of Arkansas, is the author of *Un nuevo reino imaginado: Las elegías de varones ilustres de indias* (Bogotá, 1999). He works on colonial Latin American culture and literature, New Granada, and film, and has had articles published in *Modern Language Notes, Thesaurus, Cuadernos de literatura, Revista universidad pontificia boliviariana*, and *Pensamiento y acción*. He codeveloped *First Encounters* (2000), a CD-ROM in English, French, and Spanish, as part of an NEH teaching-with-technology program. Restrepo is working on a critical anthology of *Las elegías de varones ilustres* and is editing a book of essays called "Dislocating Modernity: Space and Subjectivity in Early Latin America" (with Nina Gerassi-Navarro).

KIRWIN R. SHAFFER, assistant professor of Latin American studies at Penn State University, Berks, is preparing a book-length manuscript on Cuban anarchism. He has published articles on this topic. His research and teaching interests focus on the cultural politics of radicals in the Caribbean and Cuba, as well as Caribbean popular culture and violence and social conflict in Latin America. He has two long-term projects under way: a history of Caribbean popular culture and a history of Spanish-speaking radicals in the United States from the last Cuban war for independence to the Spanish civil war (1890s–1930s).

GUSTAVO VERDESIO, associate professor of Spanish at the University of Michigan, is the author of *Forgotten Conquests: Re-reading New World History from the Margins* (Temple UP, 2001) and the editor (with Alvaro F. Bolaños) of *Colonialism Past and Present* (SU of New York P, 2002). His research and teaching interests include the Latin American colonial period, pre-Columbian cultures, theory, and cultural studies. He is currently editing an issue of the journal *Dispositio/n* on Latin American subaltern studies. He has a book in progress on pre-contact indigenous territorialities and material cultures.

WORKS CITED

Abu-Lughod, Lila. "The Interpretation of Culture(s) after Television." Ortner 110–35.

Ades, Dawn. *Art in Latin America*. New Haven: Yale UP, 1989.

Adler, Nancy J. *International Dimensions of Organizational Behavior*. 3rd ed. Cincinnati: South-Western Coll., 1997.

Adorno, Rolena. *Guamán Poma: Writing and Resistance in Colonial Peru*. Austin: U of Texas P, 1986.

———. "Nuevas perspectivas en los estudios coloniales hispanoamericanos." *Revista de crítica literaria latinoamericana* 14.28 (1988): 11–28.

Aguilera Rojas, Javier, ed. *La ciudad hispanoamericana: Sueño de un orden*. Madrid: Centro de Estudios Históricos de Obras Públicas y Urbanismo, 1989.

———. *Fundación de ciudades hispanoamericanas*. Madrid: MAPFRE, 1994.

Alencar, José de. *Iracema*. Trans. Isabela Burton. London: Bickers, 1886.

Almeida, Bira. *Capoeira, a Brazilian Art Form: History, Philosophy, and Practice*. Berkeley: North Atlantic, 1986.

Almeida, Paulo Roberto de, Rubens Antônio Barbosa, and Marshall C. Eakin, eds. *O Brasil dos brasilianistas: Um guia dos estudos sobre o Brasil nos Estados Unidos, 1945–2000*. São Paulo: Paz e Terra, 2002.

Alonso, Carlos J. "Cultural Studies and Hispanism: Been There, Done That." *Siglo XX / Twentieth Century* 14.1–2 (1996): 137–51.

Altamirano, Ignacio. *El Zarco; La navidad en las montañas*. 1901. Mexico City: Porrúa, 1995.

Althusser, Louis. "Ideology and Ideological State Apparatuses (Notes towards an Investigation)." *"Lenin and Philosophy" and Other Essays*. Trans. Ben Brewster. London: New Left, 1971. 121–73.

Amado, Jorge. *Gabriela, cravo e canela*. São Paulo: Martins, 1958. Trans. as *Gabriela, Clove and Cinnamon*. Trans. James L. Taylor and William Grossman. Austin: Bard, 1998.

———. *O país do Carnaval*. Rio de Janeiro: Schmidt, 1931.

———. *Tenda dos milagres*. São Paulo: Martins, 1969. Trans. as *Tent of Miracles*. Trans. Barbara Shelby Merello. Introd. Ilan Stavans. Madison: U of Wisconson P, 2003.

American Me. Dir. Edward James Olmos. Universal, 1992.

Amores perros. Dir. Alejandro González Iñarritu. Mexico City. Altavista Films, 2000.

Anaya, Rudolfo A. *Bless Me, Ultima*. Berkeley: Tonatiuh-Quinto Sol, 1972.

———. *Zia Summer*. New York: Warner, 1996.

Anderson, Benedict. *Imagined Communities: Reflections on the Origin and Spread of Nationalism*. 1983. Rev. ed. London: Verso, 1991.

Anderson, Danny J. "Cultural Studies and Hispanisms." *Siglo XX / Twentieth Century* 14.1–2 (1996): 5–13.

Andrade, Mário de. *Macunaíma*. Trans. E. A. Goodland. New York: Random, 1984.

Andrade, Oswald de. *Obras completas*. Vol. 6. *Do Pau-Brasil à antropofagia e às utopias: Poesias reunidas*. Rio de Janeiro: Civilização Brasileira, 1970–.

———. "Oswald de Andrade's Cannibalist Manifesto." Ed. Leslie Bary. *Latin American Literary Review* 19.38 (1991): 35–47.

Anzaldúa, Gloria. *Borderlands / La Frontera: The New Mestiza*. 2nd ed. San Francisco: Aunt Lute, 1999.

Appadurai, Arjun, ed. *Globalization*. Durham: Duke UP, 2001.

Arenal, Electa, and Stacey Schlau. *Untold Sisters: Hispanic Nuns in Their Works*. Albuquerque: U of New Mexico P, 1989.

Arguedas, José María. *El zorro de arriba y el zorro de abajo*. Lima: Horizonte, 1988.

Armstrong, Piers. "Interdisciplinary Discipline: Postmodern Academics, Course Conception Trends and the Situation of Brazilian Studies." *Fagulha* 6.1 (1998): 2–10 <http://www.brasaus.org/fagulha/fagulha6-1.htm>.

———. *Third World Literary Fortunes: Brazilian Cultural Identity and Its International Reception*. Lewisburg: Bucknell UP; London: Associated UP, 1999.

Arrom, Silvia. *The Women of Mexico City, 1790–1857*. Stanford: Stanford UP, 1985.

Arrom, Silvia, and Servando Ortoll. *Riots in the Cities: Popular Politics and the Urban Poor in Latin America*. Wilmington: Scholarly Resources, 1996.

At Play in the Fields of the Lord. Dir. Hector Babenco. MCA Universal Home Video, 1991.

Augé, Marc. *Los no lugares: Espacios del anonimato*. Barcelona: Gedisa, 1998.

Avelar, Idelber. "The Clandestine Ménage à Trois of Cultural Studies, Spanish, and Critical Theory." *Profession 1999*. New York: MLA, 1999. 49–58.

Averill, Gage. *A Day for the Hunter, a Day for the Prey: Popular Music and Power in Haiti*. Chicago: U of Chicago P, 1997.

Azevedo, Aluísio. *A Brazilian Tenement*. Trans. Harry W. Brown. New York: Fertig, 1976.

Baker, Houston A., Jr., Manthia Diawara, and Ruth H. Lindeborg, eds. *Black British Cultural Studies: A Reader*. Chicago: U of Chicago P, 1996.

Bakhtin, Mikhail. *Rabelais and His World*. Cambridge: MIT P, 1968.

Balderston, Daniel. *El deseo, enorme cicatriz luminosa*. Caracas: Excultura, 1999.

———, ed. *Erotismo y escritura*. Spec. issue of *Revista iberoamericana* 65.187 (1999): 263–440.

Balderston, Daniel, and Donna J. Guy, eds. *Sex and Sexuality in Latin America*. New York: New York UP, 1997.

Barragán de Toscano, Refugio. *La hija del bandido*. 1880. Mexico City: México, 1934.

Barren Lives (Vidas Secas). Dir. Nelson Pereira Dos Santos. Brazil, 1963.

Barrett, Leonard E. *The Rastafarians: Sounds of Cultural Dissonance*. Boston: Beacon, 1998.

Barroso, Ary. "Aquarela do Brasil." Rio de Janeiro, 1939.

Barthes, Roland. "The Photographic Message." *A Barthes Reader*. Ed. Susan Sontag. Toronto: McGraw, 1983. 194–210.

———. "Semiology and Urbanism." *Semiotic Challenge*. Berkeley: U of California P, 1994. 191–201.

Bartra, Roger. *La jaula de la melancolía: Identidad y metamorfosis del mexicano*. Mexico: Grijalbo, 1987.

Beckles, Hilary, and Brian Stodart, eds. *Liberation Cricket: West Indies Cricket Culture*. Manchester: Manchester UP, 1995.

Behague, Gerard. *Music and Black Ethnicity: The Caribbean and South America*. Miami: North-South Center, 1994.

Benedetti, Mario. "El presupuesto." *Montevideanos*. 1959. Mexico City: Nueva Imagen, 1978. 11–17.

Benjamin, Walter. *Illuminations*. New York: Schocken, 1969.

Benveniste, Emile. *Problems in General Linguistics*. Trans. Mary Elizabeth Meek. Coral Gables: U of Miami P, 1971.

Berenguer, Carmen. "Santiago metro." *Huellas de siglo*. Santiago: Manieristas, 1986. 19.

Bergmann, Emilie L., and Paul Julian Smith, eds. *¿Entiendes? Queer Readings, Hispanic Writings*. Durham: Duke UP, 1995.

Berrian, Brenda F. *Awakening Spaces: French Caribbean Popular Song, Music, and Culture*. Chicago: U of Chicago P, 2000.

Beverley, John. *Against Literature*. Minneapolis: U of Minnesota P, 1993.

———. " 'By Lacan': From Literature to Cultural Studies." 1992. Beverley, *Against Literature* 1–22.

———. "Estudios culturales y vocación política." *Revista de crítica cultural* 12 (1996): 46–53.

———. "Hybrid or Binary? On the Category of 'the People' in Subaltern and Cultural Studies." Beverley, *Subalternity* 85–113.

———. "Sobre la situación actual de los estudios culturales." *Asedios a la heteroge-*

neidad cultural. Ed. José Antonio Mazzotti et al. Philadelphia: Asociación Internacional de Peruanistas, 1996. 456–74.

———. *Subalternity and Representation: Arguments in Cultural Theory*. Durham: Duke UP, 1999.

Birringer, Johannes. "Homosexuality and the Revolution: An Interview with Jorge Perugorría." *Cineaste* 21.1–2 (1995): 21. *ROM 355, Spring 2000: Romance Languages Cinemas: Screening the Body*. Ed. José Colmeiro. Michigan State U. 6 Mar. 2003 <http://www.msu.edu/~colmeiro/perugorria.html>.

Black Orpheus [Orfeu negro]. Dir. Marcel Camus. France, 1958.

Blanco, José Joaquín. "Altamirano: Las letras mesiánicas." *Crónica literaria*. Mexico City: Cal y Arena, 1996. 41–51.

Blount, Jeb. "Gerencia: Recién llegados." *Revista Latin Trade* Apr. 1997: 67–69.

Borges, Jorge Luis. *Fervor de Buenos Aires*. Buenos Aires: Impresor Serrantes, 1923.

———. *Selected Poems*. Ed. Alexander Coleman. New York: Viking, 1999.

Bourdieu, Pierre. *Outline of a Theory of Practice*. Trans. Richard Nice. Cambridge: Cambridge UP, 1977.

Brantlinger, Patrick. *Crusoe's Footprints: Cultural Studies in Britain and America*. New York: Routledge, 1990.

Broughton, Simon, ed. *World Music*. London: Rough Guides, 1994.

Brown, Diana DeGroat. *Umbanda: Religion and Politics in Urban Brazil*. New York: Columbia UP, 1994.

Browne, Ray B. "The Voices of Popular Culture in History." *Perspectives: American Historical Association Newsletter* 35.5 (1997): 26+.

Brunner, José Joaquín. *Bienvenidos a la modernidad*. Santiago: Planeta Chilena, 1994.

Buena Vista Social Club. Prod. Road Movies Filmproduktion. Artisan Entertainment, 1999.

Buffington, Robert. *Criminal and Citizen in Modern Mexico*. Lincoln: U of Nebraska P, 2000.

Burdick, John. *Blessed Anastácia: Women, Race, and Popular Christianity in Brazil*. New York: Routledge, 1998.

Bürger, Peter. *Theory of the Avant-Garde*. Trans. Michael Shaw. Minneapolis: U of Minnesota P, 1985.

Burgos, Julia de. *Song of the Simple Truth: Obra completa poética*. Trans. Jack Agüeros. Willimantic: Curbstone, 1997.

Burns, Bradford, ed. *A Documentary History of Brazil*. New York: Knopf, 1966.

———. *A History of Brazil*. 3rd ed. New York: Columbia UP, 1993.

Byram, Michael, and Veronica Esarte-Sarries. *Investigating Cultural Studies in Foreign Language Teaching*. Clevedon, Eng.: Multilingual Matters, 1990.

Byram, Michael, Veronica Esarte-Sarries, and Susan Taylor. *Cultural Studies and Language Learning: A Research Report*. Clevedon, Eng.: Multilingual Matters, 1991.

Caballero Calderón, Eduardo. "Por los caminos de Suramérica." *Obras*. Vol. 1. Medellín: Bedout, 1963. 273–394.

Cabeza de Baca, Fabiola. *We Fed Them Cactus.* 1954. 2nd. ed. Albuquerque: U of New Mexico P, 1994.

Cabrera Infante, Guillermo. *Tres tristes tigres.* Barcelona: Seix Barral, 1967.

El callejón de los milagros. Dir. Jorge Fons. Mexico. WinStar TV and Video, 1995.

Campanella, Tommaso. *City of the Sun.* 1602. Berkeley: U of California P, 1981.

Campbell, Horace. *Rasta and Resistance: From Marcus Garvey to Walter Rodney.* Trenton: Africa World, 1987.

Campuzano, Juan R. *Ignacio Altamirano: Constructor de la nacionalidad y creador de la literatura mexicana.* Mexico City: Federación Editorial Mexicana, 1986.

Canasta de cuentos mexicanos. Dir. Julio Bracho. Churubusco Azteca, 1956.

Cantú, Norma E. *Canícula: Snapshots of a Girlhood en la Frontera.* Albuquerque: U of New Mexico P, 1995.

Canudos Revisited. U of Wisconsin, Milwaukee, Center for Latin Amer., 1990.

Capital Sins: Authoritarianism and Democratization, The Americas. Program 2. WGBH, Boston, and Channel 4, UK, 1993.

Captain Ron. Dir. Thom Eberhardt. Touchstone Pictures. Buena Vista Pictures, 1992.

Cardenal, Ernesto. *Los ovnis de oro (poemas indios)* [Golden UFOs]. Mexico: Siglo Veintiuno, 1988.

Cardoso, Eliana, and Ann Helwege. *Latin America's Economy: Diversity, Trends, and Conflicts.* Cambridge: MIT P, 1995.

Carpentier, Alejo. *La ciudad de las columnas.* 2nd ed. Barcelona: Bruguera, 1985.

———. *The Kingdom of This World.* New York: Knopf, 1957.

Castañeda, Mireya. "The Dogma of Humberto Solás." *Granma International* 23 July 2000: 3.

Castañeda, Quetzil E. "Installing, Enfolding, Evoking, Performing: Notes on a New Ethnography of Evocation." *Monograph of the Field School in Experimental Ethnography.* Vol. 1 (1997). N.p.

———. *In the Museum of Maya Culture.* Minneapolis: U of Minnesota P, 1996.

———. "Paradigms of Fieldwork: Perils of Experimentality and the Problem of the Research Problem." Unpublished ms.

Castells, Manuel. *La cuestión urbana.* 15th ed. Mexico: Siglo XXI, 1999.

———. "The Dependent City and Revolutionary Populism: The *Movimiento Inquilinario* in Veracruz, Mexico, 1922." *The City and the Grassroots.* Berkeley: U of California P, 1983. 37–48.

Castillo, Debra A. *Easy Women: Sex and Gender in Modern Mexican Fiction.* Minneapolis: U of Minnesota P, 1998.

———. "The Tropics of the Imagination: 'Quetzacoatl and All That.' " *Tropicalizations: Transcultural Representations of Latinidad.* Ed. Frances R. Aparicio and Susana Chávez-Silverman. Hanover: UP of New England, 1997. 67–98.

Castro, Casimiro. *México y sus alrededores.* 1855. México: Valle de México, 1972.

Castro, Felipe. *La rebelión de los indios y la paz de los españoles.* Mexico: Instituto Nacional Indigenista, 1996.

Castro-Klarén, Sara. "Literacy, Conquest, and Interpretation: Breaking New Ground on the Records of the Past." *Social History* 23.2 (1998): 133–45.

Ceballos, Ciro B. "Un adulterio." *Un adulterio*. 1903. Mexico City: Premiá–Secretaría de Educación Pública, 1982. 11–47.

Certeau, Michel de. "Walking in the City." *The Practice of Everyday Life*. Berkeley: U of California P, 1984. 91–110.

Chabram, Angie. "Chicana/o Studies as Oppositional Ethnography." *Cultural Studies* 4(1990): 228–47.

———. "Conceptualizing Chicano Critical Discourse." *Criticism in the Borderlands: Studies in Chicano Literature, Culture, and Ideology*. Ed. Héctor Calderón and José David Saldívar. Durham: Duke UP, 1991. 127–48.

Cham, Mbye B., ed. *Ex-Iles: Essays on Caribbean Cinema*. Trenton: Africa World, 1992.

Chanan, Michael. *The Cuban Image: Cinema and Cultural Politics in Cuba*. Bloomington: Indiana UP, 1986.

———. *Twenty-Five Years of the New Latin American Cinema*. London: British Film Inst., 1983.

Chang, Kevin O'Brien, and Wayne Chen. *Reggae Routes: The Story of Jamaican Music*. Philadelphia: Temple UP, 1998.

Chávez-Silverman, Susana, and Librada Hernández, eds. *Reading and Writing the Ambiente*. Madison: U of Wisconsin P, 2000.

Chesnut, Andrew. *Born Again in Brazil: The Pentecostal Boom and the Pathogens of Poverty*. New Brunswick: Rutgers UP, 1997.

Chevannes, Barry. *Rastafari: Roots and Ideology*. Syracuse: Syracuse UP, 1994.

———, ed. *Rastafari and Other African-Caribbean Worldviews*. New Brunswick: Rutgers UP, 1998.

Chutney in Yuh Soca: A Multicultural Mix. Prod. Arts Council Film. Filmmakers Library, n.d.

Cieza de León, Pedro. *El señorío de los Incas*. Madrid: Historia 16, 1988.

Clendinnen, Inga. *The Aztecs: An Interpretation*. Cambridge: Cambridge UP, 1997.

Clifford, James. "Introduction: Partial Truths." Clifford and Marcus 1–26.

———. *The Predicament of Culture*. Cambridge: Harvard UP, 1988.

Clifford, James, and George E. Marcus, eds. *Writing Culture: The Poetics and Politics of Ethnography*. Berkeley: U of California P, 1986.

Codex Borgia. New York: Dover, 1993.

Codrescu, Andrei. *Ay Cuba! A Socio-erotic Journey*. New York: St. Martin's, 1999.

Coe, Michael. *The Maya*. 5th ed. London: Thames, 1993.

Colón, Cristóbal. *Los cuatro viajes*. Madrid: Alianza, 2000.

Colors. Dir. Dennis Hopper. Orion, 1988.

Condé, Maryse. *Crosing the Mangrove*. New York: Doubleday, 1995.

Cook, David Noble. *Born to Die: Disease and New World Conquest, 1492–1650*. Cambridge: Cambridge UP, 1998.

Cool Runnings. Dir. John Turteltaub. Walt Disney Studios. Buena Vista Pictures, 1993.

Cooper, Carolyn. " 'Lyrical Gun': Metaphor and Role Play in Jamaican Dancehall Culture." *Massachusetts Review* 35.3–4 (1994): 429–47.

Cortázar, Julio. "El perseguidor." *Los relatos.* Vol 3. Madrid: Alianza, 1988. 220–74.

Cortázar, Julio, and Alicia D'Amico-Sara Facio. *Buenos Aires, Buenos Aires.* Buenos Aires: Suramericana, 1968.

Cortés, Hernán. *Cartas de relación.* México: Porrúa, 1992.

———. *Letters from Mexico.* Trans. Anthony Pagden. New Haven: Yale UP, 1986.

Countryman. Dir. Dickie Jobson. Island, 1982.

Cuba's Boys of Summer. Prod. CNN Presents. Time/Warner, 1996.

¡Cuba Va! The Challenge of the Next Generation. Dir. Gail Dolgin and Vincente Franco. Videocassette. Cuba Va Film Project, 1993.

Culler, Jonathan. "Changes in the Study of the Lyric." *Lyric Poetry: Beyond New Criticism.* Ed. Chaviva Hošek and Patricia Parker. Ithaca: Cornell UP, 1985. 38–54.

———. *Structuralist Poetics: Structuralism, Linguistics, and the Study of Literature.* Ithaca: Cornell UP, 1975.

Cultural Studies and Hispanism. Spec. issue of *Siglo XX / Twentieth Century* 14 (1996): 1–240.

Curran, James, David Morley, and Valerie Walkerdine, eds. *Cultural Studies and Communications.* London: Arnold, 1996.

da Cunha, Euclides. *Os sertões.* 1902. São Paulo: Brasiliense, 1985. Trans. as *Rebellion in the Backlands.* Trans. Samuel Putnam. Chicago: U of Chicago P, 1957.

Cuzco, la ciudad y su gente. Videocassette. Project for Intl. Communication Studies, U of Iowa, 1990.

Damon, Maria. *The Dark End of the Street.* Minneapolis: U of Minnesota P, 1993.

Dancehall Queen. Dir. Rick Elgood and Don Letts. Videocassette. Hawk's Nest Productions, 1997.

Daniel, Yvonne. *Rumba: Dance and Social Change in Contemporary Cuba.* Bloomington: Indiana UP, 1995.

Danticat, Edwidge. *Krik? Krak!* New York: Vintage, 1996.

Danzón. Dir. María Novaro. Mexico. Videovisa, 1991.

Darío, Rubén. *Obras completas.* 5 vols. Madrid: Aguado, 1950–55.

Davalos, KarenMary. "Chicana/o Studies and Anthropology: The Dialogue That Never Was." *Aztlán* 23.2 (1998): 13–45.

Davidson, Cynthia C., ed. *Anybody.* Cambridge: MIT P, 1997.

———, ed. *Anyplace.* Cambridge: MIT P, 1995.

Davis, Wade. *The Serpent and the Rainbow.* New York: Touchstone, 1997.

de la Campa, Román. *Latin Americanism.* Minneapolis: U of Minnesota P, 1999.

del Sarto, Ana. "Cultural Critique in Latin America or Latin American Cultural Studies?" *Journal of Latin American Cultural Studies* 9.3 (2000): 235–47.

Devereaux, Leslie. "An Introductory Essay." *Fields of Vision: Essays in Film Studies, Visual Anthropology, and Photography*. Ed. Devereaux and Roger Hillman. Berkeley: U of California P, 1995. 1–18.

Díaz Ayala, Cristóbal. *The Roots of Salsa: The History of Cuban Music*. Bayside: Zinn, 2000.

Díaz del Castillo, Bernal. *Historia verdadera de la conquista de la Nueva España*. Mexico City: Porrúa, 1994.

Dissens. Ed. Santiago Gómez Castro. Instituto de Estudios Sociales y Culturales Pensar. Pontificia U Javeriana. Bogotá. 1 Dec. 2000 <http://www.javeriana.edu.co/pensar/dr.html>.

Divine Horsemen: The Living Gods of Haiti. Prod. Mystic Fire. Mystic Fire Video, 1985.

Domanella, Ana Rosa, and Nora Pasternac, eds. *Las voces olvidadas*. Mexico City: Colegio de México, 1991.

Dorfman, Ariel. *The Empire's Old Clothes: What the Lone Ranger, Babar, and Other Innocent Heroes Do to Our Minds*. New York: Pantheon, 1983.

Doyle, Michael Scott, T. Bruce Fryer, and Ronald Cere. *Exito comercial: Prácticas administrativas y contextos culturales*. 3rd ed. Fort Worth: Harcourt, 2001.

Duby, Georges, ed. *Histoire de la vie privée*. Paris: Seuil, 1999.

Dunn, Christopher. "Afro-Bahian Carnival: A Stage for Protest." *Afro-Hispanic Review* 11.1–3 (1992): 11–20.

———. *Brutality Garden: Tropicália and the Emergence of a Brazilian Counterculture*. Chapel Hill: U of North Carolina P, 2001.

Dunn, Christopher, and Charles A. Perrone, eds. *Brazilian Popular Music and Globalization*. Gainesville: U of Florida P, 2001.

During, Simon, ed. *The Cultural Studies Reader*. New York: Routledge, 1993.

Eagleton, Terry. *The Idea of Culture*. Oxford: Blackwell, 2000.

Eakin, Marshall C. *Brazil: The Once and Future Country*. New York: St. Martin's, 1997.

Easthope, Anthony. *Literary into Cultural Studies*. London: Routledge, 1991.

Emerging Powers: Mexico. Dir. Leslie Clark. Wall Street Journal Video, 1996.

The Emperor's Birthday. Volcano Films. Filmmakers Library, n.d.

Ercilla y Zúñiga, Alonso de. *La araucana*. Ed. Marcos Augusto Moríngo and Isaías Lerner. Madrid: Castalia, 1979.

La estrategia del caracol. Dir. Sergio Cabrera. Colombia. Argentina Home Video, 1993.

Evans, Karen U. H. "Business Language: What Is It All About?" *CLEAR News* 3.1 (1999): 1, 6–7.

Fash, William. *Scribes, Warriors and Kings: The City of Copan and the Ancient Maya*. London: Thames, 1991.

Fernández de Lizardi, José Joaquín. *El periquillo sarniento*. 1816. Mexico City: Proxema, 1979. Trans. as *The Itching Parrot*. Trans. and introd. Katherine Anne Porter. Garden City: Doubleday, 1942.

Fischer, Michael M. J. "Ethnicity and the Post-modern Arts of Memory." Clifford and Marcus 194–233.

Fisher, Glen. *International Negotiation: A Cross-Cultural Perspective*. Chicago: Intercultural, 1980.

Florentine Codex. Santa Fe: School of Amer. Research, 1950.

Foster, David William. *From Mafalda to Los Supermachos: Latin American Graphic Humor as Popular Culture*. Boulder: Rienner, 1988.

———. *Gay and Lesbian Themes in Latin American Writing*. Austin: U of Texas P, 1991.

———. *Sexual Textualities*. Austin: U of Texas P, 1997.

Foster, David William, and Roberto Reis, eds. *Bodies and Biases*. Minneapolis: U of Minnesota P, 1996.

Foucault, Michel. "Of Other Spaces." *Diacritics* 16 (1986): 22–27.

Franco, Jean. *Critical Passions: Selected Essays*. Durham: Duke UP, 1999.

———. *Plotting Women: Gender and Representation in Mexico*. New York: Columbia UP, 1989.

———. "Remapping Culture." *Americas: New Interpretive Essays*. Ed. Alfred Stepan. Oxford: Oxford UP, 1992. 172–88.

———. "What's in a Name?: Popular Culture Theories and Their Limitations." *Studies in Latin American Popular Culture* 1 (1982): 5–14.

French, John D. *Sharing the Riches of Afro-Brazilian History and Culture: Undergraduate and Graduate Teaching Syllabi and Handouts*. Working Paper. Durham: African and African-Amer. Studies Program at Duke U (paper 1); Consortium in Latin Amer. Studies at the U of North Carolina, Chapel Hill, and Duke U (paper 34), 2002.

Freyre, Gilberto. *Casa Grande e Senzala*. Rio de Janeiro: Maia e Schmidt, 1933.

———. *The Mansions and the Shanties: The Making of Modern Brazil*. Trans. Harriet de Onís. New York: Knopf, 1963.

———. *The Masters and the Slaves: A Study in the Development of Brazilian Civilization*. Trans. Samuel Putnam. New York: Knopf, 1956.

Frías, Heriberto. "Las inseparables." *Los piratas del boulevard (desfile de zánganos y víboras sociales y políticas en Mexico)*. Mexico City: Botas, 1916. 137–39.

Fryer, T. Bruce, and Gail Guntermann. *Spanish and Portuguese for Business and the Professions*. Lincolnwood: Natl. Textbook, 1998.

Fuentes, Carlos. "Malintzin de las maquilas." *La frontera de cristal*. Mexico City: Alfaguara, 1995. 129–60.

Fuery, Patrick, and Nick Mansfield. *Cultural Studies and Critical Theory*. Melbourne: Oxford UP, 2000.

Galende, Federico. "Un desmemoriado espíritu de época: Tribulaciones y desdichas en torno a los estudios culturales (Una réplica a John Beverley)." *Revista de crítica cultural* 13 (1996): 52–55.

Galloway, Vicki, Angela Labarca, and Elmer A. Rodríguez. *Saldo a favor: Intermediate Spanish for the World of Business*. New York: Wiley, 1998.

Gamboa, Federico. *Santa.* 1903. Mexico City: Grijalbo, 1979.

Garber, Marjorie, Paul B. Franklin, and Rebecca L. Walkowitz, eds. *Field Work: Sites in Literary and Cultural Studies.* New York: Routledge, 1996.

García, Marco-Aurélio, and Michael M. Hall. "Urban Labor." *Modern Brazil: Elites and Masses in Historical Perspective.* Ed. Michael L. Conniff and Frank D. Mc-Cann. Lincoln: U of Nebraska P, 1989. 161–91.

García Canclini, Néstor. *La ciudad de los viajeros: Travesías e imaginarios urbanos, México, 1940–2000.* Mexico City: Grijalbo, 1996.

———. *Consumidores y ciudadanos: Conflictos multiculturales de la globalización.* Mexico City: Grijalbo, 1995.

———. *Culturas híbridas: Estrategias para entrar y salir de la modernidad.* Mexico City: Grijalbo, 1989. Trans. as *Hybrid Cultures: Strategies for Entering and Leaving Modernity.* Trans. Christopher L. Chiappari and Silvia L. Lopez. Minneapolis: U of Minnesota P, 1995.

———. "La épica de la globalizacion y el melodrama de la interculturalidad." New Perspectives in/on Latin America: The Challenge of Cultural Studies. U of Pittsburgh, Mar. 1998.

———. "Los estudios culturales: Elaboración intelectual del intercambio América Latina–Estados Unidos." *Papeles de Montevideo* 1 (1997): 45–58.

———. *La globalización imaginada.* Buenos Aires: Paidós, 2000.

García Espinosa, Julio. "For an Imperfect Cinema." *Reviewing Histories: Selections from New Latin American Cinema.* Ed. Coco Fusco. Buffalo: Hallwalls, 1987.

García Márquez, Gabriel. *Cien años de soledad.* Bogotá: Círculo de Lectores, 1980. Trans. as *One Hundred Years of Soltitude.* Trans. Gregory Rabassa. New York: Harper, 1967.

Garcilaso de la Vega, El Inca. *Comentarios reales.* 2 vols. Caracas: Ayacucho, 1976.

Garden of the Forking Paths: Dilemmas of National Development. WGBH, Boston, and Channel 4, UK. Annenberg–CPB Collection, 1993.

Gilbert, Alan. *The Latin American City.* 2nd ed. London: Latin Amer. Bureau, 1998.

Giroux, Henry A. *Impure Acts: The Practical Politics of Cultural Studies.* New York: Routledge, 2000.

Giroux, Henry A., and Peter McLaren, eds. *Between Borders: The Pedagogy and the Politics of Cultural Studies.* New York: Routledge, 1994.

Giroux, Henry A., with Patrick Shannon, eds. *Education and Cultural Studies: Toward a Performative Practice.* New York: Routledge, 1997.

González Echevarría, Roberto. *The Pride of Havana: A History of Cuban Baseball.* London: Oxford UP, 1999.

González Rodríguez, Sergio. "Lectura y censura sexual en México, 1900–1990." *Los amorosos.* Ed. González Rodriguez. Mexico City: Cal y Arena, 1996. 13–58.

Graff, Gerald. *Beyond the Culture Wars: How Teaching Conflicts Can Revitalize American Education.* New York: Norton, 1992.

Graffiti. Dir. Matthew Patrick. 1985. Stone Center for Latin Amer. Studies, Tulane U.

Granillo Vázquez, Lilia. "La abnegación maternal, sustrato fundamental de la cultura femenina en México." *Identidades y nacionalismos: Una perspectiva interdisciplinaria*. Coord. Granillo Vázquez. Mexico City: U Autónoma Metropolitana–Azcapotzalco/Gernika, 1993. 195–255.

Gringo in Mañanaland: A Musical. Prod. DeeDee Halleck. 1995.

Grossberg, Lawrence. "The Circulation of Cultural Studies." Storey, *What* 178–86.

———. "Introduction: Bringin' It All Back Home—Pedagogy and Cultural Studies." Giroux and McLaren 1–28.

Grossberg, Lawrence, Cary Nelson, and Paula Treichler, eds. *Cultural Studies*. New York: Routledge, 1992.

Gruzinski, Serge. *Painting the Conquest: The Mexican Indian and the European Renaissance*. Paris: UNESCO, 1992.

Grzegorczyk, Marzena. "From Urb of Clay to the Hypodermic City: Improper Cities in Modern Latin America." *Journal of Latin American Cultural Studies* 7.1 (1998): 55–74.

Guantanamera. Dir. Tomás Gutiérrez Alea. Instituto Cubano de Arte e Industria Cinematográficos. New Yorker Films, 1994.

Guback, Thomas, and Tapio Varis. *Transnational Communication and Cultural Industries*. Reports and Papers on Mass Communication 92. Paris: UNESCO, 1982.

Guerra-Cunningham, Lucía, ed. *Splintering Darkness: Latin American Women Writers in Search of Themselves*. Pittsburgh: Latin Amer. Literary Review, 1990.

Guilbault, Jocelyne. *Zouk: World Music in the West Indies*. Chicago: U of Chicago P, 1993.

Guillermoprieto, Alma. *Samba*. New York: Vintage, 1991.

Gunn, Giles, ed. *Globalizing Literary Studies*. Spec. issue of *PMLA* 116.1 (2001): 1–272.

Gutiérrez, Ramón. *Arquitectura y urbanismo en Iberoamérica*. Madrid: Cátedra, 1997.

Haberly, David. *Three Sad Races*. Cambridge: Cambridge UP, 1983.

Haiti: Killing the Dream. Dir. Katharine Kean and Rudi Stern. Videocassette. Mystic Fire Video, 1992.

Haitian Pilgrimage. Prod. Green Valley Films, 1992.

Hall, Stuart. "The Emergence of Cultural Studies and the Crisis of the Humanities." *October* 53 (1990): 11–23.

———. "Encoding, Decoding." *Culture, Media, Language: Working Papers in Cultural Studies, 1972–1979*. Ed. Hall, Dorothy Hobson, Andrew Love, and Paul Willis. London: Hutchinson, 1980. 128–38.

———. "The Local and the Global: Globalization and Ethnicity." A. King 19–40.

Hanchard, Michael, ed. *Racial Politics in Contemporary Brazil*. Durham: Duke UP, 1999.

The Harder They Come. Dir. Perry Henzell. International Films. Xenon Entertainment, 1972.

Hardoy, Jorge, and Ana Hardoy. "The Plaza in Latin America: From Teotihuacan to Recife." *Cultures* 5.4 (1978): 59–92.

Harris, Philip R., and Robert T. Moran. *Managing Cultural Differences: High Performance Strategies for a New World of Business.* Houston: Gulf, 1991.

Hartman, Geoffrey H. *The Fateful Question of Culture.* New York: Columbia UP, 1997.

Havana. Dir. Sydney Pollack. Universal Pictures, 1990.

Hejinian, Lyn. Presentation. Conf. on Poetry and Pedagogy: The Challenge of the Contemporary. Bard Coll., New York. 24–27 June 1999.

Hemming, John. "Extermination or Protection." *Amazon Frontier: The Defeat of the Brazilian Indians.* London: Macmillan, 1987. 467–81.

Hernández, Abdel. "Languages of Fieldwork in Act Installation." Conf. of Amer. Anthropological Assn. Chicago. 19 Nov. 1999.

Hernández, Abdel, and Surpik Angelini, curators. Artists in Trance: Workshop on Intercultural Work with the Other. Rice U. Jan.-Apr. 1997.

Hernández, Deborah Pacini. "Dancing with the Enemy: Cuban Popular Music, Race, Authenticity, and the World-Music Landscape." *Studies in Latin American Popular Culture* 12 (1993): 110–25.

Hibbert, Christopher. *Cities and Civilization.* New York: Welcome Rain, 1996.

Hijuelos, Oscar. *The Mambo Kings Play Songs of Love.* New York: Harper, 1989.

Hill, Donald. *Calypso Calaloo: Early Carnival Music in Trinidad.* Gainesville: UP of Florida, 1993.

Hirsch, E. D. *Cultural Literacy.* New York: Vintage, 1988.

Hoberman, Louisa, and Susan Socolow, eds. *Cities and Society in Colonial Latin America.* Albuquerque: U of New Mexico P, 1986.

Holanda, Sérgio Buarque de. *Raízes do Brasil.* Rio de Janeiro: Olympio, 1936.

———. *Visão do paraíso; Os motivos edênicos no descobrimento e colonização do Brasil.* Rio de Janeiro: Olympio, 1959.

Holiday in the Sun. Dir. Steve Purcell. Dualstar Video. Warner Home Video, 2001.

How Stella Got Her Groove Back. Dir. Kevin Rodney Sullivan. Fox, 1998.

How Tasty Was My Little Frenchman (Como Era Gostoso o Meu Francês). Dir. Nelson Pereira Dos Santos. Brazil, 1971.

Huerta, Efraín. "Juárez-Loreto." *Poesía completa* 301–02.

———. "Meditación y delirio en el metro." *Poesía completa* 299–300.

———. *Poesía completa.* Ed. Martí Soler. Mexico City: Fondo de Cultura Económica, 1988.

Hyslop, John. *Inka Settlement and Planning.* Austin: U of Texas P, 1990.

Imaiz, Eugenio. *Utopías del renacimiento.* Mexico City: Fondo de Cultura Económica, 1994.

Inca: Secrets of the Ancestors. Dir. Tom Simon. 1995.

The Incas. Dir. Anna Benson-Gyles and Marian White. PBS, 1988.

Incidents of Travel in Chichén Itzá. Dir. Jeffrey Himpele and Quetzil E. Castañeda. Watertown: Documentary Educ. Resources, 1997.

Indiana Journal of Hispanic Literatures 13 (1998).

In the Shadow of the Incas. Videocassette. Dir. Gottfried Kirchner. Films for the Humanities. Princeton, 1993.

Irwin, Robert McKee. *"El Periquillo Sarniento* y sus cuates: El 'éxtasis misterioso' del ambiente homosocial en el siglo XIX." *Literatura mexicana* 9.1 (1998): 23–44.

Irwin, Robert McKee, Edward J. McCaughan, and Michelle Rocío Nasser, eds. *The Famous 41.* New York: Palgrave, 2003.

I Walked with a Zombie. Dir. Jacques Tourneur. RKO, 1943. Turner Home Video, n.d.

Jahn, Brian, and Tom Weber, eds. *Reggae Island: Jamaican Music in the Digital Age.* Boulder: Da Capo, 1998.

Jakobson, Roman. "Closing Statement: Linguistics and Poetics." *Style in Language.* Ed. Thomas A. Sebeok. Cambridge: MIT P, 1958. 350–434.

———. *Lingüística y poética.* Madrid: Cátedra, 1988.

James, C. L. R. *Beyond a Boundary.* Durham: Duke UP, 1993.

Jameson, Fredric. "On Cultural Studies." *Social Text* 34 (1993): 17–52.

———. *Postmodernism; or, The Cultural Logic of Late Capitalism.* Durham: Duke UP, 1991.

Jameson, Fredric, and Masao Miyoshi, eds. *The Cultures of Globalization.* Durham: Duke UP, 1998.

Jelin, Elizabeth. "The Minefields of Memory." *NACLA: Report on the Americas* 32.2 (1998): 23–29.

Jesús, Carolina María de. *Child of the Dark.* New York: Mentor, 1963.

Jiménez, José Olivio. *Antología crítica de la poesía modernista hispanoamericana.* Madrid: Hiperión, 1985.

Johnson, David E., and Scott Michaelsen. "Border Secrets: An Introduction." *Border Theory: The Limits of Cultural Politics.* Ed. Michaelsen and Johnson. Minneapolis: U of Minnesota P, 1997. 1–39.

Johnson, Randal, and Robert Stam, eds. *Brazilian Cinema.* Enl. ed. New York: Columbia UP, 1995.

Johnson, Richard. "What Is Cultural Studies Anyway?" Storey, *What* 75–114.

Joseph, Gilbert, and Mark Szuchman, eds. *I Saw a City Invincible: Urban Portraits of Latin America.* Wilmington: Scholarly Resources, 1996.

Kaliman, Ricardo. "What Is 'Interesting' in Latin American Cultural Studies." *Journal of Latin American Cultural Studies* 7.2 (1998): 261–72.

Kincaid, Jamaica. *A Small Place.* New York: Penguin, 1988.

King, Anthony D., ed. *Culture, Globalization, and the World-System: Contemporary Conditions for the Representation of Identity.* Minneapolis: U of Minnesota P, 1997.

King, John. *Magical Reels: A History of Cinema in Latin America.* 2nd ed. London: Verso, 2000.

Kowalski, Jeff, ed. *Mesoamerican Architecture as a Cultural Symbol.* New York: Oxford UP, 1999.

Kramsch, Claire. *Context and Culture in Language Teaching.* Oxford: Oxford UP, 1993.

———. "The Cultural Discourse of Foreign Language Textbooks." *Toward a New Integration of Language and Culture.* Ed. Alan J. Singerman. Middlebury: Northeast Conf. on the Teaching of Foreign Langs., 1988. 63–88.

———. *Language and Culture.* Oxford: Oxford UP, 1998.

Lamas, Marta. *Cuerpo: Diferencia sexual y género.* Mexico City: Taurus, 2002.

Lange, Dale L., Carol A. Klee, R. Michael Paige, and Yelena A. Yershova, eds. *Culture as the Core: Interdisciplinary Perspectives on Culture Teaching and Learning in the Language Curriculum.* Minneapolis: Center for Advanced Research on Lang. Acquisition Working Papers Ser. 11, 1998.

Lara, Agustín. *Serie Platino.* BMG Music, 1997.

Lara y Pardo, Luis. *La prostitución en México.* Paris: Bouret, 1908.

Larsen, Neil. "Aesthetics and the Question of Colonial 'Discourse.' " Larsen, *Reading* 103–09.

———. "Brazilian Critical Theory and the Question of Cultural Studies." Larsen, *Reading* 205–16.

———. "The Cultural Studies Movement in Latin America: An Overview." Larsen, *Reading* 189–96.

———. "Cultural Studies Questionnaire." *Journal of Latin American Cultural Studies* 7.2 (1998): 245–48.

———. *Reading North by South.* Minneapolis: U of Minnesota P, 1995.

The Last Supper. Dir. Tomás Gutiérrez Alea. Instituto Cubano de Arte e Industria Cinematográficos. Tricontinental Film Center, 1976.

Latin American Subaltern Studies Group. "Founding Statement." 1992. *Disposition* 19.46 (1994): 1–11.

Leis, Raúl. "Contra el baká: Cultura y educación, en la tarea común de despertar a los durmientes." *Casa de las Américas* 26.153 (1985): 63–75.

Leitch, Vincent B. *Cultural Criticism, Literary Theory, Poststructuralism.* New York: Columbia UP, 1992.

Lent, John A., ed. *Caribbean Popular Culture.* Bowling Green: Bowling Green UP, 1990.

León Portilla, Miguel. *El reverso de la conquista.* Mexico City: Mortiz, 1987.

———, ed. *Visión de los vencidos: Relaciones indígenas de la conquista.* Mexico: U Nacional Autónoma, 1959.

Levine, Lawrence W. *The Opening of the American Mind: Canons, Culture, and History.* Boston: Beacon 1996.

Levine, Robert M., and John J. Crocitti, eds. *The Brazil Reader: History, Culture, Politics.* Durham: Duke UP, 1999.

Light Memories of Rio (Rio de memórias). Interior Producoes e Embrafilme. Cinema Guild, Brazil, 1990.

Limón, José E. *Dancing with the Devil: Society and Cultural Poetics in Mexican American South Texas.* Madison: U of Wisconsin P, 1994.

Lockhart, James. *The Nahuas after the Conquest: A Social and Cultural History of the Indians of Central Mexico, Sixteenth through Eighteenth Centuries.* Stanford: Stanford UP, 1992.

López de Gómara, Francisco. *Historia de la conquista de México.* Mexico City: Porrúa, 1988.

Lovelace, Earl. *The Dragon Can't Dance.* Essex, Eng.: Longman, 1979.

———. *Salt.* New York: Persea, 1998.

Lowell, Lewis J. *Ring of Liberation: Deceptive Discourse in Brazilian Capoeira.* Chicago: U of Chicago P, 1992.

MacCormack, Sabine. *Religion in the Andes: Vision and Imagination in Early Colonial Peru.* Princeton: Princeton UP, 1991.

Machado de Assis, Joaquim Maria. *"The Devil's Church" and Other Stories.* Trans. Jack Schmitt and Lorie Ishimatsu. Austin: U of Texas P, 1977.

Las madres de la Plaza de Mayo. Dir. Susana Muñoz and Lourdes Portillo. 1985. Stone Center for Latin Amer. Studies, Tulane U.

Malpass, Michael A., ed. *Provincial Inca: Archaeological and Ethnohistorical Assessment of the Impact of the Inca State.* Iowa City: U of Iowa P, 1993.

Mambo Kings. Dir. Arne Glimcher. Warner, 1992.

Manuel, Frank, and Fritzie Manuel. *Utopian Thought in the Western World.* Cambridge: Cambridge UP, 1979.

Manuel, Peter Lamarche, ed. *Caribbean Currents: Caribbean Music from Rumba to Reggae.* Philadelphia: Temple UP, 1995.

———. *East Indian Music in the West Indies: Tan-Singing, Chutney, and the Making of Indo-Caribbean Culture.* Philadelphia: Temple UP, 2000.

———. *Essays on Cuban Music: North American and Cuban Perspectives.* Blue Ridge Summit: UP of America, 1992.

Marcus, George E. "Afterword: Ethnographic and Anthropological Careers." Clifford and Marcus 262–66.

Marcus, George E., and Michael M. J. Fischer. *Anthropology as Cultural Critique: An Experimental Moment in the Human Sciences.* Chicago: U of Chicago P, 1986.

Martí, José. *Ismaelillo; Versos libres; Versos sencillos.* Ed. Ivan Schulman. Madrid: Cátedra, 1990.

———. *Política de nuestra América.* Mexico: Siglo XXI, 1982.

Martín-Barbero, Jesús. *De los medios a las mediaciones: Comunicación, cultura y hegemonía.* 2nd ed. Mexico: G. Gili, 1991.

Martínez, Elena. *Lesbian Voices from Latin America.* New York: Garland, 1996.

Mas Fever: Inside Trinidad Carnival. UC Berkeley Center for Media and Independent Learning, 1989.

Mattelart, Armand. *Transnationals and the Third World: The Struggle for Culture.* Westport: Bergin, 1983.

Mayers, Kathleen, ed. *Word from New Spain: The Spiritual Autobiography of Madre María de San José.* Liverpool: Liverpool UP, 1993.

Mazzotti, José Antonio. *Coros mestizos del Inca Garcilaso: Resonancias andinas.* Lima: Otorongo Producciones; Fondo de Cultura Económica, 1996.

Medina Cano, Federico. "El centro comercial: Una burbuja de cristal." *Revista universidad pontificia bolivariana* [Medellín] 46.142 (1997): 21–49.

Melhuus, Marit, and Kristi Anne Stølen, eds. *Machos, Mistresses, Madonnas: Contesting the Power of Latin American Gender Imagery.* London: Verso, 1996.

Meyer, Karl E. *Teotihuacan.* New York: Newsweek, 1973.

Mignolo, Walter. "Cultural Studies Questionnaire." *Journal of Latin American Cultural Studies* 7.1 (1998): 111–19.

———. *The Darker Side of the Renaissance: Literacy, Territoriality. and Colonization.* Ann Arbor: U of Michigan P, 1995.

———. "La lengua, la letra, el territorio (o la crisis de los estudios literarios coloniales)." *Dispositio* 11.28–29 (1986): 135–60.

———. *Local Histories / Global Designs: Coloniality, Subaltern Knowledges, and Border Thinking.* Princeton: Princeton UP, 2000.

Mignolo, Walter, and Elizabeth Hill Boone, eds. *Writing without Words: Alternative Literacies in Mesoamerica and the Andes.* Durham: Duke UP, 1994.

Miracles Are Not Enough: Continuity and Change in Religion. WGBH, Boston, and Channel 4, UK. Annenberg–CPB Collection, 1993.

Mi Vida Loca / My Crazy Life. Dir. Allison Anders. Cineville, 1994.

Molloy, Sylvia. "Presidential Address 2001: Crossings." *PMLA* 117 (2002): 407–13.

Molloy, Sylvia, and Robert McKee Irwin, eds. *Hispanisms and Homosexualities.* Durham: Duke UP, 1998.

Monsiváis, Carlos. "Bolero: A History." *Mexican Postcards.* London: Verso, 1997. 166–95.

———. "Ortodoxia y heterodoxia en las alcobas (hacia una crónica de costumbres y creencias sexuales en México)." *Debate feminista* 6.11 (1995):183–210.

Moraes, Vinicius de. *Orfeu da conceição: Tragedia carioca.* Rio de Janeiro: Dois Amigos, 1956.

More, Thomas. *Utopia.* 1516. London: Penguin, 1961.

Moreiras, Alberto. *The Exhaustion of Difference: The Politics of Latin American Cultural Studies.* Durham: Duke UP, 2001.

———. "The Order of Order: On the Reluctant Culturalism of Anti-Subalternist Critiques." *Journal of Latin American Cultural Studies* 8.1 (1999): 125–45.

———. "The Secret Agency of Disillusionment." *Latin American Literary Review* 20.40 (1992): 70–74.

———. "A Storm Blowing from Paradise: Negative Globality and Latin American Cultural Studies." *Siglo XX / Twentieth Century* 14.1–2 (1996): 59–84.

Mowitt, John. "Survey and Discipline: Literary Pedagogy in the Context of Cultural Studies." *Class Issues: Pedagogy, Cultural Studies, and the Public Sphere.* Ed. Amitava Kumar. New York: New York UP, 1997. 48–64.

Mumford, Lewis. *The Culture of Cities.* New York: Harcourt, 1938.

Mundy, Barbara E. *The Mapping of New Spain: Indigenous Cartography and the Maps of the* Relaciones geográficas. Chicago: U of Chicago P, 1996.

Murphy, Joseph M. *Santería: African Spirits in America.* Boston: Beacon, 1993.

Murphy, Peter F. "Cultural Studies as Praxis." *College Literature* 19.2 (1992): 31–43.

Mutis, José Celestino. *Diario de observaciones.* 2 vols. Bogotá: Minerva, 1957–58.

Myers, Helen. *Music of Hindu Trinidad: Songs from the India Diaspora.* Chicago: U of Chicago P, 1998.

Nelson, Cary. *Repression and Recovery: Modern American Poetry and the Politics of Cultural Memory, 1910–1945.* Madison: U of Wisconsin P, 1989.

Neruda, Pablo. "Alturas de Macchu Picchu." *Canto general.* Barcelona: Bruguera, 1980. 25–37.

No nacimos pa' semilla. Dir. Alonso Salazar. Bogotá. CINEP, 1990.

Nora, Pierre. *Realms of Memory: The Construction of the French Past.* 3 vols. New York: Columbia UP, 1997.

Novinger, Tracy. *Intercultural Communication: A Practical Guide.* Austin: U of Texas P, 2001.

Off the Streets, into Art: Slave Ship. Dir. Anna Penido and David Sonnenschein. Crystal Vision Prods., 1993.

Olodum. *Best Of Olodum.* Conti–Continental–Warner, 1997.

Los olvidados. Dir. Luis Buñuel. Mexico, 1950. Madera Cinevideo, 1989.

Omari, Mikelle Smith. *From the Inside to the Outside: The Art and Ritual of Bahian Candomblé.* Los Angeles: Museum of Cultural History, UCLA, 1984.

Oña, Pedro de. *Arauco domado.* 1596. Madrid: Cultura Hispánica, 1944.

Orfeo negro [Black Orfeus]. Dir. Marcel Camus. France. 1959. Voyager, 1986.

Orfeu. Dir. Carlos Diegues. Brazil. Globo Filmes, 2000.

Orme, William A., Jr. *Understanding NAFTA: Mexico, Free Trade, and the New North America.* Austin: U of Texas P, 1996.

Ortiz, Fernando. *Contrapunteo del tabaco y el azúcar.* 1940. *Cuban Counterpoint: Sugar and Tobacco.* Trans. Harriet de Onís. Durham: Duke UP, 1995.

Ortner, Sherry, ed. *The Fate of "Culture": Geertz and Beyond.* Berkeley: U of California P, 1999.

Pales Matos, José Luis. *Selected Poems.* Houston: Arte Publico, 2000.

Paredes, Américo. *George Washington Gómez.* Houston: Arte Público, 1990.

———. "On Ethnographic Work among Minority Groups: A Folklorist's Perspective." *New Scholar* 6 (1977): 1–32.

———. *With His Pistol in His Hand: A Border Ballad and Its Hero.* Austin: U of Texas P, 1958.

Paredes, Raymund A. "The Evolution of Chicano Literature." *Three American Literatures: Essays in Chicano, Native American, and Asian-American Literature for Teachers of American Literature.* Ed. Houston A. Baker, Jr. New York: MLA, 1982. 33–79.

Parle, Dennis J. "Managing an Advanced Business Spanish Course with Business Majors and Native Speakers." *Global Business Languages* (1996): 81–93.

Parra, Nicanor. "Los vicios del mundo moderno." *Antipoemas: Antología, 1944– 1969*. Barcelona: Seix Barral, 1972. 38–41.

Pascal, Nanettte R., and María P. Rojas. *Relaciones comerciales*. Lexington: Heath, 1996.

Patai, Daphne. "Vera: A Woman Speaks." Summ 188–94.

Patrizi, Francesco. *La citta felice*. 1553. Venice: Griffo, 1968.

Paulson, Wiliam R. *The Noise of Culture*. Ithaca: Cornell UP, 1988.

Paz, Octavio. "Los hijos de la Malinche." 1950. *El laberinto de la soledad*. Mexico City: Fondo de Cultura Económica, 1989. 59–80.

Perrone, Charles. "Nationalism, Dissension and Politics in Contemporary Brazilian Music." *Luso-Brazilian Review* 39.1 (2002): 65–78.

Pettavino, Paula J., and Geralyn Pye. *Sport in Cuba: The Diamond in the Rough*. Pittsburgh: U of Pittsburgh P, 1994.

Piglia, Ricardo. *Ciudad ausente*. Buenos Aires: Suramericana, 1993.

Pixote. Dir. Heitor Babenco. Embrafilm, Brazil. Columbia Home Video, 1981.

Pohl, John M. D. *The Politics of Symbolism in the Mixtec Codices*. Nashville: Vanderbilt U Pubs. in Anthropology, 1994.

Poma de Ayala, Felipe Guamán. *Nueva corónica y buen gobierno*. 3 vols. Lima: Fondo de Cultura Económica, 1993.

Ponce, Mary Helen. *Hoyt Street: Memories of a Chicana Childhood*. New York: Doubleday, 1993.

Portrait of Castro's Cuba. Turner, 1991.

Prado, Paulo. *Retrato do Brasil: Ensaio sobre a Tristeza Brasileira*. Rio de Janeiro: Briguiet, 1931.

Pratt, Mary Louise. "*I, Rigoberta Menchú* and the 'Culture Wars.' " *The Rigoberta Menchú Controversy*. Ed. Arturo Arias. Minneapolis: U of Minnesota P, 2001. 29–48.

Project on Business Environment and Social Responsibility. U of Colorado. 6 Mar. 2003 <http://www.colorado.edu/IBS/EB/PBESR/index.html>.

Puig, Manuel. *El beso de la mujer araña*. Barcelona: Seix Barral, 1976.

———. *La traición de Rita Hayworth*. Barcelona: Seix Barral, 1995.

Quilombo. Dir. Carlos Diegues. Brazil. New Yorker Films, 1984.

Quintana, Alvina E. *Home Girls: Chicana Literary Voices*. Philadelphia: Temple UP, 1996.

Quiroga, José. *Tropics of Desire: Interventions from Queer Latin America*. New York: New York UP, 2000.

Rama, Angel. *La ciudad letrada*. Hanover: Del Norte, 1984. *The Lettered City*. Trans. John Charles Chasteen. Durham: Duke UP, 1996.

———. *Transculturación narrativa en América latina*. Mexico City: Siglo XXI, 1982.

Ramos, Graciliano. *Barren Lives*. Trans. Ralph Edward Dimmick. Austin: U of Texas P, 1965.

Ramos, Julio. "A Citizen Body: Cholera in Havana (1833)." *Disposition* 19.46 (1994): 179–95.

Recuerdos de mi barrio: El Vergel, asentamientos espontáneos de Cali, Colombia. Dir. John Gray and John Van Oudenallen. Center for Latin Amer., U of Wisconsin, Milwaukee, 1993.

Regis, Louis. *The Political Calypso: True Opposition in Trinidad and Tobago.* Gainesville: UP of Florida, 1999.

Rhys, Jean. *Wide Sargasso Sea.* New York: Norton, 1966.

Rice, Laura. "Trafficking in Philosophy: Lines of Force in the City-Text." *City Images: Perspectives from Literature, Philosophy, and Film.* Ed. Mary Ann Caws. New York: Gordon, 1991. 221–39.

Richard, Nelly. "Intersectando Latinoamérica con el latinoamericanismo: Saberes académicos, práctica teórica y crítica cultural." *Revista iberoamericana* 63.180 (1997): 345–61.

———. Introducción. *Residuos y metáforas: Ensayos de crítica cultural sobre el Chile de la transición.* Santiago: Cuarto Propio, 1998. 11–23.

Riedemann, Clemente. "La especiulación de lo pretérito." Riedemann, *Karra Maw'n* 60.

———. *Karra Maw'n y otros poemas.* Valdivia: El Kultrún, 1995.

———. "Parque Arauco." Riedemann, *Karra Maw'n* 72.

Robledo, Angela Inés, ed. *Jerónima Nava y Saavedra: Autobiografía de una monja venerable.* Cali: Centro Editorial U del Valle, 1994.

Rodrigo D: No futuro. Dir. Victor Gaviria. Colombia. 1989. King Video, 1991.

Romero, José Luis. *Latinoamérica: Las ciudades y las ideas.* Buenos Aires: Siglo XXI, 1976.

Rosaldo, Renato. *Culture and Truth: The Remaking of Social Analysis.* Boston: Beacon, 1989.

———. "Imperialist Nostagia." Rosaldo, *Culture* 68–87.

Roumagnac, Carlos. *Crímenes sexuales y pasionales.* Mexico City: Bouret, 1906.

———. *Los criminales en México.* Mexico City: El Fénix, 1904.

Rowe, William, and Vivian Schelling. *Memory and Modernity: Popular Culture in Latin America.* London: Verso, 1991.

Rucker, Mark, and Peter Bjarkman. *Smoke: The Romance and Lore of Cuban Baseball.* New York: Total–Sports Illustrated, 1999.

Sahagún, Bernardino de. *Florentine Codex: General History of the Things of New Spain.* Trans. Arthur J. Anderson and Charles E. Dibble. Santa Fe: School of Amer. Research, 1950.

Said, Edward. *Orientalism.* New York: Vintage, 1978.

———. "Traveling Theory." *The World, the Text, and the Critic.* Cambridge: Harvard UP, 1983. 226–47.

Salazar, Alonso. *No nacimos pa' semilla* [Born to Die in Medellín]. Bogotá: CINEP, 1990.

Saldívar, David. *Border Matters: Remapping American Cultural Studies.* Berkeley: U of California P, 1997.

Samper, Miguel. *Selección de escritos.* Bogotá: Colcultura, 1977.

Santa. Dir. Antonio Moreno. Mexico, 1931.

Santa Cruz Pachacuti, Juan de. *Relación de antigüedades de este Reino del Perú*. Ed. Carlos Araníbar. Lima: Fondo de Cultura Económica, 1995.

Santí, Enrico Mario. "Latinamericanism and Restitution." *Latin American Literary Review* 40 (1992): 88–96.

Santiago, Silviano. "Apesar de dependente, universal." *Vale quanto pesa*. Rio de Janeiro: Paz e Terra, 1982. 13–24.

———. "O entre-lugar do discurso latino-americano." *Uma literatura nos trópicos: Ensaios sobre dependência cultural*. São Paulo: Perspectiva, 1978. 11–29.

Sarlo, Beatriz. "Cultural Studies Questionnaire." *Journal of Latin American Cultural Studies* 6.1 (1997): 85–92.

———. *Escenas de la vida posmoderna: Intelectuales, arte y videocultura en la Argentina*. Buenos Aires: Ariel, 1994.

———. "Los estudios culturales y la crítica literaria en la encrucijada valorativa." *Revista de crítica cultural* 15 (1997): 32–38. Rpt. as "Cultural Studies and Literary Criticism at the Crossroads of Values." *Journal of Latin American Cultural Studies* 8.1 (1999): 115–24.

———. *Una modernidad periférica: Buenos Aires: 1920 y 1930*. Buenos Aires: Nueva Visión, 1988.

Sarmiento, Domingo F. *Facundo*. 1845. Madrid: Alianza, 1988.

Sartor, Mario. "The Latin American City: Pre-Columbian Ancestry, the Founding Laws, and Tradition." *Zodiac* 8 [Milan] (1992–93): 15–47.

Savishinsky, Neil J. "Transnational Popular Culture and the Global Spread of the Jamaican Rastafarian Movement." *New West Indian Guide* 68.3–4 (1994): 259–81.

Schele, Linda, and David Freidel. *A Forest of Kings: The Untold Story of the Ancient Maya*. New York: Morrow, 1990.

Schepper-Hughes, Nancy. "Everyday Violence." *Summ* 194–202.

Schiller, Herbert, ed. *The Ideology of International Communication*. New York: Inst. for Media Analysis, 1992.

Schwarz, Roberto. *Misplaced Ideas: Essays on Brazilian Culture*. London: Verso, 1992.

The Serpent and the Rainbow. Dir. Wes Craven. MCA–Universal, 1988.

Silva, Armando. *Imaginarios urbanos*. 4th ed. Bogotá: Tercer Mundo, 2000.

Simon, Paul. *Rhythm of the Saints*. CD Album. Warner, 1990.

Skidmore, Thomas E. *Fact and Myth: Discovering a Racial Problem in Brazil*. Notre Dame: Helen Kellogg Inst. for Intl. Studies, U of Notre Dame, 1992.

Skidmore, Thomas E., and Peter H. Smith. *Modern Latin America*. 5th ed. New York: Oxford UP, 2001.

Smith, Paul. *Discerning the Subject*. Minneapolis: U of Minnesota P, 1988.

Smith, Paul Julian. *Vision Machines: Cinema, Literature and Sexuality in Spain and Cuba, 1983–1993*. Critical Studies in Latin Amer. and Iberian Culture. London: Verso, 1996.

Solano, Francisco. *Ciudades hispanoamericanas y pueblos de indios*. Madrid: Consejo de Investigaciones Científicas, 1990.

Sommer, Doris. *Foundational Fictions.* Berkeley: U of California P, 1993.

Spalding, Karen. *Huarochirí: An Andean Society under Inca and Spanish Rule.* Stanford: Stanford UP, 1984.

Spivak, Gayatri. "Can the Subaltern Speak?" *Marxism and the Interpretation of Culture.* Ed. Cary Nelson and Lawrence Grossberg. Urbana: U of Illinois P, 1988.

Staden, Hans. *Hans Staden: The True History of His Captivity, 1557.* Trans. Malcolm Letts. London: Routledge, 1928.

Stern, Steve. *Peru's Indian Peoples and the Challenge of Spanish Conquest: Huamanga to 1640.* Madison: U of Wisconsin P, 1982.

Stolzoff, Norman. *Wake the Town and Tell the People: Dancehall Culture in Jamaica.* Durham: Duke UP, 2000.

Storey, John. *Cultural Studies and the Study of Popular Culture: Theories and Methods.* Athens: U of Georgia P, 1996.

——, ed. *What Is Cultural Studies? A Reader.* London: Arnold, 1997.

Strawberry and Chocolate. Dir. Tomás Gutiérrez Alea. Instituto Cubano de Arte e Industria Cinematográficos. Miramax, 1993.

Sturm, Fred Gillette. "Religion." *Modern Brazil: Elites and Masses in Historical Perspective.* Ed. Michael L. Conniff and Frank D. McCann. Lincoln: U of Nebraska P, 1989. 246–64.

Sugar Cane Alley. Dir. Euzhan Palcy. NEF Diffusion. New Yorker Films, 1983.

Summ, G. Harvey, ed. *Brazilian Mosaic.* Wilmington: Scholarly Resources, 1995.

Telles, Edward. "Ethnic Boundaries and Political Mobilization among African Brazilians: Comparison with the U.S. Case." Hanchard 82–97.

——. "Race, Class and Space in Brazilian Cities." *International Journal of Urban and Regional Research* 19.3 (1995): 395–406.

Tenda dos Milagres. Dir. Nelson Pereira Dos Santos. Brazil, 1977.

Titu Cusi Yupanqui. *Relación de la historia del Perú* Ed. Luis Millones. Lima: El Virrey, 1985.

Tolman, Jon, gen. ed. *Brazil Slide Series.* Albuquerque: Latin Amer. Inst., U of New Mexico, 1988.

"Tomás Gutiérrez Alea: Interview with the Cuban Director." *UNESCO Courier* 7 (1995) : 53–56.

Torres García, Joaquín. *Constructive City with Universal Man.* 1942. Manolita Piña del Río, Montevideo.

——. "Escuela del Sur." 1935. *Art Museum of the Americas.* May 2002. 6 Mar. 2003 <http://www.museum.oas.org/permanent/constructivism/torres_garcia/ writingsby.html>.

The Toured: The Other Side of Tourism in Barbados. UC Berkeley Center for Media and Independent Learning, 1992.

Toussaint, Manuel. *Pintura colonial en México.* Mexico City: U Autónoma de México, 1982.

Travels: Iquitos. Dir. Paul Yule and Randy Harries. Berwick Universal Pictures Prod., 1989.

Traven, Bruno. "Canastitas en serie." *Canasta de cuentos mexicanos.* Mexico City:

Compañía General de Ediciones, 1956. 9–28. Trans. as "Assembly Line." *The Night Visitor and Other Stories.* Introd. Charles Miller. New York: Hill, 1966. 73–88.

Trigo, Abril. "Why I Do Cultural Studies." *Journal of Latin American Cultural Studies* 9.1 (2000): 73–93.

Tulane Univ. Latin Amer. Library. Photographic Archives. 16 June 2002 <http://www.tulane.edu/latinlib/lalphoto.html>.

Ulrich, Jutta Norris. "Putting Language before Business: The Business Case Study in the Foreign Language Classroom." *Foreign Language Annals* 33.2 (2000): 230–36.

Univ. of Hawai'i Art Gallery. *José Guadalupe Posada: My Mexico.* 16 June 2002 <http://www.hawaii.edu/artgallery/posada.html>.

University of Hawai'i at Mānoa 2002–2003 Catalog. 4 Mar. 2003 <http://www.catalog.hawaii.edu/>. Path: General Information; The University of Hawai'i.

Vaca, Nick C. "The Mexican-American in the Social Sciences: 1912–1935." *El Grito* 3.3 (1970): 3–24.

———. "The Mexican-American in the Social Sciences: 1936–1970." *El Grito* 4.1 (1970): 17–51.

Vanden, Harry E., and Gary Prevost. *Politics of Latin America: The Power Game.* Oxford: Oxford UP, 2002.

Vargas Llosa, Mario. *The Storyteller.* Trans. Helen Lane. New York: Farrar, 1989.

Vargas Machuca, Bernardo de. *Milicia indiana.* Caracas: Ayacucho, 1994.

Varis, Tapio. "The International Flow of Television Programs." *Journal of Communication* 34 (1984): 143–52.

Vasconcelos, José. "Nacionalismo y universalismo filosóficos." 1931. *El ensayo hispanamericano del siglo XX.* Ed. John Skirius. 2nd ed. Mexico City: Fondo de Cultura Económica, 1989. 104–19.

Veloso, Caetano, and Gilberto Gil. *Tropicália 2.* WEA/Atlantic/Nonesuch, 1994. Musical recording.

La vendedora de rosas. Dir. Victor Gaviria. Colombia. Alfa Video, 1998.

Verdesio, Gustavo. "Colonialism Now and Then: Colonial Latin American Studies in the Light of the Predicament of Latin Americanism." *Colonialism Past and Present: Reading and Writing about Colonial Latin American Texts Today.* Ed. Alvaro F. Bolaños and Verdesio. Albany: State U of New York P, 2002. 1–17.

———. "Reflexiones sobre el estatus de la estética en los estudios literarios: El caso de la actual 'crisis de paradigma' en los estudios colonials." *Papeles de Montevideo* 1.1 (1997): 111–20.

Villaverde, Cirilo. *Cecilia Valdés.* Mexico City: Porrúa, 1995.

Voices of the Orishas. Videocassette. U of California Extension Center for Media and Independent Learning. Berkeley, 1995.

Waters, Anita M. *Race, Class, and Political Symbols: Rastafari and Reggae in Jamaican Politics.* New Brunswick: Transaction, 1985.

Week-End in Havana. Dir. Walter Lang. Fox, 1941.

Wide Sargasso Sea. Dir. John Duigan. Sargasso Prods. New Line Studios, 1993.

Willdorf, Nina. "How to Be Gay (and Controversial)." *Chronicle of Higher Education* 4 Sept. 2000: A12.

Williams, Raymond. *The Country and the City*. Oxford: Oxford UP, 1973.

———. *Keywords: A Vocabulary of Culture and Society*. New York: Oxford UP, 1976.

Worlds Apart. Prod. Barraclough Carey. BBC Television; Turner Broadcasting System. Ambrose Video. New York, 1992.

Xica (or *Xica Da Silva*). Dir. Carlos Diegues. New Yorker Video, 1976.

Yawar Mallku. Dir. Jorge Sanjinés. Bolivia, 1968. New Yorker Films, 1969.

Yergin, Daniel, and Joseph Stanislaw. *The Commanding Heights: The Battle for the World Economy*. 1998. New York: Touchstone, 2002.

Yúdice, George. "Civil Society." *Social Text* 45.14 (1995): 1–25.

———. "Cultural Studies Questionnaire." *Journal of Latin American Cultural Studies* 6.2 (1997): 217–32.

———. "Estudios culturales y sociedad civil." *Revista de crítica cultural* 8 (1994): 44–53.

———. "Posmodernidad y valores." *Revista de estudios hispánicos* 32 (1998): 399–414.

———. "Postmodernity and Transnational Capitalism." *On Edge: The Crisis of Contemporary Latin American Culture*. Ed. Yúdice, Jean Franco, and Juan Flores. Minneapolis: U of Minnesota P, 1992. 1–28.

Zadek, Simon, and Pauline Tiffen. " 'Fair Trade': Business or Campaign?" *Development: Journal of the Society for International Development* 3 (1996). 21 Nov. 2000 <http://www.waw.be/sid/dev1996/zadek.html >.

Zavala, Iris. *El bolero: Historia de un amor*. Madrid: Alianza, 1991.

INDEX OF NAMES